Valuegrowth Investing

A disciplined approach to investment

[handwritten note:] ALL THERE IS TO INVESTING IS PICKING GOOD STOCKS
AT GOOD TIMES AND STAYING WITH THEM AS LONG

GLEN ARNOLD *[handwritten:]* AS THEY REMAIN GOOD COMPANIES.
BUFFETT P171

FINANCIAL TIMES

Prentice Hall

An imprint of Pearson Education

London · New York · San Francisco · Toronto · Sydney
Tokyo · Singapore · Hong Kong · Cape Town · Madrid
Paris · Milan · Munich · Amsterdam

PEARSON EDUCATION LIMITED

Head Office:
Edinburgh Gate
Harlow CM20 2JE
Tel: +44 (0)1279 623623
Fax: +44 (0)1279 431059

London Office:
128 Long Acre
London WC2E 9AN
Tel: +44 (0)20 7447 2000
Fax: +44 (0)20 7240 5771
Website: www.financialminds.com

First published in Great Britain in 2002

© Pearson Education Limited 2002

The right of Glen Arnold to be identified as Author
of this Work has been asserted by him in accordance
with the Copyright, Designs and Patents Act 1988.

This publication is designed to provide accurate and authoritative information
in regard to the subject matter covered. It is sold with the understanding that
neither the authors nor the publisher is engaged in rendering legal, investing,
or any other professional service. If legal advice or other expert assistance is required,
 the service of a competent professional person should be sought.

The publisher and contributors make no representation, express or implied, with
regard to the accuracy of the information contained in this book and cannot accept
any responsibility or liability for any errors or omissions that it may contain.

ISBN 0 273 65625 2

British Library Cataloguing in Publication Data
A CIP catalogue record for this book can be obtained from the British Library

10 9 8 7 6 5 4 3 2 1

Typeset by Northern Phototypesetting Co. Ltd, Bolton
Printed and bound in Great Britain by Biddles Ltd, Guildford & King's Lynn

The Publishers' policy is to use paper manufactured from sustainable forests.

Valuegrowth Investing

Dedicated to my two sons, Charles and Lawrence,
undoubtedly the best investments ever made

Disclaimer

Neither the author nor the publisher can accept responsibility for any loss occasioned to any person who either acts or refrains from acting as a result of any statement in this book. Readers should note that the author is not recommending the purchase or sale of any particular financial security – references to companies are made for illustration.

Acknowledgements

I would like to thank the following investors (and/or their publishers) for permitting the use of copyright material:

Warren Buffett
David Dreman
Philip Fisher
Benjamin Graham
Peter Lynch
Charles Munger
John Neff.

I am also very grateful to ABN Amro, Barclays Capital, Professor Elroy Dimson, Professor Paul Marsh, Professor Mike Staunton, John Train and Janet Lowe for allowing the use of copyright material. Christopher Arnold, my father, who kindly took time out from his busy routine to read through an early draft of the book, made suggestions for improvement that were extremely valuable. He is also responsible, together with my mother, Brenda Arnold, for sparking my interest in things financial from an early age. I thank them both. Andrew King, a friend, also spent a great deal of time reading an early draft. Again the suggestions made led to significant improvement. Lesley (my wife) for her steadfast support, and for switching roles from school teacher to typist at times of crisis. Sarah Mitchell for typing most of the book – this was a task for the brave only given my atrocious handwriting. Jonathan Agbenyega, a commissioning editor with faith enough to start the process of turning ideas into a book and the professionalism to see it through to a successful conclusion.

Contents

Contents

Introduction

A Challenge

A few years ago I found myself in a position to start work trying to answer an important question: 'what are the crucial elements leading to the successful analysis of shares?' The task was a daunting one. There are many that would say it is impossible to devise an easy-to-understand evaluation technique that can cope with the variety and complexity of modern companies. A general framework to identify under-priced shares could not be devised, the nay-sayers, and my own nagging small voice, would proclaim.

There are two possible routes that could be taken on a quest of this nature. The first is to immerse oneself in the academic literature on share analysis. As a teacher of finance I had some familiarity with share valuation models, and as a result knew that this route would prove largely unfruitful. Don't misunderstand me, these models do serve a purpose. They are useful for appreciating the variables that should be included in a valuation formula to calculate share value, e.g. future earnings per share. The problem is that they are little help in figuring out the factors that create the actual input number, e.g. *what it is that determines* the future earnings per share.

The second route (the one I took) is to conduct a study of the key elements used by the world's most respected investors. We can learn from the experience of people who, through a lifetime of endeavour, have gained insight into stock price behaviour, and who have displayed enviable performance records. There are some investors who seem to stand head-and-shoulders above the crowd. It might be possible, I reasoned, to observe the range of factors that all the great investors look for when evaluating a company and its shares. If these common elements can be put into a set of rules or a framework, and combined with modern strategic analysis and financial techniques, then I may be able to produce something of value.

The result of that work is set down in this book. Looking at it from a purely selfish viewpoint, I now have something of great value to me – I have developed my own coherent investment philosophy that will guide all future personal investments. I hope readers will find a set of principles that they can employ successfully.

'Valuegrowth' investing is an easily comprehended investment philosophy based on sound principles. At the core of this philosophy is a focus on the business that underlies the share. Investors must value a share by examining the potential for a business to generate 'owner earnings'. It is the present value of these owner earnings that gives a share its intrinsic value. The crucial factors determining intrinsic value are the strength and durability of the company's economic franchise, the quality (honesty and competence) of its managers and its financial position.

The outstanding investors of the last century have been more than willing to explain their philosophies and guiding principles. Far from being fearful that other investors will emulate them, and thus destroy their 'competitive edge', they seem mystified that so few people take the time to understand what, to them, seem self-evident truths. These masters, such as Warren Buffett, Philip Fisher, Benjamin Graham, John Neff, Charles Munger and Peter Lynch have bent

> ..... **The present value of owner earnings gives a share its intrinsic value.** ....

over backwards to explain in essays, books and speeches the key elements of their approaches. Just as importantly they have vociferously denounced those ideas and approaches that destroy investor value, or at least, distract attention and divert energy from the real issues.

My day job throughout the period spent exploring investment philosophies was that of a university lecturer and professor, in which I taught finance and strategy. In some ways this worked against my quest. For example much of the academic literature on stock markets focuses on the 'Efficient market hypothesis' (EMH) that, in effect, says it is impossible for ordinary investors using publicly available information (i.e. they are not insiders) to out-perform the market index, except by chance. Or as it is put more picturesquely: to outperform a chimpanzee selecting a broadly based portfolio of shares. (This has been tried; generally the chimp did better than professional investors.)

Many finance theorists solemnly believe that this hypothesis reflects reality. Statistical analysis has been conducted and the 'evidence' is believed to show that the modern sophisticated markets of the developed world are good at pricing stocks. There is an old joke in the academic world concerning a professor of finance who wholeheartedly believed the efficient market hypothesis to be true. One day the professor was walking towards the lecture theatre with a few students. A student abruptly interrupted the conversation to declare that there was a 20 dollar bill lying on the floor. The professor told the student not to bother to stoop down 'because if it really had been there someone would have picked it up by now'.

Even within the academic literature doubts have emerged about the EMH: shares bought on simple value principles appear to out-perform the market average; small company shares have given exceptionally high returns (for some periods, at least), and bubbles in the stock market are a serious challenge to the EMH.

Naturally, if we turn to the practitioners we get scorn poured on the whole notion of EMH. Warren Buffett said:

> I'm convinced that there is much inefficiency in the market…When the price of a stock can be influenced by a 'herd' on Wall Street with prices set at the margin by the most emotional person, or the greediest person, or the most depressed person, it is hard to argue that the market always prices rationally. In fact, market prices are frequently nonsensical… There seems to be some perverse human characteristic that likes to make easy things difficult. The academic world, if anything, has actually backed away from the teaching of value investing over the last 30 years. It's likely to continue that way. Ships will sail around the world but the Flat Earth Society will flourish.[1]

Benjamin Graham, arguably the most influential thinker on investment in the 20th Century, took a similarly scolding view:

> Evidently the processes by which the securities market arrives at its appraisals are frequently illogical and erroneous. These processes…are not automatic or mechanical, but psychological for they go on in the minds of people who buy and sell. The mistakes of the market are thus the mistakes of groups of masses of individuals. Most of them can be traced to one or more of three basic causes: exaggeration, oversimplification, or neglect.[2]

My academic work led to the study and teaching of modern strategy analysis. This had a particular focus on the resource-based view of the firm – a discipline developed in the 1990s. Using these tools and frameworks it is possible to analyze a firm's economic (or industry) environment and competitive position within its environment.

This knowledge is a wonderful complement to some of the guiding principles followed by the successful investors. For example, Warren Buffett talks of the strength of the firm's 'economic franchise' as being of key importance in assessing its long term value, and Peter Lynch searches for niche businesses with exclusive franchises and high barriers to entry.

After spending many years reading and thinking about the various investment methods I eventually formulated the Valuegrowth approach. Putting value and growth into one word is intended to signify that the value investment approach is not opposite to, or inimical to, the growth

> **To separate growth and value is ridiculous.**

approach. An investor selecting a share for qualities of value should, as part of the assessment, analyze its growth potential. On the other hand, an investor judging a so-called growth stock will not pay *any* price, and so will look to purchase at a low price relative to its future

prospects. To separate growth and value is ridiculous. I cannot put the point any more effectively than Warren Buffett:

> Most analysts feel they must choose between two approaches customarily thought to be in opposition; 'value' and 'growth'. Indeed, many investment professionals see any mixing of the two terms as a form of intellectual cross-dressing.
>
> We view that as fuzzy thinking (in which, it must be confessed, I myself engaged some years ago). In our opinion the two approaches are joined at the hip; growth is *always* a component in the calculation of value, constituting a variable whose importance can range from negligible to enormous and whose impact can be negative as well as positive.
>
> In addition, we think the very term 'value investing' is redundant. What is investing if it is not the act of seeking value at least sufficient to justify the amount paid? Consciously paying more for a stock than its calculated value – in the hope that it can soon be sold for a still higher price – should be labelled speculation (which is neither illegal, immoral nor – in our view – financially fattening).
>
> Whether appropriate or not, the term 'value investing' is widely used. Typically, it connotes the purchase of stocks having attributes such as a low ratio of price to book value, a low price-earnings ratio, or a high dividend yield. Unfortunately, such characteristics, even if they appear in combination are far from determinative as to whether an investor is indeed buying something for what it is worth and is therefore truly operating on the principle of obtaining value in his investments. Correspondingly, opposite characteristics – a high ratio of price to book value, a high price-earnings ratio, and a low dividend yield – are in no way inconsistent with a 'value' purchase.
>
> Similarly, business growth, *per se*, tells us little about value. It's true that growth often has a positive impact on value, sometimes one of spectacular proportions. But such an effect is far from certain. For example, investors have regularly poured money into the domestic airline business to finance profitless (or worse) growth. For these investors, it would have been far better if Orville

had failed to get it off the ground at Kitty Hawk: the more the industry has grown the worse the disaster for the owners.

Growth benefits investors only when the business in point can invest at incremental returns that are enticing – in other words, only when each dollar used to finance the growth creates over a dollar of long-term market value. In the case of a low return business requiring incremental funds, growth hurts the investor. ... The investment shown by the discounted-flows-of-cash calculation to be the cheapest is the one that the investors should purchase – irrespective of whether the business grows or doesn't, displays volatility or smoothness in its earnings, or carries a high price or low in relation to its current earnings and book value.[3]

The Valuegrowth method draws on the ideas and techniques of seven distinct investment approaches. These are explained and contrasted early in the book. So, at the very least, if the reader is not content with my conclusions that Valuegrowth is best, he or she may choose to be guided by the principles set out in one or more of the progenitor approaches.

The book is divided into two parts. Part One describes stock selection philosophies developed in the 20th Century, from Benjamin Graham's current asset value approach (buying at less than two-thirds the value of working capital), to Philip Fisher's bonanza stock investing, focusing on technology growth shares.

Knowing the fundamental principles behind good investment practice is merely the first step – and the easiest. There are plenty of books on the market describing these ideas but they never seem to take the reader on to establishing practical techniques that the investor can use. This is what Part Two is designed to do. It brings together the most sophisticated elements of these approaches with modern strategic appraisal techniques to develop the Valuegrowth method. This has seven key elements:

- a business you understand
- a strong and durable economic franchise
- operated by honest and competent people
- financial strength
- available at a very attractive price
- low diversification
- holding for the very long term.

Valuegrowth investing is a demanding discipline. To do the task properly requires dedication and freedom from time consuming distractions. The financial press is full of such wasteful ephemera: short-term market moves, monetary policy panic, share price momentum figures and so on. Throughout the book investors will be reminded not to make investing too difficult. There has to be a focus on the business. That is, after all, what an investor is buying: a piece of a business. So avoid equations with Greek letters in them, forget charts and graphs, leave aside mathematical formulas and asset allocations rules, ignore the market moods, fads and fashions. Be very sceptical about tipsters, brokers' recommendations and forecasters. Leave turnaround situations alone and don't be tempted by those firms that offer jam tomorrow, but will have no profit to show for the next few years, and are currently trading on a multiple of turnover.

> There has to be a focus on the business.

The book also provides guidance on the frame of mind needed for a successful valuegrowth investor, for example: don't gamble, control your emotions, be patient, set reasonable goals and admit and learn from your mistakes.

The private investor reading this may be thinking that they could not possibly compete with the professional fund managers, or achieve the same returns as the great investors. This is unreasonable self-deprecation. All the successful investors say that institutional fund managers suffer from some important disadvantages compared with the dedicated private investor.

Fund managers with hundreds of millions of dollars to invest suffer from a terrible wealth withering disease: liquidity-itis. They generally restrict their analysis and purchases to those firms which have a sufficiently large free float of shares to permit millions of dollars worth of investment and, perhaps more importantly to them, disinvestment without moving the share price. As a result their investment universe tends to consist only of company stocks (and other financial assets) that have the quality of high liquidity. This 'fetish of liquidity'[4] leads to large numbers of smaller and medium stocks being ignored by analysts, brokers and fund managers. There is often a high degree of ignorance of the small and medium stocks, except for the *hot* sectors of the day. Even within the ranks of large companies, shares fall out of fashion and become ignored by the professional investors. You are far more likely to find bargains in the relatively under-analyzed areas of the market.

Furthermore, in these areas the aware private investor has a competitive edge. Imagine the difficulty facing the institutional investor. They are often compelled to hold hundreds of stocks. This may be due to the requirements of the funds' constitution or the rules for that type of institution (e.g. pension fund rules). These rules make some sense, up to a point. It would be unacceptable for a fund manager acting as a custodian of workers' retirement funds to place that money in one basket. However, the fundamentally sound rationale behind portfolio theory and the benefits of diversification can be taken too far, and this tendency can give the private investor (or the non-conventional fund manager) an opportunity. Because institutional investment vehicles tend to end up with hundreds of stocks the funds are bound to suffer from the problems of what I call 'diminishing marginal attractiveness'. This can be illustrated if you imagine yourself having the responsibility of investing $2 billion. What would you do? Well, you might start by listing, in order of attractiveness the stocks that you judge to be good buys. You know the list has to be a large one because you simply could not invest a high proportion of this fund in one stock without losing the sought-after quality of liquidity. So let's assume you settle on 100 stocks ($20 million per stock on average) as the minimum number needed. The first one on the list would be your number one choice for appreciation – an over-looked bargain. The second stock would still have a high attraction, but would be less attractive than the first. That is, the marginal (next) stock would have a diminished attractiveness. So each stock down the list would exhibit diminished marginal attractiveness compared with the previous one. So the 90th stock is considerably less attractive than the 10th stock. Ultimately, as the portfolio gets larger the performance will tend to the merely mediocre (and that is before expenses!).

The private investor, on the other hand, can afford to avoid plunging too far down the diminishing marginal attractiveness curve. Investments can be concentrated on the top ten, or, if you are prepared to accept slightly more risk, on the top five selections.

There is another respect in which the institutional fund manager is at a disadvantage. Stuck in their offices in the financial district, dealing with the day-to-day business of holding 100, 200 or 1,000 stocks, they are pushed for time to gain personal knowledge of the businesses they buy a piece of, or those that they might like to buy. Imagine the constant noise of takeover bids for elements of the portfolio, or all the annual meetings, or management crises. It must be deafening and highly distracting. 'Many a fortune has slipped through men's fingers by engaging in too many occupations at once.'[5] The private investor has the benefit of being able to stand back from the hubbub of the financial markets, and to go down to the shopping mall and experience buying a shirt from a new retail chain which, although small now, could revolutionize the selling of shirts; or to take time to ask children about the latest craze; or to attend trade shows where you can talk to competitors and customers of firms whose shares you are thinking of purchasing. It is the knowledge that comes from everyday experiences, by you and, as related to you by others, of the company's product or service that can often gain you the competitive edge. No amount of balance sheet analysis or macro economic forecasts while sitting in a New York skyscraper will tell you that McDonalds produce great hamburgers and have high approval rating from their customers (if you were investing in the 1950s), or that Intel (in the 1970s) have a great team of technologists much respected by their peers. But, if you are a small investor with an interest in restaurants or computer technology you can find out these key facts. The Wall Street manager is generally too busy or too distracted by the latest fashion in the markets. The manager's personal awareness has to be spread thinly whereas the private investor can specialize and focus; 'When a man's undivided attention is centred on one object, his mind will constantly be suggesting improvements of value'[6]; or, as Azariah Rossi, a 16th Century Italian physician put it: 'None ever got ahead of me except the man of one task'.

Fund managers may also suffer from a short-term focus. Their ability is often judged through the use of quarterly performance tables. Few fund trustees or mutual fund holders would cry 'sack him' if one quarter was relatively poor, but by the time five or six poor quarters have passed, the manager might need to start brushing up the old curriculum vitae. The leading investors discussed in this book agree that a period of several quarters is far too short to appraise performance in the fickle markets of today, with their slow reaction to underlying fundamental value. Many fund managers would concur. But sadly, they are aware that their shoulders are being peered over, forcing many to behave in a short-termist fashion. They are simply unable to hold for the long term.

In contrast to these frustrated long-termists a high proportion of funds are run by people who think that the best way to outperform is to trade in the market looking to benefit from short-term trends, momentum or the current flavour of the month. These managers often believe in the 'greater fool' method of investing, in which the objective of the game is to pass on a share which is currently of great interest to the market speculators and traders after making a return on the 'investment' without really bothering to understand the fundamentals of the business. Eventually, of course, in this game of high stakes pass-the-parcel an investor pays a very high price, after being attracted by the upward price momentum of the past. Then the music stops, as the market starts to chase the next big story, and the greater fool suffers.

Institutions also have a tendency to 'churn' – buying and selling shares frequently. They incur high transaction costs reducing the effective annual returns. A buy and hold strategy can make private investors wealthy rather than their brokers and advisers. Another important advantage the private investor possesses is the ability to leave the market for a while. 'Don't just do something, stand there.'[7] You don't have to be in the stock market all the time. There are occasions when cash can be a valuable asset. This flexibility is much reduced for institutions.

The professional managers as a group show a strong tendency to form a consensus view. This may be due to cultural homogeneity, similarity of data sources or dominance of a few 'lead steers'. Whatever the cause, a lemming-like mentality can develop, and the shares of companies are excessively bid-up or sold off. These extreme occasions present opportunities for the patient investor able to cut himself or herself off from the crowd, think independently and really get to grips with understanding the underlying businesses.

To cap all these arguments we have the accumulating evidence that explodes a popular myth: active professional institutional fund managers do not, on average, perform better than the market index. This observation, backed up by mountains of academic research, is severely damaging for the investment industry, and therefore does not receive much publicity. But, if you dig into academic studies, you will find, time and again, evidence of poor returns, especially after transaction and management costs – these people, it seems, must be paid a great deal for dull performance, just like many CEOs.

The image of these managers being emotionally anchored and rational beings, who coolly evaluate stocks, buying when the supposedly less informed, less experienced and less emotionally controlled general public is selling in stock market panic; or who sell stocks when the over-excited private investor is piling in and pushing the market to mania levels is plain wrong. Of course there are some private investors who behave like this, but the evidence is that irrationality is as prevalent, if not more so, among professional fund managers. David Dreman comments that Securities and Exchange Commission evidence clearly shows that:

> The much abused and supposedly emotional individual investor sold securities near the 1968 market top and sold at the market bottom of both 1970 and 1974. The institutional investor on the other hand, bought near market tops and sold at the bottoms. In the 1987 crash the individual investor was scarcely involved. The market panic in the third quarter of 1990 ... demonstrated once again that professional, not individual, investors were the largest, and most desperate sellers.[8]

He goes on:

> The same pattern shows clearly with mutual funds.... Rather than supporting stocks when prices plummet, they get trampled at the exit. When prices soar, they buy aggressively. The pros seem to judge the market direction poorly.[9]

In sum: do not feel intimidated by the 'professional'. Peter Lynch and Warren Buffett call the professional investors the oxymorons. Armed with sound principles, the right emotional attitude and a modicum of intelligence, you can outperform the highly paid managers who suffer from severe constraints created by the institutional setting, by cognitive errors and by a range of social maladies, including herd mentality.

Do not feel intimidated by the 'professional'.

The chapters that follow are not addressed to the complete novice. It is assumed that the reader has some acquaintance with the simpler concepts and terminology of finance and investment.

This is intended to be more than a descriptive work. It tries to convey fundamental concepts, provide practical methods and sound reasoning to guide investment selections. Theory is introduced where it is of practical benefit. However, this is kept to a minimum, not only because the reader should not be overburdened with complexity or technical methods, which are more trouble than they are worth, but, more importantly, because much of the modern theory has limited practical value.

The standards and techniques detailed are within the capabilities of all reasonably intelligent and informed investors. They are definitely not the exclusive preserve of the professional investor. Indeed being a trained 'professional' may be a distinct disadvantage in the acquisition of the skills and attitude of the Valuegrowth investor.

One aim of the book is to provide defences, in the form of principles and the strengthening of an appropriate attitude of mind, against the mood swings of the market and against the superficial and the temporary:

> To invest successfully over a lifetime does not require a stratospheric IQ, unusual business insights, or inside information. What's needed is a sound intellectual framework for making decisions and the ability to keep emotions from corroding that framework.[10]

For those of us less than intellectually gifted, Peter Lynch offers further hope:

> In terms of IQ, probably the best investors fall somewhere above the bottom 10 per cent but also below the top 3 per cent. The true geniuses it seems to me, get too enamoured of the theoretical cogitations and are forever betrayed by the actual behaviour of stocks, which is more simple-minded than they can imagine.[11]

I hope this book will be useful in guiding you to a sound intellectual framework for making decisions, to keep emotions from corroding that framework and to understanding the actual behaviour of shares.

Notes

1 Buffett, W. (1984) 'The Super Investors of Graham and Doddsville' an edited transcript of a talk given at Columbia University in 1984. Reproduced in *Hermes*, magazine of Columbia Business School, autumn 1984 and in the reprinted version of Benjamin Graham's *The Intelligent Investor* (1973), published by Harper Business. This material is copyrighted and is reproduced with the permission of the author.

2 Graham, B. and Dodd, D. (1934), p. 585.

3 Buffett, W. (1992). This material is copyrighted and is reproduced with the permission of the author.

4 Keynes (1936).

5 A quote from the great entertainer and writer Phinaeus T. Barnum. *The Life of P.T. Barnum*, New York: Redfield, 1885.

6 *Ibid.*

7 Attributed to Alfred Hitchcock.

8 Dreman, D. 1998, p. 32.

9 *Ibid.*, p. 33.

10 Buffett, W. in the introduction to Benjamin Graham's 4th revised edition of *The Intelligent Investor* (1973) Harper Business, written for the reprinted version in 1997. This material is copyrighted and is reproduced with the permission of the author.

11 Lynch, P. (1990), p. 69.

PART ONE

Investment
►philosophies

1

Peter Lynch's niche investing

Peter Lynch is the most outstanding fund manager of the latter part of the 20th Century. From May 1977 to May 1990 he was the portfolio manager of Fidelity's Magellan Fund. Over this 13-year period a $1,000 investment rose to be worth $28,000, a rate of return that is way ahead of the field at 29.2 per cent per annum. Furthermore, the Fund's performance was consistent – in only two of those years did it fail to beat the S&P 500. The fund grew from an asset base of $18 million to one of more than $14 billion. It was not only the best performing fund in the world; it also became the biggest. There were 1 million shareholders in 1990, when Lynch quit, at the age of 46, to devote more time to his family.

Lynch looks for a combination of characteristics, some of which are similar to those required by the other investors examined in this book, e.g. a business with a strong competitive position, and financial strength. Others are significantly different, e.g. he often looks for a lousy industry and buys the best firm in that industry. He is very insistent that private investors can outperform the professional fund manager. The private investor can develop a number of advantages over the professional if he or she applies common sense with a little research and sticks to companies they know about. For Lynch, 'Investing is not complicated. If it gets too complicated, go on to the next stock'.[1]

> The private investor can develop a number of advantages over the professional.

Lynch was born in 1944, a son of an industrious former mathematics professor who later became a senior auditor. He grew up in a family that generally distrusted stocks, as did most of the US in the 1950s. People would say 'never get involved in the market, it's too risky. You'll lose all your money', as they remembered the dark days of the 1930s. As it turned out, the 1950s were an excellent period in which to invest: 'this taught me not only that it is difficult to predict markets, but also that small investors tend to be pessimistic and optimistic at precisely the wrong times'.[2]

When Lynch was ten his father died from a brain tumour. To help the family finances he caddied (part-time) at a golf course. He would listen to the golfers' conversations, particularly when they spoke about investments. He discovered that many of them had made exciting returns and the young Lynch began to lose his fear of the stock market.

At Boston College he avoided science, maths and accounting. He concentrated on the arts with history, psychology and political science. He also studied meta-physics, logic, religion and Greek philosophy. He was later to state that stock picking is much more an art than a science. A logical commonsense approach, rather than mathematical precision, is the key.

> People who have been trained to rigidly quantify everything have a big disadvantage … All the math you need in the stock market…(Chrysler's got $1 billion in cash, $500 million in long-term debt, etc.) you get in the fourth grade. Logic is the subject that's helped me the most in picking stocks, if only because it taught me to identify the peculiar illogic of Wall Street. Actually Wall Street thinks just as the Greeks did. The early Greeks used to sit around for days and debate how many teeth a horse has. They thought they could figure it out by just sitting there, instead of checking the horse. A lot of investors sit around and debate whether a stock is going up, as if the financial muse will give them the answer, instead of checking the company.[3]

The first stock Lynch bought was Flying Tigers Airlines for $7 a share in 1963. It was this stock which sparked in him a passion for making ten times his money. It was a multi-bagger that put him through graduate school. Within two years Flying Tiger hit $32¾. 'It proved to me that the big-baggers existed, and I was sure there were more of them from where this one had come'.[4]

When he was a caddy, Lynch met D. George Sullivan, the President of Fidelity. When he reached his senior year at Boston College (and before moving on to Wharton) he asked Sullivan for a summer job at Fidelity, which he was granted against stiff competition. He was put to work researching companies and writing reports. He learned how to examine a company's business in some depth. His experience of the real world of investment gave him a sceptical eye to what was being taught on his MBA course at Wharton. 'It seemed to me that most of what I learned at Wharton, which was supposed to help you succeed in the investment business, could only help you fail…. Quantitative analysis taught me that the things I saw happening at Fidelity couldn't really be happening. I also found it difficult to integrate the efficient market hypothesis…. It also was obvious that the Wharton professors who believed in quantum analysis and random walk weren't doing nearly as well as my new colleagues at Fidelity, so between theory and practice, I cast my lot with the practitioners…. My distrust of theorizers and prognosticators continues to the present day.'[5]

Wharton was not a complete waste of time; some of the courses were rewarding, and, best of all, he met his future wife Carolyn on Campus. Whilst in the army (1967–9) he tried rash speculation in the stock market and learned a few lessons from the hard knocks. On returning from Korea he joined Fidelity as a research analyst. By 1974 he was director of research and, in 1977, took over the Magellan Fund. Eleven years previously the fund was worth $20 million, but the crisis of the early 1970s had led to a steady outflow of money. Customer redemptions had reduced the fund to $6 million by 1976. It was merged with another fund to give it a viable size. It was this $18 million that Lynch took charge of. The directors of Fidelity put a lot of trust in Lynch by giving him a wide discretion to select stocks. This paid off handsomely. By the late 1980s the fund was worth more than the GNP of most countries in the world.

THE PRIVATE INVESTOR VERSUS THE PROFESSIONAL FUND MANAGER

For a fund manager, Lynch is astonishingly scathing about the profession. His rule number one is to:

> stop listening to the professionals! Twenty years in this business convinces me that any normal person using the customary 3 per cent of the brain can pick stocks just as well, if not better, than the average Wall Street expert … investing, where the smart money isn't so smart, and the dumb money isn't really as dumb as it thinks. Dumb money is only dumb when it listens to the smart money. In fact, the amateur investor has numerous built in advantages that, if exploited, should result in his or her outperforming the experts, and also the market in general.[6]

He agrees that there are some exceptional fund managers – how could he not, considering that he is one himself? But the majority are 'run-of-the-mill fund managers, dull fund managers, comatose fund managers, sycophantic fund managers, timid fund managers, plus other assorted camp followers, fuddy-duddies and copycats hemmed in by the rules'.[7] This leaves the door wide open for the amateur who commits himself or herself to a 'small amount of study' to outperform '95 per cent of the paid experts … plus have the fun of doing it'.[8]

So what is it that the oxymorons do wrong? Why do they perform so badly compared with the market or the switched-on amateur? The first observation Lynch makes is that the profession has an unwritten law that states that it is okay to fail in a commonly accepted conventional way, but that you will lose your job if you try to be unconventional in order to out-perform and then fail. The unconventional action may be right for investors, and taken over a number of attempts the successes will out-weigh the failures, but the fact that a poor result can ruin a career means that bold action is never taken. If mediocre results come from following well-established practice, and mediocre results are not punished because the majority of fund managers perform at the same level, then the manag-er has no incentive to try the more adventurous approach – one slip and disaster looms:

> With survival at stake, it's the rare professional who has the guts to traffic in an unknown La Quinta [one of Lynch's best investments]. In fact, between the chance of making an unusually large profit on an unknown company and the assurance of losing only a small amount on an established company, the nor-mal mutual fund manager, pension-fund manager, or corporate-portfolio man-ager, would jump at the latter. Success is one thing, but it's more important not to look bad if you fail. There's an unwritten rule on Wall Street: 'You'll never lose your job losing your client's money in IBM'. If IBM goes bad and you bought it, the clients and the bosses will ask: 'What's wrong with that damn IBM lately?' But if La Quinta Motor Inns goes bad, they'll ask: 'What's wrong with you?' That's why security-conscious portfolio managers don't buy La Quinta Motor Inns when two analysts cover the stock and it sells for $3 a share. They don't buy Wal-Mart when the stocks sell for $4, and it's a dinky store, in a dinky little town in Arkansas, but soon to expand. They buy Wal-Mart when there's an outlet in every large population center in America, fifty analysts fol-low the company, and the chairman of Wal-Mart is featured in *People* Maga-zine.... By then the stocks sells for $40.[9]

Even if an individual fund manager is willing to take reasoned risks for clients against all the social and political obstacles, the institutional rules and regulations may prevent it. Committees may create lists of stocks for the managers to choose from. If the list contained dynamic and exciting companies that is fine, but too often only those that satisfy all 30 committee members are included: 'If no great book or symphony was ever written by committee, no great portfolio has ever been selected by one, either'.[10] The committee members hardly know the firms they are including or exclud-ing. They certainly haven't visited the companies or investigated their future potential, 'they just take what they are given and pass it along'.[11]

The rules imposed on the free-thinking managers are remarkable for their arbitrary nature. For example, all companies with unions might be disallowed; or companies regarded as 'non-growth'; or specific industries (e.g. oil or utilities) are excluded.

The Securities and Exchange Commission (SEC) rules also encourage mediocrity, as funds cannot invest more than 5 per cent of their assets in a particular stock. This leads to the larger funds being forced to put the bulk of their money into the biggest 500 companies, paying little attention to the other 10,000 publically quoted in the US. Some funds add to the managers' burden of restriction by having a rule forbidding purchase of shares below a market capitalization of say, $100 million. Thus the 'portfolios are wedded to the 10 per cent gainers, the plodders, and the regular Fortune 500 bigshots that offer few pleasant surprises'.[12]

Fund managers are simply not looking to buy the stocks with the best prospects, their primary concern is with projecting the right image and covering their backs should something go wrong, such as a stock they have rejected going up.

> Whoever imagines that the average Wall Street professional is looking for reasons to buy exciting stocks hasn't spent much time on Wall Street. The fund manager most likely is looking for reasons *not* to buy exciting stocks, so that he can offer the proper excuses if those existing stocks happen to go up. 'It was too small for me to buy' heads a long list, followed by 'there was no track record', 'it was a non-growth industry', 'unproven management'... 'the competition would kill them'... These may be reasonable concerns that merit investigations, but often they're used to fortify snap judgment and wholesale taboos.[13]

The tendency to ignore small and medium-sized company stocks comes in for particular criticism because, with rare exceptions 'big companies don't have big stock moves'.[14] The smallest companies are the ones that are going to give you the 4- or 10-baggers in a few years. So holding everything else constant, if you want to perform exceptionally well you will do better with small companies. The professionally invested funds are almost automatically excluded from this possibility.

Particular vitriol is reserved for the practice of investing in companies that the fund manager has not taken the time to understand.

> There seems to be an unwritten rule on Wall Street: If you don't understand it, then put your life savings into it. Shun the enterprise around the corner, which can at least be observed, and seek out the one that manufactures an incomprehensible product... a company that makes the 'one megabit S-Ram, C-mos...bipolar risc...floating point, data I/O array processor, optimizing

compiler, 16 mega....' Gig my gigahertz and whetstone my mega flop, if you couldn't tell if that was a racehorse or a memory chip you should stay away from it.[15]

Wall Streeters are always watching each other to see if there is a new trend to follow. They lack individualism and strength of character to take the initiative and make the first move. A stock is not regarded as attractive 'until a number of large institutions have recognized its suitability and an equal number of respected Wall Street analysts ... have put it on recommended lists. With so many people waiting for others to make the first move, it's amazing that anything gets bought'.[16] Lynch describes a number of instances where the analysts and managers jumped on the bandwagon when it was too late. For example, when The Limited went public in 1969 just one analyst followed the firm. It wasn't until 1974 that this person was joined by a second analyst, and it took until 1981 for enough interest to be generated in the stock for six analysts to follow it. Dunkin' Donuts was a 25-bagger between 1977 and 1986 and yet until 1984 no major firms followed it. Even then, between 1984 and 1989, only two turned their attention to it. When Stop and Shop was on the verge of going from $5 to $50 only one analyst took an interest. In contrast, IBM had 56 brokerage analysts covering it.

One of the potential explanations for stocks being largely ignored is that they fail to fall neatly into analysts' categories. Thus a company which does not fall into one of the standard industry classifications may be worthy of further study by the private investor, as the oxymorons leave it undervalued. Lynch did well with Service Corporation International, a funeral service company, which was unstudied and unappreciated by Wall Street (until it was too late).

Lynch believes that the herd on Wall Street charge about, being pushed by those adjacent to them whispering the latest gossip, hot tip or pointing out the new revolutionary industrial sector. 'You have to understand the minds of the people in our business. We all read the same newspapers and magazines and listen to the same economists. We're a very homogenous lot, quite frankly'.[17] You should not follow what some fund manager is buying, even Peter Lynch, he advises, because:

(1) he might be wrong! (A long list of losers from my own portfolio constantly reminds me that the so-called smart money is exceedingly dumb about 40 per cent of the time); (2) even if he's right, you'll never know when he's changed his mind about a stock and sold; and (3) you've got better sources, and they're all around you.[18]

So, if the professional fund managers are generally incapable of performing well where does that leave the amateur? In a very good position, according to Lynch. 'Going it alone … that's where the ten-baggers come from, beyond the boundaries of accepted Wall Street cogitation'.[19] The private investors' edge comes from the knowledge they are able to accumulate about specific companies and industries. They are able to observe great growth prospects long before the professionals get to hear about them. Investors can first encounter ten-baggers quite close to home. For example, in the shopping mall or at work: 'the average person comes across a likely prospect two or three times a year – sometimes more'.[20] Anything that is really useful to know about a company is available to the private investor. 'All the pertinent facts are just waiting to be picked up … what you can't get from the annual report, you can get by asking your broker, by calling the company, by visiting the company, or by doing some grassroots research, also known as kicking the tyres'.[21] Lynch says that despite spending hour after hour conversing with CEOs, financial analysts and colleagues in the mutual fund business, the best investments are usually stumbled upon in everyday life. This is how he discovered some of his big winners: Taco Bell – 'I was impressed with the burrito on a trip to California';[22] La Quinta Motor Inns – 'Somebody at the rival Holiday Inn told me about it';[23] Apple Computer – 'my kids had one at home';[24] Dunkin' Donuts – 'I loved the coffee'.[25] Naturally, these reasons are not sufficient to purchase the stocks, 'the discovery is not a buy signal … what you've got so far is simply a lead to a story that has to be developed'.[26]

Lynch thinks that the best place to look for multi-baggers is in the most boring places. Better yet, boring and unpleasant! These sectors of the economy attract little attention from analysts and companies may become severely underpriced:

> A company that does boring things is almost as good as a company that has a boring name, and both together is terrific. Both together are guaranteed to keep the oxymorons away until finally the good news compels them to buy … when it becomes trendy and overpriced, you can sell your shares to the trend-followers.[27]

There are also stocks which are out-of-favour, even larger non-boring ones, and therefore under-priced. These could be stocks that were once popular but the professionals have abandoned them after a bad patch.

THE CHARACTERISTICS OF GOOD NICHE STOCKS

Lynch selected stocks for the gigantic Magellan Fund from six different categories (slow growers, stalwarts, cyclicals, fast growers, turnarounds and asset plays). To develop skills in analyzing all these distinct types of stocks is very demanding. We will focus on Lynch's favourite category: the fast growing small to medium-size firm operating a niche business with high potential. These are aggressive enterprises that will grow at 20 to 25 per cent a year. 'If you choose wisely, this is the land of the 10- to 40-baggers, and even the 200-baggers. With a small portfolio, one or two of these can make a career'.[28] The main elements for a niche company are shown in Fig. 1.1.

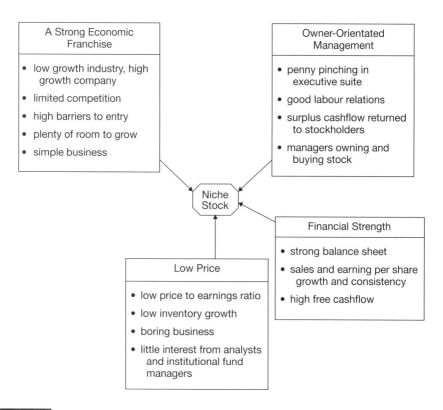

Figure 1.1 Lynch's niche investing

Strong economic franchise

The first factor is a strong economic franchise. Lynch believes that a company is more likely to exploit its superior competitive position sustainably in a slow growing industry. In fact, he would prefer it if the industry had no growth at all (e.g. funeral services).

> There's nothing thrilling about a thrilling high-growth industry, except watching the stocks go down… (e.g.) computers in the 1980s … for every single product in a hot industry, there are a thousand MIT graduates trying to figure out how to make it cheaper in Taiwan. As soon as a computer company designs the best word-processor in the world, ten other competitors are spending $100 million to design a better one, and it will be on the market in eight months. This doesn't happen with bottle caps, coupon-clipping services, oil-drum retrieval, or motel chains … In a no-growth industry especially one that is boring and upsets people, there's no problem with competition. You don't have to protect your flanks from potential rivals because nobody else is going to be interested. This gives you the leeway to continue to grow, to gain market share.[29]

There are plenty of examples of fast growing companies in slow growing industries: Anheuser Busch in drink, SCI in funerals, Wal-Mart in retail distribution, Marriott in hotels. These are companies that succeeded in one place and were then able to duplicate the winning formula over and over again on a wider geographic base. This type of expansion can result in very rapid advances in earnings. While the attention of the Press, Wall Street and corporate executives is focused on the fascinating battles for dominance in the well known fast growing 'industries of tomorrow' (e.g. computers, telecommunications, internet) the highly competent niche businesses are quietly building up a head of steam to dominate their sectors. The illusory goldmines of the fast growing sectors attract many entrants to the industries ('in business, imitation is the sincerest form of battery'[30]), whereas in a lousy industry the weak drop out and the strong take a larger market share. Lynch maintains that it is preferable to hold a stock in a company which is able to capture an increasingly large share of a stagnant market than to hold a company which is struggling to protect a dwindling share of an ostensibly exciting market. 'In business, competition is never as healthy as total domination'.[31]

It is apparent that some investors confuse two concepts of growth. The first is growth in sales for the industry. This will lead to growth in the more important form – growth of earnings for a particular firm in that industry – only if certain conditions are present, the most important of which is that any high profits are not competed away. Indeed in most high growth industries there is great uncertainty as to the potential for translating the growth in sales into earnings growth. This uncertainty alone should put off investors, especially when they consider that there are simpler, more predictable industries where the competitive threats are easier to assess.

There are a number of clues to the strength of the economic franchise, e.g. if the company is able to raise prices year after year without losing customers; earnings per share have risen steadily; the company has duplicated its success in city after city; it is not selling a high proportion of its output to one customer; the firm has a clear local monopoly.

> I'd much rather own a local rock pit than own Twentieth Century-Fox, because a movie company competes with other movie companies and the rock pit has a niche … if you've got the only gravel pit in Brooklyn you've got a virtual monopoly … due to the weight of rocks, aggregates are an exclusive franchise … There's no way to overstate the value of exclusive franchises to a company or its shareholders … Once you've got an exclusive franchise in anything, you can raise prices.[32]

The ideal niche company would be engaged in a simple business. It is much easier to understand the 'story' of the simple business and draw conclusions on the strengths of the firms. Also, the management are less likely to make mistakes. If it is a company that any idiot could run, that is regarded as a great positive sign 'because sooner or later any idiot probably is going to be running it'.[33]

Indicators of owner orientated management

It is crucially important that the managers are operating the business in the interests of the owners and not for themselves. Lynch used a number of indicators for judging the degree of owner-orientation.

Managers should be penny-pinchers in the executive suite: 'the extravagance of any corporate office is directly proportional to management's reluctance to reward shareholders'.[34] Lynch thought it was great when he visited Taco Bell's headquarters and found it stuck behind a bowling alley. It was a 'grim little bunker'.[35] At Crown, Cork and Seal the president's office had faded linoleum and shabby furniture. The office did not overlook areas of green lawn, but the can lines. These are companies with the right priorities. 'Rich earnings and a cheap headquarters is a great combination'.[36] The warning flashes appear if the executive suite has fine antiques and expensive wood panelling.

Good management treats staff with respect and fairness. 'They reject the corporate caste system that creates white-collar Brahmins and blue-collar untouchables. Their workers are well paid and have a stake in the companies' future'.[37]

A company that is reluctant to reward shareholders by buying back shares or raising the dividend when it has cash flow surplus to its investment needs is likely to have poor management. Reducing the number of shares can have a wonderful effect on earnings per share and the stock price. Some managements prefer to expand the company with foolish acquisitions at inflated prices. Lynch calls this disworsification. Hersh Shefrin tells a story about a visit Lynch made to Apple Computers, one of the stocks in the Magellan portfolio. Bob Saltmarsh, Apple's treasurer, says that he found Lynch very different from other fund managers. 'His questions were different. They were more focused and insightful. In particular, he stayed away from techno-questions, and told me: "I only buy what I understand".'[38] Apple had been through a good period, sales had doubled and it had $700–800 million in cash. Lynch asked the same question nine or ten different ways. Saltmarsh was uncertain as to what Lynch really wanted to know so he asked him just what he was getting at. 'Will you be another G.M.? Is that money burning a hole in your pocket? Will you stick to your knitting, or will you go off and try something that you don't understand.'[39]

Lynch liked to see managers buying their company's stocks. 'When insiders are buying like crazy, you can be certain that at a minimum, the company will not go bankrupt in the next six months.'[40] The ownership of a large quantity (relative to salary) of stock encourages managers to make rewarding shareholders the first priority. The converse, managers selling stocks, should not be taken to be a negative signal, however. There are many reasons for selling – school fees, house purchase etc. – but there is only one reason that insiders buy: 'They think the stocks price is undervalued and will eventually go up'.[41]

Financial strength

Investors should never contemplate investing in a company without understanding its finances. A strong balance sheet is essential. 'The biggest loses in stocks come from companies with poor balance sheets.'[42] The first test is to see if the company is solvent – that is, does it have the ability to pay debts as they fall due. Lynch looked for quite a large margin of safety in this and preferred companies with little or no debt and a lot of cash. 'More than anything else, it's debt that determines which companies will survive and which will go bankrupt in a crisis.'[43] He paid particular attention to the debt structure as well as the overall amount of debt. To have most of the debt in short-term loan form or with capital repayment dates bunched together can be dangerous. If debt is increasing relative to cash that is a sign of deteriorating prosperity. If, however, the amount of cash is growing while the debt levels are static or falling it is a sign of strength. Cash exceeding debt is very favourable.

> ...... **Never contemplate investing in a company without understanding its finances.** ......

Other key information, available from an examination of the accounts, includes the extent to which both sales *and* earnings per share are moving in the right direction. Also, you can observe whether the firm produces enough cash to invest in all the potential value enhancing projects without needing to ask shareholders for money. If a company needs large amounts of cash injected in order that it can make cash, you, as a stockholder, aren't going to get very far. Another bad sign is the piling up of inventories: 'when inventories grow faster than sales, it's a red flag'.[44]

Low price

Lynch wrote that valuing a stock as part of a business is no more difficult than analyzing the value of a local launderette, pharmacy or apartment building. 'Although it's easy to forget sometimes, a share of stock is not a lottery ticket. It's part ownership of a business.'[45] In the same way that you would not pay a large multiple of last year's earnings for a launderette unless you anticipate sustained high growth in those earnings, you should reject stocks on high price – earnings ratios, unless future earnings growth is estimated to be high:

> With very few exceptions, an extremely high p/e ratio is a handicap to a stock, in the same way that extra weight in the saddle is a handicap to a racehorse. A company with a high p/e must have incredible earnings growth to justify the high price that has been put on the stock.[46]

Lynch offers a rule of thumb to judge price-earnings ratios:

> the p/e ratio of any company that's fairly priced will equal its growth rate [in earnings]… if the p/e ratio is less than the growth rate, you may have found yourself a bargain… in general, a p/e ratio that's half the growth rate is very positive and one that is twice the growth rate is very negative.[47]

When thinking about these words we must bear in mind that Lynch was investing in an era of relatively high inflation, and therefore nominal growth rates would have been in double figures. In an environment in which inflation is in the region of 2–3 per cent we cannot expect nominal earnings growth for the average stock in the long run to be more than nominal GDP growth, i.e. 2–3 per cent per year of real growth plus 2–3 per cent of inflation. In such an environment Lynch's rule of thumb becomes unusable. What we can say is that a niche investor would avoid stocks with high P/Es relative to medium term growth estimates.

Lynch provided a list of the five basic ways in which a corporation can increase earnings:

- costs can be reduced
- prices raised
- new markets entered
- greater penetration of existing markets
- closure, revitalization or disposal of losing operations.

Fundamentally, earnings growth depends on the strategic positioning of the firm and the skills of its managers. These are qualitative factors, difficult to translate into neat mathematical estimates of future earnings. Understanding the firm's competitive environment and the ability of managers is vital to any evaluation of a stock.

Factors which help produce a low stock price relative to future earnings include that it is a boring business overlooked by the Wall Street analysts and fund managers, or, it could simply be too small to register on their radar.

Once all the information needed for the analysis (economic franchise, management quality, financial strength and low price) is gathered Lynch would impose an important discipline on himself and his subordinates. He would require that the mass of detail be boiled down to a few salient points. The key variables leading to a buy recommendation had to be presented in a 'two minute monologue'. Long reports with pages of appendices are all very well, but the art of investment is being able to home-in on the crucially important factors – and these are easy to get across in two minutes, if the case is strong enough. If more than two minutes is needed then perhaps the investment is too complicated and clouded in uncertainties to be considered any further.

OTHER FACTORS IN MANAGING A PORTFOLIO

Diversification

The Magellan Fund held up to 1,400 different stocks at one time. It had 15,000 different stocks over the 13 years it was controlled by Peter Lynch. Does this mean that he was in favour of a high degree of diversification? Not a bit of it. Lynch was largely forced into holding so many stocks because the fund was so large and the SEC rules insisted that the fund not hold more than 10 per cent of the stocks of a given company, and not more than 5 per cent of the fund's assets in any one company. Generally, half of the fund was invested in 100 stocks and two-thirds in 200 stocks. Only 1 per cent of the money was split between 500 stocks which were then monitored for possible additional investment later. The irony of Lynch's position is that he ran an extremely diversified fund, but maintained that investors (those managing funds of thousands, or millions, of dollars, rather than billions) should diversify to only a small degree. The exact extent of that diversification varies in his writing, but it was never more than twelve stocks.

Consider these quotes:

> The smallest investor can follow the Rule of Five and limit the portfolio to five issues. If just one of those is a 10-bagger and the other four combined go nowhere, you've still tripled your money.[48]

> The part-time stock picker probably has time to follow 8–12 companies, and to buy and sell shares as conditions warrant. There don't have to be more than five companies in the portfolio at any one time.[49]

The crucial consideration is allowing enough time to be able to develop and maintain a high level of knowledge about each of the companies. 'Owning stocks is like having children – don't get involved with more than you can handle.'[50] All stocks in the portfolio have to pass some stiff tests and you will not know if they pass the tests unless you are able to spend time analyzing them. The private investor simply will not have the analytical edge over Wall Street if he/she spreads intellectual resources thinly. The point at which you step over the boundary between investing in an informed way and speculating is different for each person:

> Maybe that's a single stock, or maybe it's a dozen stocks. ... There's no use diversifying into unknown companies just for the sake of diversity. A foolish

diversity is the hobgoblin of small investors. That said, it isn't safe to own just one stock, because in spite of your best efforts, the one you choose might be the victim of unforeseen circumstances. In small portfolios I'd be comfortable owning between three and ten stocks.[51]

Know the facts

When the investor takes the heart-stopping, and, at the same time, exhilarating decision to invest a large proportion of a fund in a stock, he or she will often hear the voices of the doubters shouting that they are wrong. The only way to overcome the fear of going against the crowd of naysayers is to know the story better than they do. The investor must check and recheck the facts in the light of the negative comments about the company. When reassured that he or she is not being foolishly optimistic then it is time to press ahead with faith that what is being bought is going to be a winner.

Continue to follow the stories

The investor must be prepared to continue to monitor the stocks held in the portfolio. Following a buy-and-forget policy can be disastrous. There are two basic questions to ask of a stock: '(1) is the stock still attractively priced relative to earnings, and (2) what is happening in the company to make the earnings go up?'[52] By learning more about the stocks you hold you can avoid making the mistake that so many investors make of selling too early. These investors experience the thrill of the price doubling or tripling and conclude that it can't possibly go any higher. But this is based on no more than the fact that it has risen a lot already and has a high (historical) P/E ratio. In reality, it is perfectly possible for a good stock to continue to advance even after an impressive rise. If the story is still strong, that is, earnings continue to improve and the fundamentals haven't changed, the stocks may yet rise a further five- or ten-fold. It simply is not possible to say, when a stock is bought, whether it will be a 6-bagger or a 12-bagger. This depends on the evolving competitive position of the firm and the quality of its management. If these fundamentals remain robust then the story is intact and you should hold on.

There is another sound reason for continuing to develop your understanding of the company and its industry. Over a period of time you will learn the key influences on earnings; what can lead to permanent impairment and what is merely a hiccup. Recessions will come and go; investing fashions will come and go. If you really understand the companies in your portfolio you will begin to recognize when the market has over-blown some temporary negative factor. Perhaps a general decline in the whole market has indiscriminately dragged down even the best stocks. Perhaps an event specific to your stocks has led to abandonment by the fickle mass of investors. Whatever the cause of the temporary price fall it provides a wonderful opportunity for the informed investor to add more stocks to the portfolio at bargain prices. 'The best stock to buy may be the one you already own.'[53]

Regular routine

There will be times when the fears of the generality of investors will get to you, and you will be scared of buying or scared into selling. A bulwark against such waves of emotion is to get yourself into a regular routine of investing and to be determined to follow the best practice no matter what. There will be years when you make returns of over 30 per cent, but there will be years when you lose 10 per cent. You have to have the strength of character to accept that this is part of the scheme of things. If you are going through a bad patch, do not reject the tried and proven method of stocks selection in favour of the current flavour of the month on Wall Street. If you expect to make 30 per cent returns year after year you can get yourself into a terrible mess. You will become frustrated in down years with your stocks. Your sense of impatience may cause you to sell your stocks at precisely the wrong moment. 'Or worse, you may take unnecessary risks in the pursuit of illusory payoffs. It's only by sticking to a strategy through good years and bad that you'll maximize your long-term gains.'[54]

Investing in the stock market is not scientific. Successful investors accept periodic losses and unexpected occurrences. Bad breaks will be given to all. The wise investor takes them on the chin and goes on searching for the next stock. 'If seven out of ten of my stocks perform as expected, then I'm delighted. If six out of ten of my stocks perform as expected, then I'm thankful. Six out of ten is all it takes to produce an enviable record on Wall Street.'[55] Many investors think of themselves as long-term holders, but in too many cases the next serious market decline (or rise in stock price) turns them quickly into panicky short-term investors, others become impatient as it seems that it is taking for ever for something to happen to their stock. The moment they give up and sell is the moment something wonderful happens.

> Success or failure will depend on your ability to ignore the worries of the world long enough to allow your investments to succeed. It isn't the head, but the stomach that determines the fate of the stock picker[56].... You can be the world's greatest expert on balance sheets or p/e ratios, but without faith, you'll tend to believe the negative headlines.....What sort of faith am I talking about? Faith that America will survive, that people will continue to get up in the morning and put their pants on one leg at a time, and that corporations that make the pants will turn a profit for the shareholders.[57]

WHAT HE AVOIDS

Lynch has a lot to say about market timing – all of it negative. He regards it as impossible to predict the direction of the market over one or two years. He also rejects technical analysis. 'I don't pay much attention to the science of wiggles.'[58] He has witnessed some amazing rises and falls in the market. Even with his vigilance and experience he says that he was unable to predict them – trying to do so is futile. He agrees with Warren Buffett that the short-term market ups and downs are irrelevant to good investing except that they might offer the opportunity to buy at a bargain price if other investors are being foolish.

> Every year I talk to the executives of a thousand companies, and I can't avoid hearing from the various gold bugs, interest rate disciples, Federal reserve watchers, and fiscal mystics quoted in the newspapers. Thousands of experts study overbought indicators, oversold indicators, head-and-shoulder patterns, put-call ratios, the Fed's policy as money supply, foreign investment, the movement of constellations through the heavens, and the moss on oak trees, and they can't predict markets with any useful consistency, any more than the gizzard squeezers could tell the Roman Emperors when the Huns would attack.... All the major advances and declines have been surprises to me.[59]

The investor must concentrate on the underlying business of the company in question and not to waste time trying to achieve the impossible. Buying or selling on the basis of predictions of market movements is likely to result in very poor performance, as the investor is likely to be pessimistic and optimistic at precisely the wrong time. These types of investors let emotion rule. They move in and out of moods of concern, complacency and capitulation at the wrong times:

He's concerned after the market has dropped or the economy has seemed to falter, which keeps him from buying good companies at bargain prices. Then after he buys at higher prices, he gets complacent because his stocks are going up. This is precisely the time he ought to be concerned enough to check the fundamentals, but he isn't. Then finally, when his stocks fall on hard times and the prices fall below what he paid, he capitulates and sells in a snit.[60]

If you need another reason for not trading in and out of the market on the basis of prediction of market trend then you need look no further than the sheer cost of all that trading – the sight of brokers and tax authorities rubbing their hands in glee is not one an investor should encourage.

Lynch is equally scathing about the work of the majority of the 60,000 economists in the US. He says that if they could be successful at forecasting two recessions in a row they'd be millionaires by now. 'As some perceptive person once said, if all the economists of the world were laid end to end, it wouldn't be a bad thing.'[61] He does make an exception for those economists who get their hands dirty by examining the nitty-gritty of industry activity, e.g. Ed Hyman looked at scrap prices, inventories and railroad car deliveries.

> Avoid the hottest stocks in the hottest industry.

Avoid the hottest stocks in the hottest industry. Those stocks receiving vast amounts of favourable publicity are often supported by nothing more than 'hope and thin air'.[62] Prices can fall just as quickly as they rose if the stock price has lost touch with the known landmarks of value. Those stocks which are not yet in the full glare of publicity but which are being whispered about by brokers and others with a weather eye out for the latest craze – the whiz bang stories, the high-tech start-ups and the bio-technological miracles – are also to be avoided. The 'whisper stocks' (those in fashionable sectors) seem to have an almost hypnotic affect on stock punters. They usually have no substance – all sizzle and no steak. 'The stockpicker is relieved of the burden of checking earnings and so forth because usually there are no earnings... there is no shortage of microscopes, PhDs, high hopes, and cash from the stock sale.'[63]

Lynch tries to remind himself, when tempted, that if the company really is that good it will be a great investment next year and the year after that. When the company has an established trading record it will be possible to see the prospects more clearly. Even companies that have proven themselves can be ten-baggers: 'when in doubt, tune in later'.[64]

Those investors that automatically sell the stocks that rise in price, but hold on to those that fall hoping that they will come out even receive particular criticism. This action is described as 'pulling out the flowers and watering the weeds'. Equally silly is the *automatic* selling of losers and holding on to winners. 'Both strategies fail because they're tied to the current movement of the stock price as an indicator of the company's fundamental value… [which] tells us absolutely nothing about the future prospects of a company.'[65] A falling price for a stock you own is only a tragedy if you sell at the lower price. If the prospects for the underlying business remain good, then a fall presents a wonderful opportunity to buy at bargain prices. 'If you can't convince yourself "when I'm down 25 per cent, I'm a buyer" and banish for ever the fatal thought, "when I'm down 25 per cent, I'm a seller", then you'll never make a decent profit in stocks.'[66] It follows that stop loss orders are illogical – so, to have a rule that any stocks down by 10 per cent will be sold will mean losing some excellent niche companies and wasting a lot of analytical effort.

Investors should never be naïve contrarians – always zigging when the market is zagging. Investors should be intelligent contrarians and pick their moment to zig when the story on a stock indicates that the market has got it wrong. 'The true contrarian … buys stocks that nobody cares about, and especially those that make Wall Street yawn.'[67]

Never buy a stock that has been promoted as the next of something. The next Microsoft or the next GE never turns out to be as great as the original. 'In my experience the next of something almost never is.'[68]

Another area of the financial market that can be time consuming and an expensive distraction is the derivatives markets. 'I've never bought a future nor an option in my entire investing career…. Warren Buffett thinks that stocks future and options ought to be outlawed, and I agree with him.'[69]

Never look at other investors' triumphs and regard them as your loss – 'If only you had bought into that stock you would have made 250 per cent return'. Don't allow this to fester in your mind because, if you do, there is a possibility that you will try to catch-up by buying risky stocks which offer fast rewards but which do not comply with sound investing criteria.

Do not reject a company from further consideration simply because the liquidity of the stock is less than perfect. The vast majority of stocks trade only a few thousand shares a day – many don't trade at all for a number of days at a time. If you confine your purchases to those that have millions of shares trading everyday you will be excluding 99 per cent of companies:

In stocks, as in romance, ease of divorce is not a sound basis for commitment. If you've chosen wisely to begin with, you won't want a divorce. And if you haven't, you're in a mess no matter what. All the liquidity in the world isn't going to save you from pain, suffering, and probably a loss of money.[70]

WHEN TO SELL

Lynch's view on when to sell is easy to state, but much more difficult to implement. The rule is to keep the investment, and even add to it, so long as the story remains sound. That is, the prospects for earnings growth indicate that the price is not over extended. 'When you've found the right stock and bought it, all the evidence tells you it's going higher, and everything is working in your direction, then it's a shame if you sell.'[71] There are at least two difficulties with this, both of them psychological. The first is if the stock price rises, the second is if the stock price is static or falls!

If it rises there is the tempting thought that you must cash-in your chips before it is too late. 'It's normally harder to stick with a winning stock after the price goes up than it is to believe in it after the price goes down.'[72] Just because a stock price has increased it does not mean it is due for a fall – the fundamentals are the determining factor, not stock price history. To cash-in at the first significant rise is to never have a ten-bagger. If the stock falls, or remains in the doldrums, a remarkable degree of patience is needed when everyone else declares that you shouldn't have bought it in the first place – what if they are right and you have made a mistake? If 12 or 24 months go by and the market has still not seen the virtues of the company, even the strongest willed and brightest analyst is likely to start to have doubts and waver. However, they should take heart, even Lynch frequently had to grit his teeth and wait for the rest of the world to recognize the promising fundamentals of a company. 'I'm accustomed to hanging around with a stock when the price is going nowhere. Most of the money I make is in the third or fourth year that I've owned something.'[73]

It all comes back to a determination to keep informed about the evolving story of the firm. Only if you are knowledgeable can you make sound decisions, including the selling decision.

If the fundamentals deteriorate and the price has increased then it may be time to contemplate switching money into a better prospect. The paradoxical combination of the price rising dramatically while the story worsens can occur in those cases where Wall Street starts to get excited too late.

'If forty Wall Street analysts are giving the stock their highest recommendation, 60 per cent of the shares are held by institutions, and three national magazines have fawned over the CEO, then it's definitely time to think about selling.'[74]

DIFFICULTIES AND DRAWBACKS OF THIS APPROACH

A superficial reading of Lynch's work makes investing sound deceptively easy. And indeed, he is very encouraging to the private investor. Beneath his basically optimistic message, however, is the constant call to understand both the business and the management thoroughly. This requires quite a serious commitment of time and mental energy. Having said that, it is clear that Lynch truly believes that it's not beyond the reach of ordinary small investors with reasonable intelligence and determination to outperform Wall Street. Perhaps they cannot achieve Lynch's amazing annual returns; they will have a higher proportion of misses to hits than he would, but, nevertheless they can do better than placing their savings in a managed mutual fund or a tracker. This positive note is struck on the assumption that the business and its environment are properly analyzed. At a minimum it would be necessary to have a knowledge of the principles of corporate strategic analysis discussed in Chapters 9 and 10.

As well as knowledge, the investor needs to have higher order personal qualities. It is very optimistic to say these are attainable by all, even after some years of investing experience.

> This is the most important question of all. It seems to me that the list of qualities ought to include patience, self-reliance, common sense, a tolerance for pain, open-mindedness, detachment, persistence, humility, flexibility, a willingness to do independent research, an equal willingness to admit to mistakes, and the ability to ignore general panic.... It's also important to be able to make decisions without complete or perfect information. Things are almost never clear on Wall Street, or when they are, then it's too late to profit from them. The scientific mind that needs to know all the data will be thwarted here. And finally, it's crucial to be able to resist your human nature and your 'gut feelings'. It's the rare investor who doesn't secretly harbour the conviction that he or she has a knack for divining stock prices.[75]

Whew! what a list of qualities. How many of us can claim this many virtues? Still, imperfect man can advance if he at least strives to be virtuous. Even Lynch frequently failed to live up to the ideal he has placed before us. His message is pick yourself up, learn from mistakes, and try to do better next time.

The investor needs to develop the capacity to delicately blend the quantitative and qualitative techniques of evaluation. To have talent in both areas is demanding.

> Stock picking is both an art and a science, but too much of either is a dangerous thing. A person infatuated with measurement, who has his head stuck in the sand of balance sheets, is not likely to succeed…. On the other hand, stock picking as art can be equally unrewarding. By art, I mean the realm of intuition and passion and right-brain chemistry… [believing in the] knack…[or following a] hunch. Those who hold this viewpoint tend to prove its validity by neglecting to do research and 'playing' the market, which results in more losses…. My stock picking method, which involves elements of art and science plus legwork, hasn't changed in 20 years.[76]

It has to be accepted that investment is a risky activity. The successful investors tilt the odds in their favour by trying to stick to tried and tested principles and to avoid making losses due to a slip in emotional control. They have been working on their knowledge and character traits for a lot longer than the rest of us. They do not reject the notion that you or I could emulate them and perform better than the average Wall Streeter, but they do insist that we get to work straightaway, and then, like the swan paddling away famously under the water, we too can serenely progress and make stock picking look easy.

> **It has to be accepted that investment is a risky activity.**

Of course, if you don't fancy all that hard work you could always approach investment the way Will Rogers did: 'don't gamble; take all your savings and buy some good stock and hold it till it goes up, then sell it. If it don't go up, don't buy it'.[77]

SUMMARY OF PETER LYNCH'S APPROACH

- The private investor can outperform the professional fund manager. Private investors have a number of advantages:

- they can be unconventional in their stock picking;
- they don't have to follow institutional rules and regulations;
- they can avoid snap judgments and wholesale taboos;
- they can buy small company stocks, where the multiple-baggers come from;
- they can take time to understand every stock in the portfolio;
- they don't have to be trend followers;
- they are able to observe companies with great growth prospects long before the professionals hear about them – in the shopping mall, at work, etc.;
- they can buy into boring and unpleasant companies at bargain prices.

- Characteristics of good niche stocks – (definition: a niche stock is a fast growing small to medium-size firm operating in a niche business with high potential – aggressive enterprises growing at 20–25 per cent per annum):
  - strong economic franchise:
    - slow growing industry, fast growing company;
    - limited competition;
    - high barriers to entry;
    - plenty of room to grow;
    - simple business;
  - owner-orientated management:
    - penny pinching in the executive suite;
    - good labour relations;
    - surplus cashflow returned to stockholders;
    - managers owning and buying stock;
  - financial strength:
    - strong balance sheet;
    - sales and earnings per share growth and consistency;
    - free cashflow;
    - low inventory growth;

- low price:
  - low price-earnings ratio;
  - boring business;
  - little interest from analysts and institutional fund managers.
- Other factors in managing a portfolio:
  - stop diversifying if you are unable to maintain a high level of knowledge about each company in the portfolio – maximum of 12, more likely 3–8, companies;
  - really know the facts so that you have the strength to go against the crowd;
  - continue to follow the stories to make sure: that the fundamentals are still in place; that you don't sell too early; you add more stock should the price fall to a bargain level;
  - stick to your regular routine. Be consistent and don't reject a good investment policy during bad patches.
- What to avoid:
  - market timing;
  - technical analysis/chartism;
  - macro economic analysis;
  - hot stocks;
  - whisper stocks;
  - pulling out the flowers and watering the weeds;
  - selling losers and holding winners automatically;
  - stop loss orders;
  - being a naïve contrarian;
  - derivatives;
  - regarding other investor triumphs as your loss, and playing catch-up;
  - being obsessed with liquidity.
- Selling policy:
  - never sell while the story remains strong (whether the stock has risen or fallen since purchase);
  - if the fundamentals deteriorate relative to the price, so that the story becomes very weak, then sell.

Notes

1   Achstatter, G., 'Fidelity's Peter Lynch. How He Conducted the Research That Made His Fund Best.' *Investor's Business Daily* (2 February 1998).
2   Lynch, P. (1990), p. 30.
3   *Ibid.*, p. 32.
4   *Ibid.*, p. 33.
5   *Ibid.* pp. 34–5.
6   *Ibid.*, pp. 13–14.
7   *Ibid.*, p. 40.
8   Lynch, P. (1994), p. 19.
9   Lynch, P. (1990), pp. 43–4.
10 *Ibid.*, p. 45.
11 *Ibid.*, p. 45.
12 *Ibid.*, p. 49.
13 *Ibid.*, p. 43.
14 *Ibid.*, p. 98.
15 *Ibid.*, p. 24.
16 *Ibid.*, p. 41.
17 *Ibid.*, p. 40.
18 *Ibid.*, p. 14.
19 *Ibid.*, p. 50.
20 *Ibid.*, p. 84.
21 *Ibid.*, p. 182.
22 *Ibid.*, p. 19.
23 *Ibid.*, p. 19.
24 *Ibid.*, p. 19.
25 *Ibid.*, p. 19.
26 *Ibid.*, p. 95.
27 *Ibid.*, p. 123.
28 *Ibid.*, p. 108.
29 *Ibid.*, p. 131.
30 *Ibid.*, p. 144.
31 Lynch, P. (1994), p. 182.
32 Lynch, P. (1990), p. 131.
33 *Ibid.*, p. 121.
34 Lynch, P. (1994), p. 86.
35 Lynch, P. (1990), p. 188.
36 *Ibid.*, p. 189.
37 Lynch, P. (1994), p. 183.
38 Shefrin, H. (2000), p. 166.
39 *Ibid.*, p. 166.
40 Lynch, P. (1990), p. 134.
41 *Ibid.*, p. 136.

42 Lynch, P. (1994), p. 306.
43 Lynch, P. (1990), p. 201.
44 *Ibid.*, p. 215.
45 *Ibid.*, p. 156.
46 *Ibid.*, p. 165.
47 *Ibid.*, p. 198.
48 Lynch, P. (1994), p. 142.
49 *Ibid.*, p. 306.
50 *Ibid.*, pp. 305–6.
51 Lynch, P. (1990), p. 242.
52 Lynch, P. (1994), p. 284.
53 *Ibid.*, p. 129.
54 Lynch, P. (1990), p. 240.
55 *Ibid.*, pp. 61–2.
56 Lynch, P. (1994), p. 19.
57 *Ibid.*, p. 45.
58 Lynch, P. (1990), p. 252.
59 *Ibid.*, p. 74.
60 *Ibid.*, p. 70.
61 *Ibid.*, p. 75.
62 *Ibid.*, p. 141.
63 *Ibid.*, pp. 151–2.
64 *Ibid.*, p. 152.
65 *Ibid.*, p. 245.
66 *Ibid.*, p. 246.
67 *Ibid.*, p. 71.
68 *Ibid.*, p. 145.
69 *Ibid.*, pp. 277–80.
70 Lynch, P. (1994), p. 120.
71 Lynch, P. (1990), p. 253.
72 *Ibid.*, p. 254.
73 *Ibid.*, p. 272.
74 *Ibid.*, p. 259.
75 *Ibid.*, p. 69.
76 Lynch, P. (1994), pp. 140–1.
77 Lynch, P. (1990), p. 37.

2

John Neff's sophisticated low price-earnings ratio investing

John Neff is a value investor. When he managed the Windsor Fund, his investment philosophy emphasized the importance of a low stock price relative to earnings. However, his approach required a stock to pass a number of tests beside the price-earnings criteria. These additional hurdles turn his approach from simple low price-earnings investing to a sophisticated one.

John Neff was in charge of the Windsor Fund for 31 years. It beat the market for 25 of those 31 years. He took control in 1964, and retired in 1995. Windsor was the largest equity mutual in the United States when it closed its doors to new investors in 1985. Each dollar invested in 1964 had returned $56 by 1995, compared with $22 for the S&P 500. The total return for Windsor, at 5,546.5 per cent, outpaced the S&P 500 by more than two to one. This was an additional return on the market of 3.15 percentage points a year after expenses. Before expenses the out-performance was 3.5 percentage points.[1] This is a very good performance especially when you consider that average fund return after expenses was less than on the S&P 500.

Neff's ability to stand against the tide of conventional market opinion and make up his own mind about a stock stems from his early experiences as well as his capacity for hard work. Even at a young age he was regarded as, to put it charitably, someone with a mind of his own. His 1st grade teacher expressed it less charitably and described him as pugnacious. 'I was never inclined to back down from an argument, even when confronted by the mantle of authority. My mother, in fact, used to claim that I ought to be a lawyer because I would argue with a signpost.'[2]

The family business went bankrupt and he learned three important lessons at a young age: '(1) when it comes to money, emotional attachment can fool you; (2) just because a company is down it is not always a wise investment, and (3) excessive drinking was not a business or a personal virtue'.[3] The first two are certainly key elements in his later investment success. The third applies in any walk of life.

In the fifth grade he traded baseball cards. Bidding for the most desirable cards could go sky high. He observed the emotional momentum or mania and thought it bizarre. Children 'bought' in the expectation of being able to sell to someone else for a higher price. He also noticed that the cards with the largest rises eventually fell the farthest – sooner or later.

In 1950 he joined his father's tiny company selling mechanical equipment to automobile dealers, service stations and farmers. This brought home the lesson that 'you don't need glamour to make a buck. Indeed, if you can find a dull business that makes money, it is less likely to attract competition'[4] – echoes of Lynch's observations?

The Navy years (1951–3) were also very instructive – mostly for the poker games after pay day. The winning sailors were the ones who developed a consistent approach, based on a good knowledge of the odds. They were strong-willed enough not to be lured into trying to win the big pots unless the probabilities were firmly on their side.

As a very able college student (1953–5) Neff took two courses taught by Dr Sidney Robbins, a disciple of Benjamin Graham (Graham is the subject of the next two chapters). Neff was able to continue his education with a degree in banking and finance from Western Reserve University while working for National City Bank in Cleveland as a securities analyst in the late 1950s. He admits that at the outset his knowledge of investment was slight. However, he proved to be a quick learner and was rapidly promoted. Eventually he grew frustrated at the restrictions placed on creative stock picking and was persuaded to move to Windsor, as a securities analyst, in 1963.

The Windsor mutual fund was downtrodden – investors were bolting for the exits. The $75 million fund had concentrated on 'small supposed growth companies without sufficient attention to the durability of growth.... [It] rode the stocks too long and got killed'.[5] After 11 months he became the first individual portfolio manager. He created an impact by taking outsized positions where he saw promising returns: 'You can diversify yourself into mediocrity'.[6]

When he retired in 1995 he reflected on his mother's comment that he would argue with a signpost. He said that he had argued with the stock market his whole career. 'Happily,' he wrote, 'I won more arguments with the market than I lost.'[7]

PRINCIPLES

So, what are the essential differences between the principles followed by most market participants and those followed by Neff?

He was always on the lookout for out-of-favour, overlooked or misunderstood stocks. These nuggets of gold always stood on low price-earnings ratios. Not only that; their prospects for earnings growth was good. The market tends to allow itself to be swept along with fads, fashions and flavours of the month. This leads to over-valuation of those stocks regarded as shooting stars, and to the under-valuation of those which prevailing wisdom deems unexciting, but which are fundamentally good stocks. Investors become caught in the clutch of group-think and *en mass* ignore solid companies. Bad news tends to weigh more heavily than good news as the investor's malaise deepens.

The way Neff saw it, if you could buy a stock where the negatives were largely known, then any good news that comes as a surprise can have a profoundly positive effect on the stock price. On the other hand if you buy into a growth story where great things are expected and built in to the price, the slightest hint of bad news can take the sizzle out of the stock.

Success in sophisticated low P/E investing requires a number of character traits. Courage is needed to buy down-and-out stocks. Other investors stare at you blankly as they try to understand your odd behaviour. You have to be prepared to accept the risk of embarrassment (a) of being different, and (b) of failing unconventionally. To fail conventionally in a particular investment is considered acceptable, but to be unconventional, and thus not to pull it off is to be regarded as dumb. Most people would rather stick with conventional wisdom and not risk ridicule:

> If you take a poll on the subject, investors will routinely claim they have sufficient courage to make an investment, no matter how unpopular. Such claims are typical of human nature, but they don't often bear scrutiny. Anyone can recognize a bargain in retrospect and then take credit later for spotting it. When shares of a stock change hands for 30 times earnings, who doesn't recall the day when shares fetched only 12 times earnings? But where were the buyers then? Most were cowering in fear of the latest news reports or piling onto the speediest growth-stock bandwagon even if its wheels were about to fall off.[8]

Perseverance is another key characteristic. To regularly, and over a long period, go against prevailing wisdom goes against instinct. Perseverance, fortitude and patience are also needed to cope with the delay there may be in benefiting from the market coming around to your point of view about a stock. Sometimes years can pass before other investors realize their mistake and start to appreciate the virtues of a good, solid company with steadily rising earnings. This is particularly true in bull markets. Neff suffered very poor relative performance in the Nifty Fifty era of the early 1970s. Investors chased up the prices of these glamour stocks that you could 'buy and forget about'. The hype came to an end with the 1973 crash. Neff kept his nerve in the up and down, and produced a sparkling performance over the long haul: 'if you can't roll with the hits and you're in too big a hurry, you might as well keep your money in a mattress'.[9]

> **Perseverance is another key characteristic.**

Sober reflection and sense of history of stock market behaviour is needed to give the investor the perspective required to assess and take intelligent risks. Without such an anchor point you are at the mercy of the winds of fashion. Over time you start to recognize the market's personality. 'It is irrational and unsentimental. It is cantankerous and hostile. At times it is forgiving and congenial. The market has good days and bad days, good years and bad years.'[10]

Neff's style of investing does not rely on a few stocks doing spectacularly well. Neff would occasionally hit home runs, but for the most part 'our scoring relied chiefly on base hits'.[11] To go home winners, investors need to be consistent and not to expect too much of any one shot. Neff used a tennis analogy to explain the requirements of consistency, persistence and patience. Some players are extremely talented and are able to adopt a playing style to win a match. They have brilliant stroke play or a winning serve, say. Most players are not like that. The best strategy for these individuals is not to try to play fantastic tennis – to go all out to win with stunning volleys. No, their best hope is to win by not losing; to keep the ball in play long enough for the opponent to make mistakes. 'Investment success does not require glamour stocks or bull markets. Judgement and fortitude were our prerequisites. Judgement singles out opportunities, fortitude enables you to live with this while the rest of the world scramble in another direction…to us ugly stocks were often beautiful.'[12]

Key elements

Windsor usually bought stocks with P/E ratios 40 to 60 per cent below the market. If these stocks also have the promise of steady earnings growth there is the potential for the appreciation to be 'turbocharged': first the P/E ratio increases when the market eventually realizes that these are good companies with solid earnings; second, the rising earnings justifies an even higher price, and the stock can appreciate 50 to 100 per cent. Imagine two companies, A and B. Both have earnings of $1 per share. However, A is a well known, thoroughly analyzed firm and so stands on a P/E ratio of 20. Company B is overlooked and in an industrial sector that is currently out-of-favour. It has a P/E ratio of 10. Not only do both firms have the same current earnings, but your rigorous analysis tells you that their earnings growth will be the same, at 8 per cent. So, after one year earnings at company A and B are both $1.08. The market continues to value A at P/E ratio of 20 and therefore the share price rises to $21.60, an 8 per cent appreciation.

Over the year the market has gradually come to realize that it has over-reacted to the difficulties in company B's industry. A re-rating has taken place. Now the market is prepared to pay a multiple of 15 on recent earnings. If earnings are now $1.08 the stock rises to $16.2. This is a 62 per cent appreciation in one year! Now, not all investments in a low P/E ratio portfolio are going to turn out to be as successful as company B stock, but evidently, it is possible to succeed in a sufficient number of cases to outperform the market. The attraction of low P/E ratio stocks is not just the potential for upside participation. They also offer good protection on the downside. Investors have forced the stock price to absorb all the bad news and so there is little positive expectation built into the price. Moderately poor financial performance is unlikely to lead to a further penalty. But any indication of improvement may lead to fresh interest. If you can sell into that fresh interest, when other investors fully recognize the underlying strengths you should produce an impressive return.

It is not enough simply to invest mechanically in all stocks with low P/Es. Rigorous analysis is also needed. For a start you need to have confidence in the earnings numbers. Accountants' numbers, such as balance sheet values and profit statements are notorious for their malleability. The analyst needs to assess the quality of the numbers presented, and then to make any adjustments considered necessary before any judgement can be applied. It may be essential to counter accounting manoeuvres by obtaining independent corroborating information. Discrepancies must be identified and explained.

The key to success in this type of investing lies in being able to distinguish between shares selling at a low P/E ratio because they are out-of-favour, overlooked or misunderstood, and those which are moribund companies with lacklustre prospects – see Fig. 2.1.

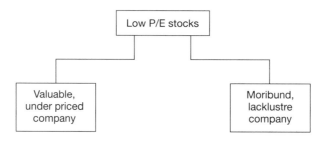

Figure 2.1   Two types of low P/E stocks

It is in this area that the sophisticated P/E ratio investor shows his/her superiority to the simple and naïve low P/E ratio investor. Figure 2.2 shows the factors that would be examined in a rigorous framework.

Modest earnings growth

Companies showing earnings growth of at least 7 per cent a year, while standing on a low P/E ratio are definitely candidates for further consideration. Historic earnings per share figures are easily obtainable, as are analysts' projections. These are a good starting point, but you need to apply your own experienced judgement because even the best Wall Street analyst has to admit that forward earnings estimates are no more than educated guesses. Companies need to show sturdy track records – preferably with persistent quarterly increases. The investor also needs to be assured that there is logical justification to expect sustainable growth at a reasonable pace. A rate of growth which is fast enough to catch the attention of the generality of investors (eventually), but not so fast as to make the stock a risky growth stock. Neff usually placed a ceiling of 20 per cent 'higher growth rates entailed too much risk for our appetite'.[13]

He tended to forecast earnings growth for five years. He regarded this as the long term for financial results, because of the potential for the competitive landscape to change within a five-year horizon.

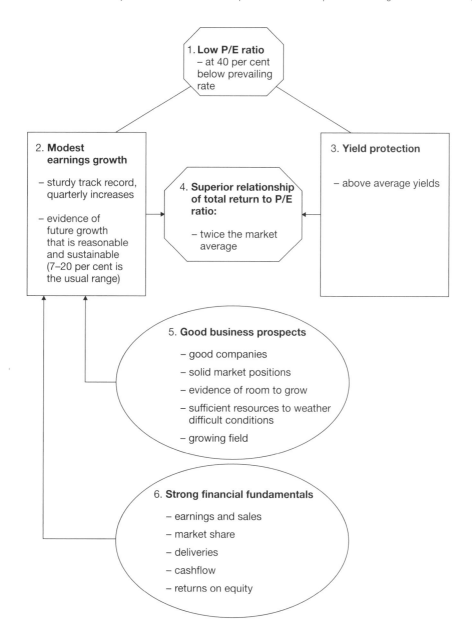

Figure 2.2 Sophisticated low price-earnings investing

Yield protection

A high dividend yield offers the benefit of a satisfactory income while the investor is waiting for the market to recognize the earnings growth potential. Also, anticipating return through growth in earnings entails more uncertainty than the return available through dividends. Dividends are rarely lowered and good companies are likely to increase the payout 'which is like learning that your bank plans to increase its passbook rate'.[14]

The Windsor Fund's out-performance of 3.15 per cent per year was largely attributable to the roughly 2 percentage points a year contributed by the superior dividend yield. Neff claimed that analysts myopically tend to evaluate stocks on the basis of earnings growth expectations almost exclusively, and therefore, investors could 'collect the dividend income for free'.[15]

He couldn't understand why a stock with earnings growth of 15 per cent plus a 1 per cent yield sold at a much higher price than a stock with 11 per cent growth and a 5 per cent yield. Because of the blinkered focus on earnings growth, the aware value investor could gain a 'free plus' (a return an investor enjoys over and above initial expectations).

Neff does not specify what he means by a 'superior yield'. Indeed, he muddies the water further by saying that at times he bought stock with a zero or a very low dividend (e.g. Intel). The implication in his writing is that he generally looked for a yield at least 2 percentage points over the average.

Total return to P/E ratio

Neff developed a rule of thumb to help him identify under-priced stocks – the total return to P/E ratio should be twice the market average. The top part of the ratio combines the growth in earnings figure with the dividend yield. This is the total return. The bottom part is the P/E ratio. It represents the amount paid to secure the total return 'a way to measure the bang for our investment buck'.[16]

$$\frac{\text{Total return}}{\text{P/E ratio}} = \frac{\text{earnings growth} + \text{yield}}{\text{price/most recently reported earnings}}$$

Investors search for the stocks that offer the highest dividend income and earnings growth prospects for the lowest price relative to current earnings. The hurdle rate Neff determined, probably after much experimentation and experience, was that the total return for a share divided by its P/E exceeds the market average ratio by two to one. Note that he does not set a fixed number for the total return to P/E ratio of 2. To obtain the hurdle rate at any one time it is necessary, first of all, to find the growth in earnings and dividend yield for the market as a whole, and to divide this by the market P/E ratio. So, for example, if the earnings growth for stocks generally is 6 per cent and the market dividend yield is 4 per cent and the historic P/E ratio for the S&P 500 is 20 then the hurdle rate for a stock would be:

$$\frac{\text{total return}}{\text{P/E ratio}} = \frac{6+4}{20} \times 2 = 1.0$$

If the market P/E ratio falls to 10 the hurdle rate will rise to 2.

The time period over which earnings growth is calculated is critical to the use of this formula. If the economy has been through an extraordinarily good period causing average earnings to rise by double digit percentages for the past five years we cannot assume that it is okay to put an earnings growth figure of, say, 15 per cent into the formula. If we did this we could end up with an unreasonably high hurdle rate. Taking a longer term view it is illogical to expect earnings for companies as a whole to continue to grow at a rate in excess of the nominal GDP. If they did, over the long run, corporate profits would take a larger and larger proportion of GDP until returns to labour and other inputs would diminish toward zero. Perhaps corporate profit will take a larger share of GDP than they do currently, but this is unlikely to be significant or continue for an extended period. A more reasonable assumption is that profit as a percentage of a nation's output is stable and therefore profits, over the long run will rise by real GDP growth plus inflation. Failing to follow the logic that there is an ultimate constraint on earnings growth may explain why in bull markets people extrapolate double digit real growth rates for the majority of stocks to an infinite horizon, thus justifying extraordinary P/E ratios. They pay the price of their irrationality when the bubble bursts.

Good business prospects

Sophisticated low P/E investing requires a combination of quantitative and qualitative analysis. The estimation of the future earnings growth rate depends on many factors that are simply not quantifiable. Much of this analysis lies in the field of corporate strategy. It is in this area that knowledge and judgement come to the fore. A set of purely mathematical or mechanical tools which can be employed to choose market-beating stocks does not exist. Rigorous analysis of the economic/industry environment and competitive position is also needed. Neff advises us to learn what makes an industry tick. 'A wise investor studies the industry, its products, and its economic structure.'[17]

There must be a sound understanding of the competitive factors, derived from a deep and high quality analysis. Such efforts are needed to ensure that weight can be placed on a judgement about the durability of earnings power – particularly under adverse conditions.

Neff was interested in 'good companies', those that have strong market positions. It seems odd that companies with powerful competitive strengths should be under-priced, overlooked and neglected, but the Windsor Fund seemed to find a more or less continuous stream of firms which the market whims had confined to the shadows, while the spotlight was on the latest glamour stock or sector.

A key question establishing the soundness of a business and its strategic plans is whether the company is a leader in its industry. You might also like to find out about the company's reputation in its industry, the growth outlook for the sector and the ability of the firm to dominate markets, products and services leading to premium prices. Also, what is the potential for the entry of new competitors, or the development of substitute products? Has the management shown good strategic thinking and implementation in the past?

Reading trade magazines is a good way of discovering developments in an industry before the news reaches Wall Street. 'Go out and kick an industry's tyres.'[18] Visit a factory or a retail outlet, try the goods. Seek out kerbside opinion about the company, its goods and its competitors. Ask people working for the firm and those outside. (This idea of obtaining knowledge by talking to a wide range of people who have had dealings with the corporation is taken to an extreme level by the investor in Chapter 5, Philip Fisher – he called it Scuttlebutt). Neff suggested trying to put a series of key questions to the CEO, or at least, the investor relations officers: 'Are the industry's prices headed up, or are they headed down? What about costs? Who are the market leaders? Do any competitors dominate the market? Can industry capacity meet demand? Are new plants under construction? What will be the effect on profitability?'[19]

Neff was looking for a company with some potential room for growth; the industrial sector should not be stagnant. The company should also have sufficient resources to weather difficult conditions.

Assessing the degree of sustainable competitive advantage of the firm and the economics of an industry is not easy. John Neff gives us some clues. Indeed, all the investors discussed in this book provide us with some glimpses of the thought processes and criteria applied to this difficult area. However, in all cases the detail of the techniques is not revealed. Perhaps they do not have a set of frameworks which they use to assess the strategic position of firms. Perhaps, they are so familiar with the business world that they have developed a sixth sense about the relative strengths of firms, and are unable to bring themselves to describe the process or provide a series of steps to guide others. Whatever the reason, these investors leave their followers floundering if they want to get past the general, first level criteria. Part Two of this book is designed to supplement these generalizations by making use of modern strategic analysis. One thing Neff did insist on was that investors should only invest in companies where there was a full understanding of the industry and the firm – Chapters 9 and 10 will help the reader to ask the right questions.

> .....The company should have sufficient resources to weather difficult conditions.......

By selecting only predictable companies in predictable industry climates, as Neff recommends, the investor has to accept that the investment returns will be less dramatic than finding the next Microsoft or Cisco Systems, but they would be more assured: 'my motto has not changed: Keep It Simple'.[20] This message is reinforced in Chapters 6 and 7 with Warren Buffett's and Charles Munger's insistence on investing only in areas within one's circle of competence.

Strong financial fundamentals

Neff believes that the way to start a company analysis is to pore over its results with a pencil and paper. It is necessary to gather 'a whole raft of numbers and facts'.[21] The analyst needs to search for confirmation or contradiction in the numbers. A good interpretation of the past or present is needed to create growth expectations that can be relied on. Company numbers and ratios should be compared with industry or market benchmarks to provide a perspective on performance. He was particularly interested in earnings and sales. Sales need to be growing to generate a healthy rise in earnings over the long run. Profit margins that are improving are sought after; this may indicate that the company has increased its pricing power. Also, companies can often fail to deliver the goods they have orders for. This may be due to some serious short-comings or because demand is out-stripping supply. If, in the latter case, it looks like the company will be able to get back on track and manage its growth profitability then the company may still be included in the portfolio.

Cashflow is a key measure (defined by Neff as retained earnings plus depreciation) because it indicates how much the company has available for reinvestment in working capital and capital items. If the investment plans cannot be financed by internally generated cashflow the firm may have to borrow or call on shareholders to contribute. Regularly putting money into a company clearly reduces shareholders returns. On the other hand, if a company has more cashflow than it can profitably invest in real assets, there could be increased dividends or stock repurchases.

Return on equity (ROE) is regarded as the best single measure of managerial performance in Neff's view. It captures the extent to which management have generated profit from the shareholder resources entrusted to them, after the debt holders have been given their return.

FINDING VALUABLE LOW P/E RATIO STOCKS

So where does John Neff get the first hint that a stock may be worth investigating? One area he looks at is the list of stocks posting new lows. Most of these companies will have poor prospects and should not be touched with a barge pole. One or two may be worth further investigation. Another list worth consulting is that of the 20 worst performers of the previous day.

Bad news can be over represented in stock prices. Look for good companies in industries which have fallen on hard times. The market has a propensity to over react and push stock prices below reasonable levels. For example, when environmental liabilities were hurting the insurance industry in the late 1980s

> **Look for good companies in industries which have fallen on hard times.**

Windsor bought into property and casualty insurers dragged down by the gloom. The Doomsday scenario did not occur and insurance company reserves were more than adequate. When Home Depot's profits slipped in 1985, due to pre opening costs and expanding overheads, the prospective P/E fell to a mere 10 (Windsor made a 63 per cent return in nine months). In the early 1980s Pier One was a well regarded retailer with a strong competitive position. This was fully recognized by the market and it sold at a high earnings multiple – too high for Windsor. However, in October 1987 investors indiscriminately sold shares. In 1988 Pier One's price fell to under eight times expected 1989 earnings. This happened despite rapid earnings growth. (Windsor doubled its money in six months.)

Companies going through dramatic change can be subject to selling pressure that is unwarranted. There may be significant changes in their products, market or management. The uncertainty associated with companies in the midst of restructuring discourages most investors and may provide an excellent opportunity for the more analytical and patient. There must be a clear rationale for believing that the company will emerge from its metamorphosis stronger. If the stock is standing on a low P/E, you have sound reason for expecting reasonable growth and it meets the other Neff criteria then take courage and go against the crowd.

Companies become overlooked because they lack the size and visibility to catch the attention of mainstream analysts. They may be 'crack' companies. That is, those engaged in a combination of industrial and commercial activities which means they are difficult to classify. They fall between the cracks of standard institutional coverage. The automobile analyst may ignore a company because a mere 30 per cent of earnings comes from the motoring industry, while the chemical industry analyst is not interested because the firm is predominantly an engineering enterprise, and so on. These crack companies can become very inefficiently valued by the market.

Companies making a gradual shift from an industry with poor economics to one with better strategic qualities can also go unnoticed for some time. This is not a dramatic restructuring such as a massive acquisition and disposal programme. This is a gradual movement of the main area of firm activity and profits. The market may still think of the firm as belonging to the old low value sector. It takes time to change perceptions. This delay in recognition presents an opportunity for the value investor.

Neff advised investors to play to their strengths. Investors, and people generally, are often very knowledgeable about a company, an industry or particular product area. If you work, or have worked in an industry, then you may have special insight into which firm is the market leader; which is growing most rapidly, and why; which has the strongest management team, culture and strategy. Knowledge can be gained by keeping your eyes and ears open. Which products are definite 'must carry' for a retailer? What products are the teenagers all talking about? Which retailers are the most effective in winning customers? The investor should also look to build on their own experiences in other areas of consumption. Perhaps you particularly liked the service you received at a new chain of automobile repair shop; or the food was good at a restaurant; or the office supply company have a culture of efficiency and friendliness combined with low prices which beats all the competition you have come across. Start with what you know and build from there.

WHAT HE AVOIDS

High transaction costs

Few mutual funds can claim to have such low expenses as the Windsor had – a mere 0.35 per cent per annum. The portfolio's turnover was kept to unusually low levels. This saving on dealing costs is complemented by the low level of operating expenses for activities such as information gathering and analysis. One of Neff's guiding rules is to keep things simple. The most important elements determining stock value can be understood without the need for expensive sophisticated equipment or people. By holding for the medium term and not going for short-term profits he reduced both transaction costs and taxes.

Excessive diversification

While all would agree that some degree of diversification is necessary, if this is taken too far investment performance is hobbled. Neff said: 'Why own, for instance, forest products companies if the market has embraced them and you can reap exceptional returns by selling them?'[22] He generally ignored market weightings and bought in areas of the market where under valuation was evident. Some sectors would be unrepresented in the portfolio, whereas others would be 'over-represented' (according to conventional logic). Normally the vast majority of the S&P 500 were not held, at any one time, by Windsor. Generally a mere four or five of these well known stocks fulfilled his requirements for inclusion. When the fund was valued at $11 billion it still only had 60 stocks. Furthermore, the largest ten accounted for almost 40 per cent of the fund. Windsor would often have 8 or 9 per cent of the outstanding shares of companies. 'By playing it safe, you can make a portfolio so pablum-like that you don't get any sizzle. You can diversify yourself into mediocrity.'[23]

Technology stocks

These were generally avoided for three reasons: (1) they are too risky; (2) they do not pass the total return to P/E ratio test; (3) Neff admitted that he had no 'discernable edge' versus other people in the market place. It is essential to have some informational and analytical advantage.

Forgetting the lessons of the past

The memory of stock market participants is notoriously short. Markets are continually foolish, being condemned to invite catastrophe by forgetting the past. A knowledge of history is essential to give the required perspective. Neff, writing in 1999, believed that speculators in 1998 and 1999 were merely the latest in a long line of amnesiacs. In the late 1990s anything ending in a .com generated great excitement. In the 1950s firms merely had to put 'tronics' on the end of their name to attract attention and to drive their share prices higher. In the 1960s it was the go-go stocks. In the late 1960s and early 1970s to be labelled one of the Nifty Fifty was to see your stock prices soar. In the 1980s oil companies were in vogue. Before these bubbles you had the new era stocks of the 1920s (does that phrase sound familiar?), and so on and so on.

> **The memory of stock market participants is notoriously short.**

Each generation believes that a few magical companies have an almost infinite capacity to grow, that the rules of economics have been rewritten and that you have to jump aboard before it is too late. The 1990s fervour was more dangerous than most because many, if not the majority, of the companies which lured the speculative dollar had no profits. They could not be called growth stocks in the traditional sense of the term. Speculators were premature in conferring growth status on companies that had good prospects only if you made massive assumptions regarding the likelihood of the entry of competitors, or the prospect for another change in technology, and, the willingness of consumers to join the revolution rather than continue to do things without the new technology. Market players tend to lose sight of the fundamentals as they are mesmerized by the rising prices. 'Windsor's critical edge amounted to nothing more mysterious than remembering the lessons of the past and how they tend to repeat themselves.'[24]

He illustrates this point wonderfully with the story about two moose hunters who hired a plane to take them to moose country in Canada. The pilot agreed to return to pick them up two days later. He said the hunters could only return with one moose for each hunter to keep the weight in the aircraft at a safe level. When the pilot returned the hunters had prepared two moose each for the flight home. The pilot said that they were to bring home only one each. 'But you said that last year,' whined one hunter. 'Then we paid an extra $1,000 and you managed to take home the four moose.' The pilot agreed. An hour into the flight the gas tanks ran low, the engine sputtered and the pilot was forced to crash land. All three managed to emerge from the plane unhurt. 'Do you know where we are?' asked one of the hunters. 'Not sure,' said the other, 'but it sure looks like where we crashed last year.'

Getting carried away with bull market hype

Markets go through cycles over time. There are occasions when investors are very risk averse. There is the phase when the emphasis is on quality. Later as confidence grows, investors look for stocks with a more speculative taint. After a period of growth the speculators fall over each other in their buying panic as the market runs well ahead of its fundamental underpinnings. 'The capacity of investors to believe in something too good to be true seems almost infinitive at times'.[25] As the fad gathers pace, people who have little familiarity with stocks get swept along with the drumbeat of the prevailing wisdom. People find the urge to 'hop on the line that moves fastest'[26] as they try to take short cuts to riches. The siren song of positive beliefs in the future drowns out the argument for a rational investment strategy based on a fundamental evaluation of stocks. Traders buy and sell on the basis of tips and superficial knowledge. The visions of overnight fortunes blind them to the illogicality of investing without sound information and calm reflective thought. People come to believe that there is gold enough for all in the same streams that earlier adventurers panned. Most of these followers go home empty handed as the wild expectations of the individual members of the mob one by one receive a slap in the face with a dose of reality. Eventually, it dawns on the masses that some players have already taken their money, as they figured things had already gone too far. Group panic begins, as everyone tries to exit at once. Predicting when these inflection points will occur is impossible so the best advice is to stay clear of stocks and markets that have lost touch with fundamentals. Don't try to play the greater-fool game – you might end up being the biggest fool.

The technical or momentum game

Neff considered it ill-advised to try and predict market movements. His approach:

> amounts to hitting behind the ball instead of anticipating market climaxes six to eighteen months ahead of the investment crowd. Poor performance often occurred as a consequence of a technical orientation that tried to predict peaks and troughs in stock charts. It assumed that where a stock has been implies where it is going.[27]

Growth stocks on high P/E ratios

The problem with stocks showing fast earnings growth is that their potential is likely to be well recognized. Indeed, on too many occasions, stocks that have attracted a market buzz have their price driven up to unrealistic heights as investors get carried away. This was clearly evident in the mania for business-to-consumer internet stocks in the late 1990s. A combination of over excitement, small free-float and the obligation of index tracker (and closet index tracker) funds to purchase high capitalization stocks drove prices to ridiculous levels, especially for those with an untested business model, no profits and without enough time having passed to be able to analyze the possibility of market entry, competition and the introduction of substitute products.

Even well established growth companies such as General Electric, Gillette, Coca-Cola and Procter and Gamble can be poor investments. Yes, they are good companies with excellent financial performances based on strong competitive positions and good management. Yes, their businesses are broadly-based, sound and global. Yes, they are safe and, almost inevitably, will be around in 20 years' time. But, no, they will not produce good returns to the stock buyer if they are purchased at a time when everyone knows these are great companies and the price is bid up to reflect this common belief. The slightest hiccup in growth or expectation of growth for these companies will see the stock sent reeling as the crowd becomes disillusioned. The lesson is that even great companies have a price ceiling. 'You can't up the ante forever. Eventually, even great stocks run out of gas.'[28] Believing that Coca-Cola is a buy at a P/E of 55, because it might go to 70 times earnings is battling against the odds. Value investors always keep the odds in their favour.

> **Value investors always keep the odds in their favour.**

Being a simple contrarian

Neff is an individual who makes up his own mind about a situation or a stock. His willingness to argue with a signpost has paid off handsomely when it comes to going against the whims and fancies of the stock market. And yet, he was never obstinate, ego-driven or simple minded in his opposition. He did not assume that the market was always wrong. He was prepared to listen to the views of others. Most importantly he did not unthinkingly and automatically take a contrarian line.

> Do not bask in the warmth of just being different. There is a thin line between being contrarian, and being just plain stubborn. I revel in opportunities to buy stocks, but I will also concede that at times the crowd is right. Eventually you have to be right on fundamentals to be rewarded….Stubborn, knee-jerk contrarians follow a recipe for catastrophe. Savvy contrarians keep their minds open, leavened by a sense of history and a sense of humour. Almost anything in the investment field can go too far, including a contrarian theme.[29]

SELLING POLICY

Windsor's success rested as much on its selling strategy as it did on its buying criteria. Neff regarded selling as the toughest investment decision. There are two reasons for selling. The first is that the fundamentals have deteriorated. Perhaps a mistake was made in the analysis of the company in the first place. Earnings or anticipated growth in earnings may, six months or a year later, prove to be much lower than the estimates used in the buying decision. Each stock in the portfolio must have a 'clearly visualized potential for growth'.[30] If the picture has deteriorated then it is best to swallow some pride and exit as expeditiously as possible. 'If the best thing we could say about a stock was that "it probably won't go down", that stock became a candidate for sale.'[31]

Clearly, it was difficult for Neff and his team, as it is for any investor, to be so self-critical as to ask themselves on a daily basis whether they were persevering with a stock because of their past enthusiasm or they had developed an affection for it, rather than because of its appreciation potential, based on earnings growth.

It is hard enough to decide when to sell your mistakes or those stocks badly affected by external factors causing the fundamentals to deteriorate. It is even more difficult to decide when to sell your successes. Neff said that these should be sold when the price approached expectations – when the stock had gone from undervalued to fairly valued. But it is not always easy to say at what point the stock has become fairly valued 'successful stocks don't tell you when it's time to sell them'.[32]

If the fundamental criteria for investment continued to hold he was content to retain shares for three, four or five years (the average holding was for three years). However, he was well aware that it was all too possible to hold on too long. 'An awful lot of people keep a stock too long because it gives them the warm fuzzies – particularly when a contrarian stance has been vindicated. If they sell it they lose bragging rights.'[33]

Also, investors are loathe to miss out on what they think will be the best part of the gain. It is galling to sell a stock and see its price rise the next day. So they hold on to avoid facing the possibility of regret. They are determined to have the last dollar from the upswing. Neff said that he was not smart enough to time sales to the peak and capture all the gain. He preferred to sell into strength and was quite content to leave some upside on the table for the buyer. The risk of being caught in a market or stock-specific downdraft was too great. To sell at fundamental value was enough, especially if the cash released could be used to purchase other stocks selling at less than fair value.

DIFFICULTIES AND DRAWBACKS WITH THIS APPROACH

Neff's approach demands a lot from the analyst. A sound knowledge of accounting, finance, strategy and economics is essential. Companies must be thoroughly investigated to determine credible earnings growth projections. You either do this properly, or not at all. It is no use following Neff half-heartedly – there lies complete failure. If you cannot devote the necessary time and mental energy, it would be better to place your money in collective investment vehicles (e.g. mutual funds) rather than merely play at sophisticated low P/E ratio investing.

As well as being time consuming and requiring technical skill the Neff way is psychologically demanding. The courage, perseverance, fortitude and patience needed may take many years to develop, even for someone predisposed to be able to develop these virtues. Sober reflection, a sense of history, consistency and judgement are qualities that are not attainable by all. Critical self examination may be needed before embarking on a Neffian adventure.

Another problem is that many, if not most, of the quoted companies would be quickly eliminated from further consideration by the simple criteria of a P/E ratio that is 40–60 per cent below the average, together with a high yield and a good total return to P/E ratio. In particular, large numbers of high growth stocks are excluded. Neff believed that such companies were too risky for him and he was uncertain of his ability to distinguish between the truly valuable (and under-priced) growth stocks and those which have been temporarily buoyed up by market enthusiasm. There are many other investors who do fish in these dangerous waters. They do so with such skill that they bag some wonderful specimens. One such investor is Philip Fisher, the subject of Chapter 5.

Neff's approach may also lead to long periods of poor performance. For example, Windsor had a terrible time in the early 1970s as investors abandoned value stocks in their rush to pump money into the Nifty Fifty. This style of investing is only suitable for those that can take at least a five-year view. If you are prepared to make the effort and possess, or are willing to develop, the character traits demanded by following this philosophy the Neff approach can be rewarding. Neff is adamant that his approach does not require genius or blinding insights, but it does require imagination, some flair and the ability to learn lessons from the mistakes made by yourself and others. Neff likes to quote Benjamin Franklin: 'Be honest; toil constantly; be patient. Have courage and self-reliance. Be ambitious and industrious. Have perseverance, ability and judgement. Cultivate foresight and imagination'. The virtues needed by good men and women in all walks of life need to be honed to a sharp point in field of investment.

KEY PRINCIPLES TO NEFF'S APPROACH

- Look for out-of-favour, overlooked or misunderstood stocks;
- Character traits of a sophisticated low P/E ratio investor:
  - courage
  - perseverance
  - fortitude
  - patience
  - sober reflection
  - sense of history
  - constancy
  - judgement.
- Price-earnings ratios 40–60 per cent below market;
- Modest earnings growth (7–20 per cent);
- High dividend yield;
- Total return to P/E ratio (greater than twice the current average);
- Good business prospects (sound strategic position);
- Strong financial fundamentals (sales, earnings, margins, delivery, cash-flow, ROE);
- Finding valuable low P/E ratio stocks:
  - stock posting new lows
  - 20 worst performers list
  - sectors/categories with a torrent of bad news
  - companies going through dramatic change
  - those lacking size and visibility (e.g. 'crack companies')
  - companies evolving improved strategies

- – the industry where you work
- – where you shop, eat, etc.
- What he avoids:
  - – high transaction costs (low turnover, keep it simple)
  - – excessive diversification
  - – technology stocks
  - – forgetting the lessons of the past
  - – getting carried away with bull market hype
  - – the technical or momentum game
  - – growth stocks on high P/E ratios
  - – being a simple contrarian.
- Selling policy:
  - – the fundamentals have deteriorated
  - – when the stocks fairly valued.

Notes

1 Neff, J. and Mintz, S. L. (1999) pp. 62 and 71. This material is used by permission of John Wiley & Sons, Inc.
2 *Ibid.*, p. 14.
3 *Ibid.*, p. 16.
4 *Ibid.*, p. 26.
5 *Ibid.*, p. 43.
6 *Ibid.*, p. 49.
7 *Ibid.*, p. xv.
8 *Ibid.*, p. 97.
9 *Ibid.*, p. xvii.
10 *Ibid.*, p. xvi.
11 *Ibid.*, p. 122.
12 *Ibid.*, p. 4.
13 *Ibid.*, p. 69.
14 *Ibid.*, p. 70.
15 *Ibid.*, p. 71.
16 *Ibid.*, p. 73.
17 *Ibid.*, p. 111.
18 *Ibid.*, p. 112.
19 *Ibid.*, p. 112.
20 *Ibid.*, p. 51.

21 *Ibid.*, p. 79.
22 *Ibid.*, p. 102.
23 *Ibid.*, p. 49.
24 *Ibid.*, p. 127.
25 *Ibid.*, p. 56.
26 *Ibid.*, p. 13.
27 *Ibid.*, p. 44.
28 *Ibid.*, p. 98.
29 *Ibid.*, p. 100.
30 *Ibid.*, p. 114.
31 *Ibid.*, p. 114.
32 *Ibid.*, p. 115.
33 *Ibid.*, p. 115.

3

Benjamin Graham: The father of modern security analysis

Benjamin Graham is regarded as the most influential of investment philosophers. Warren Buffett said he was the 'smartest man I ever knew'.[1] Buffett owes a great deal to Graham. When he was a 19-year-old student at the University of Nebraska he read Graham's second great book *The Intelligent Investor*, and said the experience was similar to that of Paul on the road to Damascus – he saw the light. Buffett was so taken with Graham's ideas that he offered to work for the Graham-Newman Co. in 1950 for nothing! Graham turned him down. Buffett later said: 'He turned me down as overvalued. He took this value stuff very seriously!'[2]

Eventually ('after much pestering'[3]), Buffett was hired in 1954, and enjoyed a great rapport with his mentor for many years. In the 1950s there were only four 'peasants' working for the tiny Graham-Newman. It is possible to trace the impressive performance of three of them after they left: Walter J. Schloss (WJS Ltd Partners), Tom Knapp of Tweedy, Browne Partners and Warren Buffett.[4] Graham did not accumulate a vast fortune himself (when he died in 1976, his estate was worth $3 million), but his ideas influenced the creation of multi-billion dollar fortunes. He had great intellectual curiosity and was less interested in money than taking on the intellectual challenge of stock selection.

Graham was the leading exponent of the value investing school of thought. By this I do not mean the simplistic, distorted and crude 'analysis' which passes for much value investing today. The current deformed and childlike methods often promoted in the financial press have no greater intellectual foundation than to buy stocks with high dividends, or buy those with low price-earnings ratios, or with low book-to-equity ratios. No, Graham's value investing was far more sophisticated than that. He looked for bargain prices but was aware that following a one-criterion philosophy would be damaging. If it was as easy as applying a mathematical single figure, everybody would be doing it and the abnormal performance would quickly be traded away.

Over 20 years (from 1936) the Graham-Newman Corporation achieved an abnormally high performance for its clients: 'The success of Graham-Newman Corporation can be gauged by its average annual distribution.

Roughly speaking, if one invested $10,000 in 1936, one received an average of $2,100 a year for the next 20 years, and recovered one's original $10,000 at the end'.[5] Graham in testimony to the senate[6] in 1955 put a slightly different figure on it: 'Over a period of years we have tended to earn about 20 per cent on capital per year'. This is much better than the return available on the market as a whole. For example, Barclays Capital[7] show the annual average real (excluding inflation) rate of return on US stocks with gross income reinvested of 7.4 per cent for those years. Even if we add back average annual inflation of 3.8 per cent[8] to the Barclays' figures to make them comparable, the Graham-Newman results are much better than the returns received by the average investor.

EARLY INFLUENCES

Benjamin Graham was born Benjamin Grossbaum in London, UK, in 1894. When he was young his family moved to the United States and shortly thereafter his father died, when Graham was eight and half years old. Perhaps Graham's early experiences, as a member of a family struggling to survive, impressed on him the need for a safety-first approach to investment (something he temporarily repressed in the heady days of the 1920s). His mother tried to boost the family income through risky investment strategies, but the result was disappointing and distressing.

Although poor, Graham had a good education and was exceptionally bright. When he graduated from Columbia University in 1914, he received offers to teach in no less than three departments: English, Philosophy and Mathematics. He declined and became a financial analyst on Wall Street. His talent quickly came to the fore and his progress was rapid, even spectacular 'a continuous advance in my standard of living'.[9] By 1925 he had left behind both his youthful poverty and his instinctive cautiousness: 'At thirty-one I was convinced that I knew it all – or at least that I knew all that I needed to know about making money in stocks and bonds – that I had Wall Street by the tail, that my future was as unlimited as my ambitions…. I was too young, also, to realize that I had caught a bad case of hubris'.[10]

On 1 January 1926, the Benjamin Graham Joint Account was established as a private investment organization. Investors put in $400,000 at the outset. Graham was joined by Jerry Newman at the end of 1926. Each year new friends were eager to place funds in the account so that by 1929 Graham and Newman were managing a fund of some $2.5 million.

Graham was articulate, engaging, logical and witty. He had all the qualities of an excellent teacher and generously put these talents to use by teaching a course called Security Analysis as a part-time assistant professor in the School of Business, Columbia – the first was in the autumn of 1927. His academic career spanned over 40 years and was to include professorships with various titles at Columbia, the New York Institute of Finance and UCLA.

By the late 1920s he had developed a reputation for finding special or bargain situations. Despite his self-admonishment, regarding his overweening self-confidence, in the late 1920s he was, by all accounts, a *relatively* safety conscious investor. His greatest strengths were seen as his intellectual independence and his highly prized integrity.

There seems to have been something of a battle between his emotions and his head at the peak of the bull market, as is demonstrated in this quote:

> I recall [Bernard] Baruch's commenting [in 1929] on the ridiculous anomaly that combined an 8 per cent rate for time-loans on stocks with dividend yields of only 2 per cent. To which I replied, 'That's true, and by the law of compensation we should expect someday to see the reverse – 2 per cent time-money combined with an 8 per cent dividend on good stocks.' My prophecy was not far wrong as a picture of 1932…. What seems really strange now is that I could make a prediction of that kind in all seriousness, yet not have the sense to realize the dangers to which I continued to subject the Account's capital.[11]

Graham later concluded that in the frenzy of 1928 and 1929 investors converted themselves into speculators. They distorted ideas of investment value and lost touch with key principles. For example, they forgot that not all good businesses offer shares that are good value, because they may be over-valued relative to those good prospects. Also, a great deal of scepticism is needed to evaluate stocks. Valuations based on projections of earnings can be very unreliable and the tangible asset base should be given more attention. In an excited environment of a speculative boom investors poured money into companies making the corporations rich but their stockholders poor. The bull market encourages 'topsy-turvy accounting policies and wholly irrational standards of value'.[12]

In the middle of 1929 the fund had $2.5 million of capital used for a long position (commitment to, or actual buying of, securities) offset by an equal dollar volume of short sales (selling of securities not currently owned). It also had $4.5 million in true long positions against which was owed $2 million. It closed 1929 with a 20 per cent loss. Worse was to follow: 50.5 per cent was lost in 1930, 16 per cent in 1931 and 3 per cent in 1932. Cumulatively, between 1929 and 1932 70 per cent of $2.5 million was gone. Despite the loss, and some investors quitting the fund, the Benjamin Graham Joint Account survived. It started 1933 with $375,000. Graham drew no salary during the Depression but worked exceptionally hard to regain investors' money. During 1933 a profit of over 50 per cent was registered, and by 1935 all past losses had been made good.

KEY ELEMENTS OF HIS PHILOSOPHY

The need for caution was seared into his mind by the experience of being whisked along with the feverish atmosphere of the 1920s, the Crash and the Great Depression. Thereafter, he insisted on a wide margin of safety. He deplored speculation. He searched for securities that were so undervalued that, in the long haul, there was only the remotest chance of losing market value.

It was Graham's emphasis on safety which Buffett finds most valuable: '[Graham] wasn't about brilliant investments and he wasn't about fads or fashion. He was about sound investing, and I think sound investing can make you very wealthy if you're not in too big of a hurry, and it never makes you poor, which is better'.[13]

During the Great Depression, Graham developed a unique approach to investment. He tried to establish in his own mind the difference between an investment and a mere speculation. The conclusion of his ruminations led him to reject the common idea that the difference lies in the type of financial instrument purchased. The length of time a security is held is also dismissed. He saw that the distinction lies in the mind of the person making the buying and selling decisions. It is the attitude of the individual that is the key. The speculator's primary concern is with anticipating and profiting from market fluctuations. In contrast 'an investment operation is one which, upon thorough analysis, promises safety of principal and a satisfactory return. Operations not meeting these requirements are speculative'.[14] The key features of an investment operation are shown in Fig. 3.1.

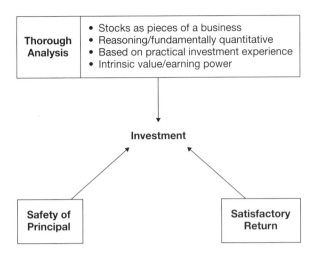

Figure 3.1 Graham's three elements for an investment operation

Note that Graham does not speak of a single stock issue or a single purchase, but, rather an investment operation. The reason for this is that:

> it is unsound to think always of investment character as inhering in an issue *per se*. The price is frequently an essential element, so that a stock … may have investment merit at one price level but not at another. Furthermore, an investment might be justified in a group of issues which would not be sufficiently safe if made in any one of them singly. In other words, diversification might be necessary to reduce the risk involved in the separate issues to the minimum consonant with the requirements of investment.[15]

Business-like investing and reasoning

The first requirement is thorough analysis, by which Graham meant studying the facts. He advised the aspiring investment analyst to view stocks as shares in an underlying business. Try to imagine that you are taking on interest in a private business. Or, better still, estimate the value as if you owned all of the enterprise. He noted that Wall Street analysts rarely consider the vital question, 'How much is the business selling for?' Yet, if anybody buying say a 10 per cent stake in a private corporation were asked to pay $100,000, the first mental process would be to multiply the price by 10 to see if the valuation for the entire business is reasonable – is it a good buy

> .....The first requirement is thorough analysis. .....

at $1 million? This business-like approach would consider the asset values being offered, the strength of the financial resources as well as the earning potential. Focusing on the underlying business enables you to avoid the error of considering only short-term prospects for the movement of the stock on Wall Street. Often short-term unfavourable factors weigh heavily on the market price of a stock. These temporary events have little bearing on the fundamental value of the business and yet Wall Street hammers the share price.

It is rather like owning a corner store that has an excellent position and is expected to continue having a strong competitive advantage and high profit for as far ahead as we can reasonably forecast. However, for the next three months trade is going to be poor because the road outside the store is going to be re-laid. It would be nonsensical to reduce the valuation of this business significantly. Its value is overwhelmingly determined by the earnings to be received way beyond the next three months. And yet, it seems that Wall Street gets hung up on temporary negative news and unreasonably depresses a stock price. Clearly, market prices are not determined by any necessarily rational or mathematical relationship to fundamental factors (at least, not in the short run) 'but through the minds and decisions of buyers and sellers'[16]... 'The prices of common stock are not carefully thought out computations, but the resultants of a welter of human reactions. The stock market is a voting machine rather than a weighing machine. It responds to factual data not directly, but only as they affect the decisions of buyers and sellers.'[17] So, if you are able to have the independence of mind to examine stock not as a short-term trading counter in a gambling game, but as an ownership share of a real business you might have a competitive edge.

Taking this independent line requires that your analysis is based in sound reasoning, that you would feel comfortable defending. It requires a critical examination of the facts about the business. It requires you to have the courage of your knowledge and experience.[18] If other people, even the majority, disagree with your conclusions you should not hesitate to condemn the popular view and act. However, only do so if you feel you are right because your data and reasoning are right. Graham describes courage as the supreme virtue in the world of securities after 'adequate knowledge and a tested judgement'.[19]

He is very careful, however, not to over-emphasize the propensity of the market to make mistakes. The independently minded and critical analyst must pay respectful attention to the judgement of the market but remain able to detach himself/herself from it when the need arises.

Intrinsic value

Intrinsic value is a concept given a great deal of weight by Graham.[20] He regarded it as an elusive concept, and the nearest he came to a definition was to say it was 'the value of the company to a private owner'.[21] It is the price at which a stock should sell if properly priced in a normal market. That is, a price justified by the facts. These facts include the assets, earnings, dividends and definite prospects.

The concept is difficult to apply in a way that will pin-down a single number. Analysts have tried. At first it was thought to be the same as book value – net asset value on the balance sheet, when the assets have been adjusted to reflect fair prices. This had the serious weakness that the book values of corporations generally have little systematic relation with earnings (and hence value). Some firms have a negative book value, but produce large profits and a high stock price; others have massive quantities of plant and machinery, factories, inventory etc., with no debt, but have poor profitability.

An alternative view, one supported by Graham, was to regard intrinsic value as being determined by its 'earning power'.[22] This is very difficult to establish with any precision. Examining past earnings (the average, trend growth, or decline) is of some use, but there must be good grounds for believing the trend to be a guide to the future if simple extrapolation is to be used. In many cases the plausibility of this assumption is weak.

Despite the difficulties it is necessary somehow to derive expectations of future earnings in which the analyst has confidence. Graham says that a precise number is not necessary; we need only establish either that the value is inadequate or that it is considerably higher than the market price. 'For such purposes an indefinite and approximate measure of intrinsic value may be sufficient.'[23] The analyst needs to work in terms of a range of approximate intrinsic value. As the uncertainty surrounding a particular stock increases the range of intrinsic values becomes larger. Graham offers the examples of $20 to $40 for Wright Aeronautical in 1922 as against $30 to $130 for Case in 1933.[24] This kind of thinking allows the investor to use the intrinsic value concept in an uncertain world. If the market price falls far below the minimum appraisal it is a 'buy'.

Margin of safety

This leads us on to perhaps Graham's most influential slogan – margin of safety. He would say that if he were challenged to distil the secret of sound investment into three words his motto would be, 'margin of safety'.[25] The traumatic experience of the boom and bust of the 1920s and 1930s caused Graham to place prime emphasis upon protection against adverse developments. The value must be well in excess of the price paid, so that even if the bought security is found to be less attractive than it appeared at the time of the analysis it is still possible to obtain a satisfactory return. Margin of safety in stock investing is analogous to the additional strength built into high rise office blocks, bridges and ships which is much more than is needed to cope with all normal, or even imaginable abnormal, events. It is a kind of insurance against untoward occurrences: 'buy securities that are *not* only *not too* high but that, on the basis of analysis, appear to be very much *too low*'.[26]

The margin of safety concept is a touchstone that distinguishes an investment operation from a speculative one. It is undoubtedly true that speculators persuade themselves on taking a chance that the odds are in their favour, and so claim that they are operating with a margin of safety. These individuals may feel a sense of superiority with regard to stock selection skills, or quality of a system. But, these claims are implausible because they have not sought out the relevant facts nor used a conclusive line of reasoning. Rather, they are based on a subjective judgement of future moves in prices – a feeling that the market, or a stock, is due to head up or down. There is no sense in which the punter is protected by a margin of safety in any meaningful sense of the phrase.

In contrast, investors base their judgements on experienced reasoning making use of statistical data; the margin of safety can be demonstrated by figures rather than relying on opinion. For example, in the 1930s Graham observed that the total value of stock of many companies was 'less than the amount of bonds that could safely be issued against its property and earning power'.[27] In other words, if you bought the company's common stock you were taking on a level of risk which was similar to that if you had bought a highly secured low default bond issued by the company, and yet the returns offered were far above that on a bond. Graham did acknowledge that the combination of good profit opportunity and safety occurs infrequently in the financial markets, however.

In more normal market conditions the secret to finding a suitable margin of safety lies in the expected earning power rather than in high asset backing. In the fourth edition of the *Intelligent Investor* (1973) Graham illustrated the concept of margin of safety by pointing out that stocks as a whole in 1972 were failing to provide such a margin. Investors had bid up price-earnings ratios to the point where even shares on relatively low-multiples were selling for over 12 times earnings, producing an earnings return (earnings/price) of 8.33 per cent: 'the excess of stock earning power over bond interest over a ten-year basis would still be too small to constitute an adequate margin of safety. For that reason we feel that there are real risks now even in a diversified list of sound common stocks. The risks may be offset by the profit possibilities ... [but] the old package of *good profit possibilities combined with small ultimate risk* is no longer available'.[28] The margin of safety had shrivelled. How prophetic Graham's words proved to be in the 1973–4 shake out. Investors in 1972, like those of 1928–9, neglected the commonsense rule that well-established standards are needed to accept stocks as having a safety element. In bull phases the market tends to make up new standards as it goes along – generally based on the current price. Regardless of how high it goes the reigning price becomes the measure of value to the unthinking speculator. Any notion of safety for such purchasers is both illusory and dangerous.

Unfortunately identifying the margin of safety with precision is not possible. There is no absolute value or complete analysis. We need to think in terms of probable protection against loss under all normal or reasonable likely conditions or variations. We are unable to provide the margin of safety for extreme contingencies. So, again Graham asks us to make use of judgement, but this judgement is based within a rational framework and facts. It lies in a stark contrast to the speculator's subjective judgement.

Satisfactory return

The final element in Fig. 3.1, to aim for a 'satisfactory return', is another crucial factor that is somewhat imprecise in Graham's writing. He warns us not to expect returns in excess of normal, unless you know as much about security values as you would about a private business that you owned outright.[29] He discourages attempts to 'beat the market' or to 'pick the winners'[30] and states 'there are no dependable ways of making money easily and quickly, either in Wall Street or anywhere else'.[31] He appears to be surprisingly pessimistic and is very different to those writers who will tell you ten ways to become a millionaire before breakfast. '"Satisfactory" is a subjective term; it covers any rate or amount of return, however low, which the investor is willing to accept, provided he acts with reasonable intelligence.'[32] Graham was trying to warn against the over-optimism and greed that can sweep individuals along, encouraging them to abandon sound investments, to speculate in stocks which appear to offer the prospect of rapid capital appreciation. Chasing these rainbows will end in naught. One of Aesop's fables tells of a dog that found a piece of meat. He picked it up and set off for home 'wait till my friends see this' thought the dog 'what a big supper I will have tonight'. On the way home, the dog had to cross a river using a bridge. He was halfway across when he looked down into the water. He stopped. There was another dog looking up at him! And it was carrying an even bigger piece of meat! 'I want that piece of meat' thought the dog, and he dropped the one he was carrying, and jumped into the water to try to snatch the meat from the other dog. 'Where has it gone?' howled the dog. The meat and the other dog had disappeared. All he could see were ripples and splashes, and his own piece of meat floating down the river. He had been looking at his own reflection. The dog went home hungry.

The irony is that Graham, following his pessimistic, safety-first approach, outperformed the market. By not aiming for unreasonably high returns, but concentrating on sound investment principles in a disciplined framework he, in fact, achieved extraordinarily abnormal results. Many of his contemporaries with high growth targets fell by the wayside.

THREE TYPES OF SHARE BUYERS

In his later work he moved away from the notion of two camps of stock purchasers; speculators and investors. This new, three-way categorization overtly permits the possibility of aiming for extraordinary performance – but only under rigorous conditions. Graham came to believe that speculative elements are present in nearly all the cases that a security analyst deals with.[33,34] In some cases the speculative element is of considerable importance. It is the task of the analyst to keep the speculative factor within minor limits. The purchaser of stock faces the substantial possibilities of profit and the potential of severe loss – these risks must be assumed by someone. Graham split the term speculation into two, each with a quite different meaning. Unintelligent speculation takes on the old meaning: buying with a lack proper knowledge and skill; risking more money than the stock-picker can afford to lose; ignoring quantitative material; placing the emphasis on the rewards of speculation rather than on the individual's capacity to speculate successfully.

Intelligent speculation, on the other hand, requires a focus on information that is quantifiable. It is based on the calculation of probabilities. By drawing on the analyst's experience, a careful weighing of the facts will lead to a measurement of the odds of success. If the odds are strongly in favour of the operation's success then to go ahead would be intelligent. The stock would have to be purchased within the range of value, found through the appraisal, to be a true intelligent speculation. For example, imagine that the calculated range for a stock is $20 to $30. If you were able to purchase at less than $20 this would be a prime Grahamite investment; between $20 and $30 you would be embarking on an intelligent speculation; paying more than $30 would be unintelligent speculation. The three approaches to stock selection are shown in Fig. 3.2.

> ...Intelligent speculation requires a focus on information that is quantifiable. ....

It is possible to reduce the risk of intelligent speculation, and even turn it into investment, by the simple device of diversification. Graham advocates the process of skilful and experienced calculation, but recognizes it is not necessary for the figures to be precise. In a portfolio 'The law of averages will take care of minor errors and of the many individual

• No analysis • All principal at risk • Returns could be very poor (unless you are lucky)	• Thorough analysis (probability based) • Some risk to principal (diversification helps reduce risk)	• Thorough analysis • Safety of principal
UNINTELLIGENT SPECULATION	INTELLIGENT SPECULATION	INVESTMENT
Unfortunately, this approach is all too common.	*Most value investment*	*Rare opportunities*

Figure 3.2 Speculation and investment

disappointments which are inherent in speculation by its very definition'.[35]

The purchaser of shares needs to undertake a critical self-examination to discover which category he or she belongs to – it is all too easy to fall into the trap of persuading yourself that you are investing, when in fact, you are unintelligently speculating, with little knowledge or analysis of the securities bought. If you truly are undertaking intelligent speculation then there is no cause to berate yourself if a particular investment fails. The failure does not prove that you were really unintelligently speculating, just so long as you genuinely undertook sufficient study and used sound judgement.

MAKE MARKET FLUCTUATIONS YOUR FRIEND

Warren Buffett said in a speech to the New York Society of Security Analysts in 1994 that if three basic ideas of Graham's are really ground into your intellectual framework he doesn't see how you could help but do reasonably well in stocks. We have dealt with two of them: (1) look at stocks as small pieces of businesses, and (2) margin of safety. The third idea which '100 years from now will still be regarded as [a] cornerstone of sound investing'[36] is to look at market fluctuations as your friend rather than your enemy – profit from folly rather than participate in it. The speculative price movements in individual stocks and the market get carried too far. Periodically, shares are ignored or decline because of unjustified popular prejudice, or undue pessimism 'in an astonishingly large proportion of the trading in common stocks, those engaged therein don't appear to know – in polite terms – one part of their anatomy from another'.[37] The good analyst sticks with his or her own judgement on earnings regardless of temporary market optimism or pessimism. This judgement would change only if the underlying factors changed. However, market movements are useful to the investor in a very practical sense. The oscillations sometimes create conditions in which prices are low relative to value, which present buying opportunities.

On other occasions, when prices are irrationally high, there should be a halt to buying, and possibly, a selling-off. Graham's disdainful view of market speculators and the opportunities they bring, with their manic-depressive behaviour, is beautifully expressed in the parable of Mr Market.[38] Imagine that in some private business you own a small share that cost you $1,000. One of your partners, named Mr Market, is very obliging indeed. Every day he tells you what he thinks your interest is worth and furthermore offers either to buy you out or to sell you an additional interest on that basis. Sometimes his idea of value appears plausible and justified by business developments and prospects as you know them. Often, on the other hand, Mr Market lets his enthusiasm or his fears run away with him, and the value he proposes seem to you a little short of silly.

If you are a prudent investor or a sensible businessman, will you let Mr. Market's daily communication determine your view of the value of a $1,000 interest in the enterprise? You may be happy to sell out to him when he quotes you a ridiculously high price, and equally happy to buy from him when his price is low. At all times you should form your own ideas of the value of your holdings, based on full reports from the company about its operations and financial position.

WHAT HE AVOIDS

This book is as much about what not to do as an investor as it is about what approaches to follow. Graham had a number of 'don'ts' on his list aside from don't unthinkingly accept general market pessimism or optimism. There are six important additional stumbling blocks to successful investment:

Forecasting the market, timing and charts

Millions, if not billions, of dollars are spent every year in attempts to forecast macro economic activity or stock market indexes. Graham paid little or no attention to any of those. He was keen to make his results largely independent of any views of the market's future by having sole reliance on a single criterion: price attractiveness. The problem with basing investment decisions on market forecasts and trying to time purchase so that you buy at the bottom and sell at the top is *not* that you are likely to be uninformed, unskilful or stupid. On the contrary, market forecasters are highly intelligent and skilful. And this is where the problem lies. It is done by so many experts that their efforts constantly neutralize each other. The net result is that the market already reflects all that these experts can say about the future. There is no reason for any typical investor to believe that he can get more dependable guidance on the market direction than count- less other speculators. It is absurd to think that the general public can ever make money out of market forecasts. If you think you can then you are making a very strong implicit assumption: you have a special talent or 'feel' for the market, a higher intelligence than your competitors. This is generally too much to ask of the ordinary investor – even a great mind like Graham's was not up to the task (a self admission).

We are all tempted to time the market because the rewards for being consistently right are enormous. But the logical grounds for believing that *anyone* can be constantly right are very weak. Market timing is time wast- ing and leaves no margin for safety: you are either right or wrong – if you are wrong money is lost.

> The only principle of timing that has ever worked well consistently is to buy common stocks at such times as they are cheap by analysis, and to sell them at such time as they are dear, or at least no longer cheap, by analysis. That sounds like timing; but when you consider it you will see that it is not really timing at all, but rather the purchase and sale of securities by the method of valuation. Essentially, it requires no opinion as to the future of the market; because if you buy securities cheap enough, your position is sound, even if the market should continue to go down. And if you sell the securities at a fairly high price you have done the smart thing, even if the market should continue to go up.[39]

The speculator, on the other hand is concerned about timing because he wants to make a quick profit – these people are, ultimately, chasing a will- o'-the-wisp.

Graham did not automatically dismiss technical analysis or chart read- ing as akin to astrology or necromancy, as many of his contemporaries did. He felt it incumbent that he put forward robust arguments against it, following a thorough examination. He came up with some rigorous rea- sons for doubting the potential of mechanical means of determining the right moments to buy or sell. His first argument is that chart reading can- not possibly be regarded as a science because its rules are not dependable. If they were it would be easy for everybody to predict prices. Everyone would time purchases and sales perfectly. The flaw in the chartists' argu- ment is that subsequent stock prices depend on human action – which is not scientifically predictable in any straightforward way. The observation that stock prices behaved in a particular way in the past and so indicate the possibility of a scientific rule for predicting the future contains the seeds of its destruction. Formulas may gain adherents because there seems to be a plausible pattern in the statistical record. But as the formula becomes more widely adopted its reliability tends to diminish. There are two reasons for this: first, the statistical record applies to one period of time and new conditions mean that the old formula does not fit. Second, once the method becomes widely known, it is adopted by great numbers of traders. The large following itself brings to an end its usefulness – it is too simple, too easy and too well known for it to last. Thus when you think you are able to make a scientific prediction of an economic event under human control the relationships change as actions invalidate the prior conclusions.

There is no *sound* theoretical basis to chart reading. The claimed theoretical base is as follows: the activities and attitudes of the market buyers and sellers is reflected in a particular stock (or the market) price chart. Therefore, we can conclude, that by studying the past record, we can predict the next move or moves. It is undoubtedly true that past share prices do reflect the activities and attitude of participants, but it does not follow that the future can be predicted from this. Studying past price patterns may teach you a great deal about the technical position of the stock, but this will not be enough for profitable trading.

Chartists generally follow the maxim that losses should be cut short and profits allowed to run. This is a very plausible argument – it avoids large losses while permitting the possibility of a large profit. There are, however, two hidden fallacies in this:

- Roulette players follow a similar system, designed to limit losses at any one session. However, over time they find that the small losses aggregate to more than the few large profits. This is only to be expected given that the mathematical odds are against them. The chartist finds that the cost of trading weights the odds against him or her.

- As a particular approach attracts more followers the losses incurred in unprofitable trades tend to increase, while the profitable events produce smaller returns. The increased number of individuals adopting the system receive signals to buy all at the same time. The competition to buy pushes up the price, thus squeezing profits. On the other hand, when the large body of adherents decide to sell they all do so at the same time thus producing a lower price.

Graham marvelled at the abandonment of common sense in buying when the price has risen and selling when the price has declined. 'This is the exact opposite of sound business sense everywhere else.'[40] He said in 1973, after over 50 years' experience he does not know of a single person who has consistently made money by this approach of 'following the market'.[41]

In the second half of the 20th Century dozens of tests were carried out by academicians to establish whether trading rules employed by technical analysts and chartists produced above average returns (this was the study of 'the weak form' of the efficient market hypothesis). The conclusions drawn from this vast literature confirmed the view that Graham reached through observation, logic, experience and intuition; there are no abnormally high returns to be had this way (at least, not on a consistent basis, after costs).

Short-term selectivity

Much of the activity of the financial district is focused on the analysis of a corporation's or an industry's near-term business prospects. The reasoning goes like this: If the results in the next 12 months are anticipated to be good the issue should be bought because when the larger profits are reported it will be possible to sell at a higher price. This may explain why so much attention is given to quarterly earnings momentum, the potential for dividend advances or some other short-term favourable development.

> I am most sceptical of this Wall Street activity ... I regard it as naive in the extreme. The thought that the security analyst, by determining that a certain business is going to do well next year has thereby found something really useful, judged by any serious standard of utility, and that he can translate his discovery into an unconditional suggestion that the stock be bought, seems to me to be a parody of true security analysis.[42]

He had three objections to this approach:

- Analysts are fallible. The forecast of next year's results may prove incorrect and the expected improvement may not take place.
- Even if the forecast is correct recent market action may have led to the prospects being already fully reflected in the price. (Sometimes the prospects are *more than* factored into the price.)
- For some reason or for no identifiable reason the price will not move the way it should.

A stock's value depends on its earning power over a long time period. The near-term should not be awarded too much weight.

> .... **A stock's value depends on its earning power over a long time period.** ....

Growth stocks

Graham defined a growth stock as one where the company *has* performed better than average (in growth of earnings per share) for a period of years and is expected to do so in the future. He pointed out that the term growth stock should not be used for companies which have an ordinary record where the investor merely *expects* it to do better than average in the future – these should be termed 'promising companies'.[43] There are a number of difficulties in finding good investments in growth stocks. First, companies with good records and apparently good prospects generally have stock that is selling at high prices. You may be entirely vindicated in your judgement of the quality of the underlying business and still do badly on the investment because the stock was so highly (over) priced when purchased. Worse still, in many cases the growth-stock investor 'has no idea of how much to pay for a growth stock' and so the 'growth stock philosophy can't be applied with reasonably dependable results'.[44] The projection of future earnings based on a past trend is full of uncertainty; modifying the trend leaves you open to the self-critical charge of arbitrariness. Too often analysts have been persuaded to extrapolate a trend forgetting to allow for the potential for the law of diminishing returns or for the impact of increasing competition to decrease the growth trajectory – or even eliminate it. A dangerous trap for the unwary is often laid at the peak of a business cycle, when there is the danger of trend projection on the very eve of a serious setback.

Most growth stocks are technologically based. Analysis of the future prospects of companies riding on the 'coattails of science'[45] is fundamentally a qualitative exercise. There are no dependable measurements and no standards by which a price may be set on future growth. 'I cannot help but feel that growth stock investment is still in the pre-scientific stage.'[46]

Paradoxically, growth stock analysis is an area where mathematical valuations are particularly prevalent, but it is the area where they are least reliable. Growth stocks' future earnings are less predictable and less tied to the hard evidence of the past. This can lead to miscalculation and serious error. The growth stock buyer contravenes the margin of safety principal.

> The market has a tendency to set prices that will not be adequately protected by a *conservative* projection of future earnings. (It is a basic rule of prudent investment that all estimates, when they differ from past performance, must err at least slightly on the side of understatement)....The margin-of-safety idea becomes much more evident when we apply it to the field of undervalued or bargain securities. We have here, by definition, a favourable difference between price on the one hand and indicated or appraised value on the other. That difference is the safety margin. It is available for absorbing the effect of miscalculations or worse than average luck. The buyer of bargain issues places particular emphasis on the ability of the investment to withstand adverse developments.[47]

Graham divided analysts into camps: those who estimate the future of a corporation and stock on the basis of prediction; and those who do so by way of protection. The prediction-based analysts have a tendency to recommend stocks with good business prospects without paying too much attention to the level of the stock price. The protection-based analysts focus on the price of the issue. This quantitative or statistical approach emphasizes the measurable relationship between selling price and earnings, assets, dividends and so forth. It is not as necessary to be enthusiastic over the firm's long-term prospects as it is 'to be reasonably confident that the enterprise will get along'.[48] Value for money is sought in concrete, demonstrable terms. Prospects and promises of the future do not compensate for a lack of sufficient value in hand.

Many analysts seek industries with the best prospects, and the best firm within those industries with the best management and other vital intangible factors. The result is high stock prices for these well-known companies, whereas there is almost complete avoidance of less promising industries and companies no matter how low the stock price falls. Sometimes the favoured stocks rise to such an extent that there is an implied belief that these companies can grow at a rapid rate indefinitely (Internet stocks in 1990s?). On the other hand, the unfavoured stocks fall to such a low level that the implication is that they are headed for extinction – analysts seem not to want them at any price. Neither belief is rational. High growth is interrupted, slowed (and often reversed) by new technology, new competition or shifting patterns of demand. Also, remarkably few large companies become extinct. 'To enjoy a reasonable chance of continued better than average results, the investor must follow policies which are (1) inherently sound and promising, and (2) are not popular in Wall Street.'[49] Note: this is not the same as simple contrarian investing, in which you simply do the opposite to the crowd. Here, your contrary opinion (if it is contrary) is based on sound and informed reasoning.

Graham did not exclude the possibility that some individual analysts could be 'smart and shrewd' enough to pick winning growth stocks that had prices which did not already reflect their prospects. But he regarded these qualities as rare, and advised investors to avoid trying to compete with these highly gifted people. (We discuss one such person Philip Fisher in Chapter 5). Instead of smart and shrewd the normal analyst should aim for 'wise'. This means, instead of brilliant insight into the future trading environment and managerial qualities of a corporation, the analyst should merely be technically competent, experienced and prudent.

Managementism

There are three levels of problems with management for the investor to be wary of. The first is out-and-out dishonesty and selfishness. Graham said that because it was impossible to 'make a quantitative deduction to allow for unscrupulous management; the only way to deal with such situations is to avoid them'.[50] The second level is honesty combined with incompetence. Stockholders can too easily take for granted that management is capable. The third level is where managers are generally honest in the ordinary sense and competent in running the business. The problem is that they are only 'human'[51] – and subject to the all too human problem of conflicts of interest. This is 'managementism'[52] at its most subtle. On all the following issues the managers are interested parties and while 'the officers of our large corporations constitute a group of men above the average in probity as well as in ability. But this does not mean that they should be given *carte blanche* in all matters affecting their own interests'.[53] The main areas of concern are:

- *Managerial compensation* Including options, bonuses as well as salaries.
- *Expansion of the business* The managers may benefit from increased salaries, power and prestige. This can be achieved particularly quickly through an acquisitions policy.
- *Information to shareholders* Managers may retain a tactical edge over the questioning shareholder by controlling the flow of information. (The justification, or excuse, for restricting the flow is that it may be of benefit to competitors.)

- *Continuance of the shareholders' investment in the company*   Occasionally shareholders would be best served if the corporation is shrunk significantly, capital withdrawn and distributed to shareholders. In extreme cases it is better to wind up the business. Few managers are prepared to countenance such action despite the ineluctable logic from the shareholders' perspective.

- *Payment of dividends*   What proportion of the money earned in a year should be passed on to stockholders? Managers have a predilection for retaining earnings, even if this capital can be used by stockholders to create more value outside of the business rather than in it. Paying out a high proportion of earnings means curtailing the resources of the enterprise, thus raising the risk of, and reducing the prestige of, the officers. There are three reasons advanced by the managers for a low payout:

1. It is good for the shareholders that a conservative policy is followed. Sometimes this makes sense, but too often a company is conservative to the point of harming shareholders' interests.

2. This business is somehow special, with special hazards, and that more care is needed. 'Since every business is a special business, it seems to me that the argument more or less answers itself. You would have to conclude that there would be no principles by which the stockholders can determine suitable treatment for themselves.'[54]

3. The stockholders don't understand the problems of the business. It is impertinent for them to suggest they know better than the management. This argument angered Graham because it implies stockholders should never have an opinion contrary to the management's, and, therefore, stockholders' control would be vitiated. Managers and stockholders should never forget that 'corporations are the mere creatures and property of the stockholders who own them; that the officers are only the paid employees of the stockholders; and that the directors, however chosen, are virtually trustees, whose legal duty is to act solely on behalf of the owners of the business'.[55]

   When a private employer hires staff he naturally looks for people he trusts. However, this does not mean he permits them to fix their own salaries or decide for him how much capital he should put into or remove from the business.

A long and complex literature has developed around the issue of dividend policy – how much to payout, and in what pattern over time (less now with more later, or more now with less later?). The reader is invited to consult any standard corporate finance text for the details of this argument.[56] Graham was ahead of his time and pre-empted the conclusion of much of this literature;

> It is customary to commend managements for 'ploughing earnings back into the property'; but in measuring the benefits from such a policy, the time element is usually left out of account. It stands to reason that if a business paid out only a small part of its earnings in dividends, the value of the stock should increase over a period of years; but it is by no means certain that this increase will compensate the stockholders for the dividends withheld from them, particularly if interest on these amounts is compounded…. In some cases the stockholders derive positive benefits from an ultraconservative dividend policy, i.e., through much larger eventual earnings and dividends. In such instances the market's judgement proves to be wrong in penalizing the shares because of their small dividend. The price of these shares should be higher rather than lower on account of the fact that profits have been added to surplus instead of having been paid out in dividends…. Far more frequently, however, the stockholders derive much greater benefits from dividend payments than from additions to surplus.[57]

Bubble stocks

Graham experienced the frustration and puzzlement that comes to the value investor in times of great stock market optimism, when prices leave values far behind. These are times when great strength of character is needed to withstand the murmurs of doubt about the value philosophy as others make effortless profit. 'Speculators often prosper through ignorance; it is a cliché that in a roaring bull market knowledge is superfluous and experience a handicap. But the typical experience of the speculator is one of temporary profit and ultimate loss… Everyone now [1959] calls himself an investor, including a huge horde of speculators.'[58] The frustration comes from believing stocks to be over priced and therefore refusing to participate in the market and then watching prices rise even higher – many of us experienced this as recently as the late 1990s.

In an interview with John Quirt in 1974, Graham explained how it is that speculators blow up a bubble:[59]

Take a stock that has earnings growth of 15 per cent per year. That's rather remarkable, but let's take it as an example. So long as the P/E just stays at its present level, the buyer will get 15 per cent returns – plus dividends if any – which will be so attractive to other investors that they will want to own that stock too, so they will buy it and in doing so they will bid up the price and hence the P/E. This makes the price rise faster than 15 per cent so the security seems even more attractive. As more and more investors become enamoured with the promised rate of return, the price lifts free from underlying value and is enabled to float freely upward creating a bubble that will expand quite beautifully until finally and inevitably it *must* burst. In other words, if you start low, you'll have a rise, and if you have a rise you'll have satisfaction and that will bring a further rise, and so on. But it won't go on forever. It may go too far but never forever.

Graham presented a wonderful illustration of the speculative mind set and the difficulty of maintaining an independent view in his tenth lecture at the New York Institute of Finance 1946–7:[60]

It reminds me of the story you all know of the oil man who went to heaven and asked St Peter to let him in. St Peter said, 'Sorry, the oil men's area here is all filled up, as you can see by looking through the gate'. The man said, 'That's too bad, but do you mind if I just say four words to them?' And St Peter said, 'Sure'. So the man shouts good and loud , 'Oil discovered in hell!', whereupon all the oilmen begin trooping out of Heaven and making a beeline for the nether regions. Then St Peter said, 'That was an awfully good stunt. Now there's plenty of room, come right in'. The oilman scratches his head and says, 'I think I'll go with the rest of the boys. There may be some truth in that rumour after all'. I think that is the way we behave, very often, in the movements of the stock market. We know from experience that we are going to end up badly, but somehow 'there may be some truth in the rumour, so we go along with the boys'.

Notes

1   Said in an interview with Janet Lowe, Omaha, 25 May 1993. Printed in Janet Lowe (1997), p. 35. © 1997 Janet C. Lowe. This material is used by permission of John Wiley & Sons Inc.

2   From an edited transcript of a talk given by Warren Buffett at Columbia University in 1984, entitled 'The Superinvestors of Graham and Doddsville'. Reproduced in *Hermes*, the magazine of Columbia Business School, autumn 1984. Also reproduced in the reprinted version of Benjamin Graham's *The Intelligent Investor* (1973), Harper Business. This material is copyrighted and is reproduced with the permission of the author.

3   *Ibid.*

4   Bill Ruane (Sequoia fund) was also a disciple after attending one of Graham's courses at Columbia in 1951.

5   Train, J. (1980), p. 98.

6   Reproduced in Lowe, J. (1999), p. 116.

7   Barclays Capital (2000) Equity-Gilt Study.

8   Implicit price deflation for GNP. US Office of Business Economics. The National Income and Product Accounts of the United States 1929–1965.

9   Graham, B. (1996), p. 163.

10 *Ibid.*, p. 190.

11 *Ibid.*, p. 252.

12 Graham, B. (1932), Forbes, 1 June.

13 Warren Buffett speech, New York Society of Security Analysts, 6 December 1994. This material is copyrighted and is reproduced with the permission of the author.

14 Graham, B. and Dodd, D. (1934), p. 54.

15 *Ibid.*, pp. 54–5.

16 *Ibid.*, p. 12.

17 *Ibid.*, p. 452.

18 Graham, B. (1973), p. 286.

19 *Ibid.*, p. 287.

20 The first use of the term intrinsic value was not by Graham. William Armstrong employed it in his 1848 pamphlet *Stocks, and Stock-jobbing in Wall Street*.

21 Graham, B. (1955), Testimony Before the Committee on Banking and Currency, United States Senate: On Factors Affecting the Buying and Selling of Equity Securities, 11 March 1955.

22 Graham, B. and Dodd, D. (1934), p. 17.

23 *Ibid.*, pp. 18–19.

24 *Ibid.*, p. 19.

25 Graham, B. (1973) p. 277.

26 Graham, B. (1946–7). Lecture 6 in the Series *Current Problems in Security Analysis*, New York Institute of Finance. Reproduced in Lowe (1999).

27 Graham, B. (1973), p. 278.

28 *Ibid.*, p. 280.

29 *Ibid.*, p. 286.

30 *Ibid.*, p. 36.

31 Graham, B. and Dodd, D. (1934), p. 613.

32 *Ibid.*, pp. 55–6.

33 Graham, B. (1946–7), Lecture 10.

34 Graham, B. (1973), p. 3.

35 Graham, B. (1946–7), Lecture 10.

36 Buffett, W. (1994), Speech to the New York Society of Security Analysts, 6 December 1994. This material is copyrighted and is reproduced with the permission of the author.

37 Graham, B. (1973), p. 13.

38 *Ibid.*, p. 108.
39 Graham, B. (1946–7), Lecture 10.
40 Graham, B. (1973), p. x.
41 *Ibid.*, p. x.
42 Graham, B. (1946–7), Lecture 7.
43 Graham, B. (1973), p. 75.
44 Graham, B. (1976), *Medical Economics.*
45 Graham, B. (1952), Proceedings of the Fifth Annual Convention. In the *Analysts Journal*, August 1952.
46 *Ibid.*
47 Graham, B. (1973), p. 281.
48 *Ibid.*, p. 199.
49 *Ibid.*, p. 13.
50 Graham, B. and Dodd, D. (1934), p. 378.
51 Graham, B., Forbes, 1 July 1932.
52 Graham, B., 'The Ethics of American Capitalism'. Speech at University of California at Los Angeles Camp Kramer Retreat, 10 November 1956.
53 Graham, B. and Dodd, D. (1934), p. 511.
54 Graham, B. (1946–7), Lecture 9.
55 Graham, B. and Dodd, D. (1934), p. 521.
56 Chapter 19 of Corporate Financial Management (Arnold, 2002) covers this topic.
57 Graham, B. and Dodd, D. (1934), pp. 329 and 337.
58 Graham, B. Speech UCLA (1959).
59 Quirt, J. (1974).
60 Reproduced in Lowe, J. (1999).

4

Benjamin Graham's three forms of value investing

Graham developed three approaches to stock selection. The first (Current asset value investing) concentrates on the asset value of the firm. The second (Defensive value investing) is a purely quantitative approach. The third (Enterprising value investing) is the least quantitatively oriented, with its emphasis on the qualitative appraisal of future earnings power.

CURRENT ASSET VALUE INVESTING

In the early 1930s Graham developed a stock market selection approach that has as its primary focus the value of the net current assets relative to the stock price. He looked for stocks, that sold at less than the value of the net current assets after deduction, not only of the current liabilities, but also the long-term liabilities. Furthermore, in the calculation of this net asset figure the fixed assets and other assets (e.g. tangibles) were assigned a value of zero.

It seems remarkable that stock prices should fall to the extent that the total market capitalization is less than the liquidation value of the firm[1] – and that is on the assumption that plant, buildings, patents, etc. are worth nothing at all! And yet it does happen – more often than we might suppose. In 1932 Graham observed[2] that over one-third of industrial stocks were selling for less than the net quick assets, i.e. net current assets minus inventory. After deducting all liabilities the value of cash and accounts receivable was greater than the market capitalization for those firms.

He gives the example of White Motors that was selling in December 1931 for $4.8 million. This was about 60 per cent of the value of its cash and equivalent alone, and was one-fifth of the net quick assets. There were dozens of companies selling for less than the value of cash in the bank. He concluded that stockholders were implying, through their refusal to buy these stocks, that the companies were worth more dead than alive.

Now, it may be thought that the early 1930s were an extraordinary period and these opportunities are unlikely to persist and so this method of investing has little validity today. However, Graham makes it clear,[3] that buying a broadly spread portfolio was not only possible but also highly profitable for over three decades, from 1923–57 (excluding 'the time of real trial in 1930–2'). 'Over a thirty-odd-year period we must have earned an average of some 20 per cent per year from this source.'[4] Graham said that this approach needed a lot of securities in a portfolio to be successful because of the likelihood of the failure of some of the stocks to live up to expectations. The portfolio often held over 100 shares. Such was the abundance of net current asset bargains that Graham generally selected stocks selling for less than two-thirds of net current assets.

In the mid-1950s this type of buying opportunity became scarce because of the bull market. There was a long fallow period in which few stocks of this kind were purchased. However, even in 1971 Graham counted 50 or more issues available at or below net current asset value. Even if all those companies reporting net losses in the previous year were excluded there were enough to make up a diversified list (although this would have been much less than the 100 or so that Graham preferred). It was not until the 1973–4 decline that the widespread availability of these bargain stocks became mind-boggling again. In January 1976[5] Graham counted over 100 stocks selling at less than net current asset value.

Graham was not prepared to accept accounting entries at face value when estimating net current asset value. He used to say that the analyst should regard liabilities as real but the assets of questionable value.[6] Liabilities are deducted at face value, assets are to be adjusted according to the schedule in Table 4.1.

Table 4.1 Adjustment factors for asset values

Type of asset	% of liquidation to book value	
	Normal range	Rough average
Current assets:		
Cash assets (including securities at market)	100	100
Receivables (less usual reserves)	75–90	80
Inventories (at lower of cost or market)	50–75	66⅔
Fixed and miscellaneous assets:		
(Real estate, buildings, machinery, non-marketable investments, intangibles, etc.)	1–50	15 (approx.)

Why do these bargains appear?

To have stocks selling persistently below liquidating value is fundamentally illogical. Errors are being committed by one or more of the following:

- the stock market in its judgement of corporations' prospects for survival, and profitability;
- the management in pursuing value destroying activities which will waste away the assets; or
- stockholders in their attitudes toward their property.

During the 1920s new-era doctrine all the tests of value were transferred to the income account and investors lost the habit of looking at the balance sheet. This thinking led to the dumping of stocks that had low or negative near-term profits. The sell-off was so severe that stock was changing hands for a fraction of the realizable value of the corporation's resources. This was driven by fear rather than necessity. The sellers for the most part seemed not to be aware of the net asset position. Those who did examine the liquidation assets justified the selling decision on the ground that liquidation value was of little practical interest since the company had no intention of liquidating. There was an anticipation of continued dissipation of firm resources.

In many cases it would be rational to be fearful that the corporation will post losses in the future, and eventually will be worth very little. But Graham posed the following question in 1932:[7] 'Is it true that one out of three American businesses is destined to continue losing money until the stockholders have no equity remaining?…. In all probability it [the stock market] is wrong, as it always has been wrong in its major judgements of the future'.

Graham was most astonished by the high level of net liquid assets of the so-called distressed shares. They had received a huge flood of cash by the exercise of subscription rights toward the end of the boom period. This not only made them cash rich, it also added greatly to the supply of stocks that intensified the market decline when the exuberance had passed and pessimism reigned. 'The same circumstance, therefore, served both to improve the *values* behind stock and to depress the *price*'.[8]

The stock market's focus on short-term trading results gave Graham a great opportunity to exploit the irrationality of the market in ignoring asset values again in the 1970s. He found well-established companies whose long-term assets, ranging from valuable land and buildings to patents and brand names, were valued at nothing. 'Pascal said that "the heart has its reasons that reason doesn't understand": for "heart" read "Wall Street".'⁹ Even in 'normal' market conditions, when the larger stocks tend to be quoted at significantly above the net current asset value, there are usually undervalued 'secondary' issues available. These stocks are subject to the waxing and waning interest of professional market operators. If interest is low the price may fail to reflect the real value of the stock. In other words, neglect (by others) can be of great benefit to the value investor.

> ..... **Neglect (by others) can be of great benefit to the value investor.** .....

Why should prices rise?

At times of market depression analysts and investors become very fearful that there is worse to come; that a high proportion of the quoted companies will struggle to survive, waste resources in the process and then die, leaving the stockholders with nothing. This is exactly what will happen to dozens, or even hundreds of corporations. Graham accepted this, but still proposed that many of the net current asset stocks were good buys. He believed that the market pessimism was indiscriminate. In the rush for the exit, investors dumped stocks for which there was good ground for believing that recovery would eventually occur, as well as the real dogs.

What was the rationale behind his belief that the majority of these value stocks will survive and produce good returns? He pointed to a number of potential developments that would prevent the management following the path of value destruction through the gradual dissipation of assets.

- *Earning power would be lifted* to the point where it was commensurate with the company's asset level. This could come about in two ways. The first is a general improvement in the industry. Graham brings our attention to the basic economic phenomenon of entry and exit to an industry to explain why corporations in an industry performing abnormally well, or abnormally badly, will not go on doing so for ever. Those with very high returns will attract competition and so their superior performance will be eroded. Often (perhaps, especially) those sectors with a rapidly rising demand will suffer the most from an even more rapid growth of supply. In the 1930s this was true of radio, aviation, electric refrigeration, bus transportation and silk hosiery. In the new millennium it is still true of aviation, which has been joined by telecommunications, the Internet, automobiles and personal computers. Conversely, in the case of a corporation selling at a large discount because of abnormally low earnings (or losses) the withdrawal of competitors from the field and the absence of new competition often eventually improves the situation to restore a normal rate of return on assets invested in the firm. The second way to lift earnings power is through a change in the company's operating policies. It is incumbent upon management to take corrective action if a stock is selling below liquidating value, if they do not do this voluntarily then they must be forced to do so by the stockholders. The changes may come about through the existing management or their replacements. The new operating policies include more efficient methods, new products, abandonment of unprofitable lines, etc. Graham tempered his optimism for change through stockholder pressure: 'It is a notorious fact, however, that the typical American stockholder is the most docile and apathetic animal in captivity'.[10]

- *A sale or merger* would take place because another corporation can make better use of the firm's assets. They should be willing to pay the liquidating value at least.

- *Complete or partial liquidation* The management of a corporation selling below liquidating value must provide a frank justification to the stockholders for continuing. If a company is not worth more as a going concern then it is in the stockholders' interest to liquidate it. If it is worth more than its liquidating value then this should be adequately communicated to the market.

From simple to sophisticated net current asset value investing

Clearly, it is not wise to purchase all stocks selling below net current assets. This is too crude. Many of these firms will become bankrupt. Graham proposed a number of additional tests to identify the most attractive net current asset stocks. These come under four headings. The first (Financial set-up) is a quantitative element whereas the other three are largely qualitative. In addition Fig. 4.1 shows two elements crucial to success in this type of investment approach, diversification and patience.

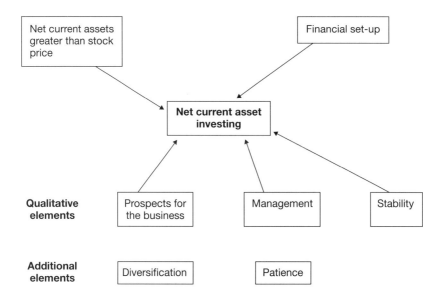

Figure 4.1 Net current asset value investing

Financial set-up

There must be a thorough analysis of the corporate income accounts. The analyst is looking for either a satisfactory level of current earnings and dividends, or a high average 'earnings power' in the past. It is wrong to rely on a projection of a past earnings trend into the future. While a past trend is a fact, a 'future trend' is only an assumption. It is impossible to be sure that the trend will not slow or go into reverse. Projecting a past trend is fundamentally psychological and arbitrary, it is not scientific.

So, if we can't carry out simple trend analysis what use are the earnings figures? Graham says that the past does give us clues to the future – never thoroughly satisfactory or reliable, and often quite useless, but, nonetheless of some value in a sufficient number of cases to make it worthwhile studying the past:

> There remains the fact that by and large a good past record offers better promise for the future than does a poor one. If a hundred enterprises are taken which had average profits of $6 per share over the past ten years, and another hundred with average profits of only $1 per share, there is every reason to expect the first group to report larger aggregate profits than the second over the *next* ten years. The basic reason therefor is that future earnings are not deter-

mined entirely by luck or by competitive managerial skill, but that capital, experience, reputation, trade contacts, and all the other factors which contributed to past earning power, are bound to exert a considerable influence on the future.[11]

Earnings power is a very important concept. It is most definitely *not* the current earnings. Graham said that it is derived from a combination of actual earnings shown over a period of years (5–10 years), and estimated future earnings. The latter are the 'average expectable earnings'[12] over some period in the future – usually five years. In examining the past and considering the future we should have in mind the average of earnings over a period of years because abnormal conditions may appertain to particular years, leading to a distorted view of earnings power due to factors like the business cycle.

> Earnings power is a very important concept.

We need to be vigilant to avoid 'booby traps in the per share figures'.[13] Earnings statements are more subject to misleading presentation than the typical balance sheet. Critical interpretation and adjustment is needed to cope with earnings figures vulnerable to arbitrary determination and manipulation. The analyst needs to separate non-recurring items from the ordinary operating results so that the underlying earning power may be more clearly estimated, 'i.e. what the company might be expected to earn year after year if the business conditions prevailing during the period were to continue unchanged'.[14] Interests in controlled or affiliated companies must be properly accounted for, as must some highly malleable elements, such as, depreciation, amortization and reserves for future losses and other contingencies. The adjustment to the published account should be designed to help answer the questions:

- What are the true earnings?
- What indication does the earnings record carry for *future* earnings power?

Other elements in the financial set-up, which may help form a view of the company's earning power and riskiness, include production and cost statistics, capacity, unfilled orders, asset make-up and liability structure. The rapid loss of quick assets is to be regarded as a very bad sign, especially if there are no definite signs of the loss ceasing.

The qualitative factors

Graham insisted that the quantitative data cannot be regarded as conclusive. They must be supported by a qualitative survey of the business. By examining the nature of the enterprise, the analyst can get some indication of the extent to which the earning power is permanent. This qualitative analysis encompasses such matters as the nature of the industry and business; the competitive position of the corporation in the industry; the operating characteristics of the company; the character of the management; the outlook for the firm, and the industry. The sources of information useful to this process vary greatly in quality and dependability. Much of it is mere opinion.

Although Graham said it was important to study the qualitative elements he did not provide many clues to help the reader examine the nature of the business and its future prospects. One is left a little sceptical that Graham actually gave the qualitative element any significant weight. The only statement I could find was the following: 'Most people have fairly definite notions as to what is "a good business" and what is not. These views are based partly on the financial results, partly on knowledge of specific conditions in the industry, and partly also on surmise or bias'.[15]

The identification of capable management is even more difficult than the analysis of firm strategy. There are few objective tests that can be applied. If the investor does not have personal knowledge of the individual managers it is often necessary to rely on reputation (which may or may not be deserved). Graham regarded a superior comparative earnings record as the most convincing indicator of high managerial ability. But, he wryly noted, 'this brings us back to quantitative data'.[16]

Philip Fisher, Charles Munger and Warren Buffett forcefully emphasize the importance of managerial competence, managerial honesty and the strength of the business franchise. They insist that the investor look out for a range of indicators and employ sophisticated investigatory techniques. These investors are content to rely on subjective analysis, whereas Graham was keen to find a more tangible/scientific measure. The deep scars inflicted in the early 1930s meant that he felt uneasy about relying on judgement. He looked for a factual base. Opinion is too vulnerable to persuasion in the passion of the moment. Thus, we have a slight contradiction in Graham's writing: qualitative factors are very important in security analysis. These, by their nature are non-quantifiable and are largely subjective, and so cannot be regarded as 'facts'. Therefore, the analyst should not place much weight on them unless they have some link to quantifiable evidence. In other words, the investor cannot trust his own judgement in the evaluation of a business' most important features: its competitive strengths and quality of management. After all, Graham would argue, investors in 1928–9 believed they could accurately predict rosy futures for many firms, and later found that they had been deluding themselves. Graham's message seems to be that qualitative factors are vital, but you need to be very cautious in interpreting the results, so you probably need to revert to quantitative facts.

Because there are so many difficulties in evaluating the prospects for the business and the quality of management Graham said that the analyst must 'guard against'[17] future changes, rather than try to guess the future better than the generality of analysts and make an abnormal profit that way. To guard against future change is to look for a company with inherent stability: 'For stability means resistance to change and hence greater dependability for the results shown in the past … it derives in the first instance from the character of the business and not from its statistical record. A stable record suggests that the business is inherently stable, but this suggestion may be rebutted by other considerations'.[18] The first port of call is the figures, but these statistics are not sufficient; qualitative considerations may completely vitiate them – perhaps a distrust of the management or inherent instability will cause rejection.

Net current asset value investing requires the holding of an extensively diversified portfolio – to reduce risk. Once bought the investor has to control urges towards impatience if stocks do not advance soon after acquisition. It may take years for the market to recognize the fundamental worth of net current asset stocks. It would be most unfortunate to sell because nothing is happening – just as you do, the chances are that the stock will be re-rated.

> .... **Do not get too hung up on the need for great precision.** ....

A word of warning in undertaking quantitative and qualitative analysis: do not get too hung up on the need for great precision. Graham liked to say that if a man was fat you did not have to know his exact weight to know that he was fat.

> A thing I would like to warn you against is spending a lot of time on over-detailed analysis of the company's and the industry's position, including counting the last bath tub that has been or will be produced; because you get yourself into the feeling that, since you have studied this thing so long and

gathered so many figures, your estimates are bound to be highly accurate. But they won't be. They are only rough estimates.[19]

If you can find a company:

- selling below net current asset value;
- run by honest and competent managers who will work hard to prevent the dissipation of assets; and
- that has shown high and stable earnings power in the past which is likely to continue in the future,

then you have found an investment bargain. Eventually the true worth of the stock will be recognized by the stock market. In the meantime, you can enjoy the high degree of safety that a stock with little chance of loss of principal possesses.

DEFENSIVE VALUE INVESTING

Graham's net current asset value investing was developed in the aftermath of the Wall Street Crash. It worked well for much of his career. However, his inquisitive, ever-active mind continued to search for other approaches to stock selection based on the fundamental principles of intrinsic value and margin of safety. He developed two other investment approaches: defensive value investing and enterprising value investing. The defensive value investor lays primary emphasis on the avoidance of serious mistakes or losses. Second, he or she is looking for a method that has a simple approach to stock selection with little effort required, e.g. a short checklist of criteria for purchasing, and the absence of a need for making frequent decisions. Third, given the first two criteria it would not be rational to expect high returns and so mere 'satisfactory results' are to be expected: 'we are sceptical of the ability of defensive investors generally to get better than average results'.[20]

Graham suggested that a follower of this approach would aim for adequate, but not excessive, diversification. This meant a portfolio of between 10 and 30 stocks – thus contributing to the simplicity and low maintenance criterion. The remainder of the guidance rules are simple-to-follow statistics about the companies (note the absence of qualitative elements):

1. *Each company should be large, prominent and important*   Small companies, generally, are subject to more than average vicissitudes. To be prominent a company should rank among the first quarter or first third in size within its industry group.
2. *A sufficiently strong financial condition*   Industrial companies should have current assets double the value of current liabilities. In addition, long-term debt should be less than the net current assets. The book value of equity (shareholders' funds) should represent at least half of the total capitalization, including all debt.
3. *Earnings and dividend stability and growth*   The company should have produced profits in each of the last ten years. Dividends should have been paid for each of the last 20 years. Earnings per share should have grown by at least one-third over the last ten years (using three-year averages at the beginning and the end).
4. *The P/E ratio should be moderate*   Graham used the limit of 15 times the average earnings of the past three years.[21] He also suggested a limit of 25 times average earnings over the last seven years, or 20 times those for the last 12 months.[22]
5. *Stock price should not be significantly above net asset value*   Graham used one-and-a-half-times the last reported book value.

There is some flexibility in points (4) and (5). If the P/E ratio is below 15 the analyst may permit a correspondingly larger asset multiplier. The rule of thumb Graham suggested was: 'the product of the multiplier [PER over last three years] times the ratio of price to book value should not exceed 22.5'.[23]

The criteria form an astonishingly strict, quantitative, almost mechanical, approach, which is significantly different to the net current asset method, with its allowance for a number of qualitative elements. It also stands in contrasts to the third method, enterprising value investing.

ENTERPRISING VALUE INVESTING

Enterprising value investing is a more aggressive approach. It involves more effort and should be expected to produce returns that are better than merely 'satisfactory'. Graham insisted that this approach did not move the stock-picker too far along the continuum away from investment and toward speculation. Only stocks which are 'certainly not over-valued by conservative measures'[24] and which meet 'objective and rational tests of underlying soundness'[25] are permitted to be considered for purchase.

Graham proposes, as a starting point, the use of the same criteria as the defensive investor but with much less inflexibility. He suggests that a considerable plus in one area would more than compensate for a deficiency elsewhere. For example, if a company failed to produce a profit three years ago but passes all the other tests well, including high average earnings, the stock may be worthy of further consideration. One key criterion which is dropped entirely is the size requirement. There is no lower limit: 'Small companies may afford enough safety if bought carefully and on a group basis'.[26] The defensive approach makes investing simple, whereas the enterprising approach requires much more time and care. The more aggressive or active investor must, through intelligent analysis, identify stocks that are both sound and attractive. As well as requiring informed judgement to weigh up the importance of key statistical data (to what extent a black mark on one factor can be offset by a considerable plus on an other), the analyst needs to estimate the average earnings over a period of years in the *future*. Furthermore, the earnings estimate should be multiplied 'by an appropriate "capitalization factor"'.[27] Unfortunately, Graham did not go into details on the subject of determining the capitalization (discount) factor.

Future earnings power estimation can be informed by knowledge of past data for physical volume, prices received, and operating margin. Assumptions then need to be made concerning future growth prospects. Clearly, enterprising investing requires much more work and thought, than the defensive approach. Because the analyst needs to thoroughly understand the corporation Graham suggests that he or she confine themselves to the:

> three or four companies whose future he thinks he knows the best, and concentrate his own and his clients' interest on what he forecasts for them …. it is undoubtedly better to concentrate on one stock that you *know* is going to prove highly profitable, rather than dilute your results to a mediocre figure, merely for diversification's sake.[28]

The reward for this extra skill and effort comes in the form of better than average returns than are available to the defensive investor. This factor alone should not cause an investor to aim at being an enterprising investor, thereby abandoning simpler techniques giving creditable rewards. It requires a high level of competence and dedication. It needs more than a trace of wisdom:

> If you merely try to bring *just a little* extra knowledge and cleverness to bear upon your investment programme, instead of realizing a little better than normal results, you may well find that you have done worse. Since anyone – by just buying and holding a representative list – can equal the performance of the market averages, it would seem a comparatively simple matter to 'beat the averages'; but as a matter of fact the proportion of smart people who try this and fail is surprisingly large.[29]

The enterprising investor must have a considerable knowledge of corporations, the stock market and security valuation. There is no series of gradations between the defensive and enterprising status. It is a grave mistake (committed by many) for an investor to try to take the middle ground. Such a compromise will end in disappointment. Graham draws an analogy with business: aspiring businessmen cannot become half-businessmen and thereby expect to achieve half the normal rate of profit.

Given that the majority of security owners can devote only a small amount of time and intellectual effort to their selections they should elect to become defensive investors and/or net current asset value investors, and to expect merely satisfactory returns. Only those with the time, discipline and knowledge should embark on the quasi-business enterprising approach.

Graham looked at risk in a different way to most market analysts. He believed that while some businesses are inherently more risky than others, the investor could more than offset his or her risk by the application of intelligent effort. So, the notion that those who are risk averse have to be content with a low return is false. Risk and return do not move proportionately to each other in a closed system – with no other influences. So an investor can achieve low-risk, not necessarily simply by accepting a low return, but by the application of more intelligent effort. High returns are primarily determined by the willingness and ability of the investor for intellectual exertion:

> The rate of return sought should be dependent … on the amount of intelligent effort the investor is willing and able to bring to bear on his task. The minimum return goes to our passive [defensive] investor, who wants both safety and freedom from concern. The maximum return would be realized by the alert and enterprising investor who exercises maximum intelligence and skill.[30]

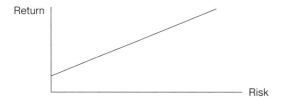

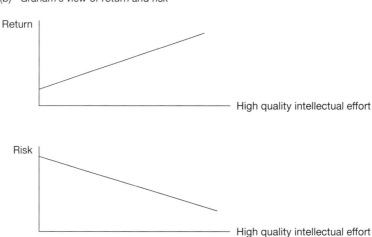

Figure 4.2   Returns and risk

In enterprising value investing the margin of safety is created through the high quality analysis of the corporation rather than the simple application of statistical tests. For this reason enterprising investors should concentrate on those corporations or industries where they have a special interest or preference. This will help give a competitive edge over other analysts – an insight others lack.

Enterprising value investing shares can be found in a number of areas of the stock market. One fruitful area for search is 'the relatively unpopular large company'.[31] The fashion tide of the market pulls speculators' attention toward the current areas of glamour, leaving other stocks stranded. The lack of interest may be due to recent unsettling news that is of a temporary nature. 'The market is fond of making mountains out of molehills and exaggerating ordinary vicissitudes into major setbacks.'[32] The larger companies going through a period of unpopularity have two advantages over smaller companies:

- they have both the capital and human intellectual resources to carry them through adversity and back to the path of a satisfactory earnings trend; and
- when the improvement starts to show through the market is likely to respond more speedily.

Despite these advantages good investments can still be found in the secondary companies. Even corporations with good past records and good prospects sometimes seem to fail to catch the imagination of the market. These stocks can suffer from protracted neglect.

Cyclical enterprises can offer value, e.g. when the immediate outlook is unfavourable, near-term profits are dropping and the stock price more than fully reflects the negative factors. The approaches of buying out-of-favour large company stocks, neglected secondary company stocks, or cyclical company stocks are three distinct categories of investment strategies. They each require different types of knowledge and temperament. It is preferable to specialize and develop appropriate specific knowledge and attributes, rather than spread intellectual and emotional resources thinly.

When to sell

Graham was prepared to hold stocks for a considerable time (indefinitely) if there was a reasonable expectation of good income and an enhancement of value. However, he would sell immediately if the stock ceased to be attractive 'either because its quality has deteriorated or because the price has risen to a level not justified by the demonstrable value'.[33]

> The true investor is scarcely ever forced to sell his shares.

He said that the true investor is scarcely ever forced to sell his shares. He or she should not permit himself or herself to be stampeded or unduly worried by market declines caused by other stock-pickers mistakes of judgement. At all times the focus should be on intrinsic value not market fluctuations and fads. While he was generally against trying to predict market surges and falls he did suggest that there are extreme situations, when the market is exceptionally high, where it is better to keep money in cash or government bonds.[34] However, these are rare events and there is a severe risk of being wrong.

Difficulties and drawbacks of Graham's approaches

There are some serious difficulties with trying to implement a Grahamite investment approach. The first comes from not fully understanding what Graham was saying, or from over-simplifying the technique. For example, some so-called followers, have developed simplistic formulas which they claim are based on Graham's methods. For example, they might have gathered historical data on stocks to establish 'value investing rules' which according to the statistical record would have produced abnormally high returns. These rules might be 'buy stocks with price-earnings ratios under two-thirds of the market average', or 'buy those on high dividend yields' or 'high book to equity ratios'. Because hypothetical out-performance occurred in the past it is automatically assumed that the magic of the formula will continue into the future to make the stock picker rich.

There are a number of derisory terms used in academic circles to describe the process of examining past data for patterns leading to a formula for success – 'torturing the data until they confess' is one. Here the 'researcher' tries out dozens of formulas on past data until he or she finds the one that gives the desired result. Along the same lines we have 'mining the data-set' until something 'useful' is found. The point the academics are making is: just because you have found some sort of statistical relationship in the numbers you have in front of you it does not mean that it is a reliable relationship on which you can make decisions about the future. It could be a pure fluke. Alternatively, perhaps it was a reliable relationship in the past but, because so many people are aware of its past existence, it no longer exists because security buyers have acted on the new information, and thus the price discounts it. Even Graham's purely quantitative approach – defensive value investing – has a long list of tests for a stock to pass before it is accepted. Graham goes further; he says this simple approach with its inattention to qualitative factors (e.g. management quality, competitive position of industry and firm, etc.) will produce merely satisfactory results and not the extraordinary returns that simple criteria value investors are looking for.

All those value funds on Wall Street or elsewhere using absurdly simple criteria are as distant from Graham's ideas as are those who chase the latest fashion in hi-tech.

Even assuming away the temptation to over-simplify Graham's principles, there are some difficult obstacles blocking the path to successful
investment. First, it is hard work. It is important to obtain high quality
data and this is not handed to the investor on a plate. A good knowledge
of accounting is needed to make the necessary adjustment for accounting
artifices. The analyst needs experience and skill to try to uncover information which has been deliberately concealed. Awareness of crucial factors such as the business environment, corporate strategy and the
behaviour of managers, are also crucial to two of his methods. These are
demanding disciplines.

Second, there are certain personality traits needed. Strength of character
is needed to resist the temptation to go with the crowd when it is panick-
ing, or when it is irrationally exuberant. Fortitude and courage are often
needed to persist when all around you appear to be doing well and you
have to wait for your harvest.

> The investor's chief problem – and even his worst enemy is likely to be himself
> … We have seen much more money made and *kept* by 'ordinary people' who
> were temperamentally well-suited for the investment process than by those
> who lacked this quality, even though they had an extensive knowledge of
> finance, accounting and stock market lore.[35]

Third, for long periods of time the methods (particularly, the net current
asset value approach) are not practicable. They would tell you to buy few
or no shares because the market is at a high level. 'My guess is the last big
time to do it Ben's way was in 1973 or 1974, when you could have done it
quite easily.'[36] This criticism by Warren Buffett seems a little harsh. It is
rare when the market is so high that it is impossible to invest using one of
the three approaches.

Fourth, value investing can be dangerous for short-term security buyers. The strongest 'buy' signals occur at times of market (and, usually, economic) recession. These tend to be periods of high volatility and the future
is seen through a fog of a depressing near-term news. Furthermore, the
value investor's buying confidence rests on two assumptions:

1. that the market price can be out of line with intrinsic value; and
2. that the disparity will correct itself.

Perhaps in the long run point (2) is true but to an investor with a short-run
investing horizon the results may be unsatisfactory. Neglect and prejudice
may result in the under-valuation persisting for an inconveniently long

time. When the price does eventually reflect the previously calculated value, it may be found that the circumstances of the firm and thus the key facts and reasoning on which the decision was reached, have changed, thereby altering the intrinsic value.

Fifth, used cigar-butts may *or may not* give you one last puff. Warren Buffett abandoned Graham's net current asset approach because:

> first, the original 'bargain' price probably will not turn out to be such a steal after all. In a difficult business, no sooner has one problem been solved than another surfaces – never is there just one cockroach in the kitchen. Second, any initial advantage you secure will be quickly eroded by the low return that the business earns. For example, if you buy a business for $8 million that can be sold or liquidated for $10 million and promptly take either course, you can realize a high return. But the investment will disappoint if the business is sold for $10 million in ten years and in the interim has annually earned and distributed only a few per cent on cost. Time is the friend of the wonderful business, the enemy of the mediocre.[37]

Buffett referred to buying a stock which is so cheap that there is an expectation of some hiccup in its fortunes to allow you to off-load the shares at a profit as the 'cigar butt' approach. 'A cigar butt found on the street that has only one puff left in it may not offer much of a smoke, but the "bargain purchase" will make that puff all profit.'[38]

Buffett followed Graham's value investing philosophy for a number of years. Berkshire Hathaway, his holding company, was itself a cigar butt. It engaged in the very unpromising textile manufacturing business in the United States. It was cheap in relation to its assets but the economics of the business were awful, and Buffett lost a lot of money on its operations. He also bought the Baltimore department store Hochschild, Kohn at a substantial discount from book value, plenty of unrecorded real estate values and a significant LIFO inventory cushion. After three years he sold at about the price he paid. His comment was that, 'It's far better to buy a wonderful company at a fair price than a fair company at a wonderful price ... when a management with a reputation for brilliance tackles a business with a reputation for bad economics, it is the reputation of the business that remains intact'.[39] In fairness to Graham it must be said that his net current asset approach *requires* a consideration of the key qualitative characteristics of the business, including an assessment of the industry economics, firm economics and strategic position. This is essential to be able to calculate earnings power. Perhaps the key to this controversy lies in the matter of emphasis: did Graham overwhelmingly emphasize the quantitative to the virtual exclusion of the qualitative as apparently suggested by Buffett, or did he give as much time to the intangible aspects of the company's position as he did to the historical facts and figures? It is difficult for us to judge this today. I have to acknowledge that Warren Buffett knew Graham and studied under his tutelage. He said, 'Ben tended to look at the statistics alone'[40] but my interpretation of Graham's writing is that qualitative factors were regarded as crucial in two of his methods: net current asset and enterprising value investing. What can be said with certainty is that with all three of Graham's methods large numbers of companies would fall at the first hurdle, because they have inadequate net assets. This means that a long list of potentially good stocks, with few tangibles but with high levels of intangible assets, are not given any further consideration. Corporations such as Disney, Coca-Cola or Washington Post (all excellent investments for Buffett) would not have got past the first stage with Graham.

Despite Buffett's move away from Graham on the specific issue of cigar butt investment he still strongly endorsed Graham's fundamental principles (e.g. intrinsic value; margin of safety; the distinction between investment, intelligent speculation and unintelligent speculation; examining the business; and not focusing on short-term stock price moves). Buffett continued to employ them and to advise anyone who would listen to follow them. He criticized universities for not teaching Graham's ideas. 'It's not difficult enough. So, instead something is taught that is difficult but not useful. The business schools reward complex behaviour more than simple behaviour, but simple behaviour is more effective.'[41]

KEY PRINCIPLES OF GRAHAM'S APPROACHES

Margin of safety: there is only the remotest chance of losing market value. Value is well in excess of price paid. The value estimate is based on facts. An insurance against untoward events.

Speculators: primarily concerned with anticipating and profiting from market fluctuations. Absence of thorough analysis, or margin of safety. Possessing the objectives of unreasonably large returns.

Investment operation:	one that, upon thorough analysis, promises safety of principal and a satisfactory return.
Thorough analysis:	view stocks as pieces of business, reasoning/fundamentally quantitative and based on practical investment experience analysis of intrinsic value and earning power.
The supreme virtues (in the world of securities analysis):	adequate knowledge tested judgement courage.
Intrinsic value:	the value of a company to a private owner. The price the stock should sell at if priced in a market which priced on the facts (assets, earnings, dividend and prospects.)
Earning power:	the main determinant of intrinsic value. The earnings capacity of a business in a normal year. Derived from historical data and future average expectable earnings. What the company might be expected to earn year after year if the business conditions continue unchanged.
Unintelligent speculation:	buying when you lack proper knowledge and skill risking more than you can afford and ignoring quantitative material.
Intelligent speculation:	focus on information that is quantifiable, calculation of probabilities, careful weighing of the facts, some risk to principal.
Make market fluctuations your friend:	remember Mr Market is a manic-depressive. Exploit the irrational price setting of the market.

Don't

- Forecast the economy or the market
- engage in market timing
- use technical analysis
- try short-term selectivity
- try selecting growth stocks

- buy promising-company stocks
- be blind to managementism
- buy in a bubble.

Net current asset value investing:	stocks selling for less than net current asset value (after deduction of all liabilities and counting fixed assets at zero) may be considered for purchase if they pass the following tests: • adequate financial set-up • good prospects for the business • honest and competent managers • stability. Also, diversification and patience are required.

Defensive value investing:	a simple stock selection method with the emphasis on the avoidance of serious mistakes and the objective of satisfactory returns. A portfolio of 10–30 stocks each passing all of the following tests:
	• a large, prominent and important company. Top 25–33 per cent in industry
	• a sufficiently strong financial current asset ratio >2
	• long term debt < net current assets
	• financial gearing < 50 per cent
	• earnings and dividend stability and growth
	    10 years of profits
	    20 years of dividends
	    eps grown by one-third in ten years
	• moderate PER
	    average of last three years < 15
	    average of last seven years < 25
	    last 12 months < 20
	• stock price < 1½ x net asset value.
	
	(The PER and stock price to net asset value criteria may be relaxed if an excellent statistic in one offsets a poor number of the other.)

Enterprising value investing:	same criteria as defensive but with more flexibility. A considerable plus may offset a black-mark elsewhere, no lower limit on size. Average future earnings power needs to be calculated. Low diversification. Above average rewards are available to those with sufficient competence and dedication.
Selling:	if the stock's quality deteriorates
	if the price rises above demonstrable value.

Problems

- misunderstanding and over-simplifying Graham's methods
- it is hard work
- virtuous and demanding personality traits are needed, e.g. strength of character, fortitude, courage
- long periods when methods are not practicable
- dangerous for short-term security buyers
- the cigar butt may not give you one last puff.

Notes

1 Net current asset value (working capital) = current assets (cash, accounts receivable, inventory) minus current liabilities. Net quick asset value = current asset minus inventory minus current liabilities.

2 Graham, B. (1932) 'Is American Business Worth More Dead Than Alive. Inflated Treasuries and Deflated Stocks: Are Corporations Milking their Owners?' Forbes, 1 June.

3 Graham quoted in Train, J. (1980), p. 103.

4 Graham, B. (1973), p. 214.

5 Train, J. (1980).

6 Graham, B. and Dodd, D. (1934), p. 495.

7 Graham, B. (1932). Forbes, 1 June.

8 *Ibid.*

9 Graham, B. (1973), p. 216.

10 Graham, B. and Dodd, D. (1934), p. 508.

11 *Ibid.*, p. 319.

12 Graham, B. (1946–7), Lecture 4.

13 Graham, B. (1973), p. 165.

14 Graham, B. and Dodd, D. (1934), p. 354.

15 *Ibid.*, p. 35.

16 *Ibid.*, p. 36.
17 *Ibid.*, p. 38.
18 *Ibid.*, p. 38.
19 Graham, B. (1946–7), Lecture 5.
20 Graham, B. (1973), p. 9.
21 *Ibid.*, p. 183.
22 He also suggested that the earnings/price ratio (the inverse of the PER) be at least as high as the current high grade bond rate.
23 Graham, B. (1973), p. 185.
24 *Ibid.*, p. 206.
25 *Ibid.*, p. 78.
26 *Ibid.*, p. 210.
27 *Ibid.*, p. 152.
28 *Ibid.*, p. 154.
29 *Ibid.*, p. xvi.
30 *Ibid.*, p. 40.
31 *Ibid.*, p. 79.
32 *Ibid.*, p. 83.
33 Graham, B. and Dodd, D. (1934), p. 321.
34 Graham, B. (1946–7), Lecture 7.
35 Graham, B. (1973), p. xv.
36 Buffett, W. quoted in Robert Lenzner 'Warren Buffett's Idea of Heaven: I don't have to work with people I don't like', Forbes 400, 18 October 1993, p. 40.
37 Buffett, W. (1989). This material is copyrighted and is reproduced with the permission of the author.
38 *Ibid.*
39 *Ibid.*
40 Buffett, W, in Anthony Bianco, 'Why Warren Buffett Is Breaking His Own Rules', *Business Week*, 15 April, 1985, p. 134.
41 Buffett, W., in Patricia E. Bauer, 'The Convictions of a Long-Distance Investor', Channels, November 1986, p. 22.

5

Philip Fisher's bonanza investing

Philip Fisher is the doyen of growth investors. He sought companies with high growth potential, but he also looked to buy at a price that gave good value. Even high earnings growth stocks fall out of favour, become overlooked and sell for less than their underlying worth from time to time. Philip Fisher concentrated his considerable talent on finding a small group of stocks that traded at low prices relative to their long-term prospects. These companies are rare, because the vast majority of companies with fast growing earnings are well recognized and highly priced; but they are well worth seeking out. Philip Fisher combined the ability to identify the fundamental factors behind a company's strength that led to above average earnings advancement with the discipline to invest only in those showing extraordinary value.

Fisher started his investment career early. His first interest was sparked when, as a boy, he listened to a conversation about stocks between his grandmother and uncle:

> A whole new world opened up to me. By saving some money, I had the right to buy a share in the future profits of any one I might choose among hundreds of the most important business enterprises of the country. If I chose correctly, these profits could be truly exciting. I thought the whole subject of judging what makes a business grow as an intriguing one, and here was a game that if I learned to play it properly would by comparison make any other with which I was familiar seem drab, meaningless and unexciting.[1]

He made a modest amount trading stocks as a teenager in the middle 1920s. To his physician father's charge that he was gambling he answered that he was 'not by nature inclined to take chances merely for the sake of taking chances',[2] but did admit (in later years) that these early dealings taught him almost nothing. The place where he did learn a lot was at Stanford University's fledgling Graduate School of Business. As a first-year student in the 1927–8 academic year he was obliged to spend one day a week visiting businesses in the San Francisco Bay area with Professor Boris Emmett. Students were able both to see the workings of the firm and, more importantly, to question the management and thereby learn the strengths and weaknesses of the business. Furthermore, because Fisher drove Prof. Emmett to and from the company sites he was able to learn more by listening to Prof. Emmett's piercing insight concerning a company.

Over time Fisher developed an ability to identify well-managed companies with a potential to grow very much beyond their present size. (In these early days the concept of a 'growth company' had not yet been verbalized by the financial community.) He also learned the importance of the selling function for a healthy business. It is not enough to have brilliant inventions and efficient manufacturing. The business needed people who were able to convince others of the value of their product if it was to control its destiny. Even more than this was required; companies need to be able to sell current products and also to be aware of, analyze and act upon the changing needs and desires of customers – in other words, marketing.

In the summer of 1928 he joined an independent San Francisco bank (later to become part of Crocker National) as a statistician – or in modern parlance, a securities analyst.[3] The assignment to undertake the 'intellectually dishonest' task of selling new issues of bonds, on which the bank made substantial commission, was not to his taste. The quality of the bonds sold were never evaluated. The customer was persuaded to buy on the basis of a 'report' which was superficial and mostly cribbed from Moody's or Standard and Poors.

In the autumn of 1928 Fisher was permitted to undertake some real analysis into radio stocks. He visited the radio departments of several retail outlets and sought opinions on the three major competitors in the industry. He was surprised by the high degree of consensus. The stock market's favourite of the day was viewed as the worst company by those who were the radio companies' customers. Another popular company RCA was just about holding its own. Philco, however was the clear winner. It had superior models, was winning market share and was highly efficient. He searched for a negative comment from a Wall Street analyst on the first company, the worst performer in the eyes of the customers, but was unable to find a single word about the troubles that were brewing. 'It was my first lesson in what was later to become part of my basic investment philosophy: reading the printed financial records about a company is never enough to justify an investment. One of the major steps in prudent investment must be to find out about a company's affairs from those who have some direct familiarity with them.'[4]

Fisher had a ringside seat at the 'incredible financial orgy'[5] of 1928–9:

> As 1929 started to unfold, I became more and more convinced of the unsound-
> ness of the wild boom … . Stocks continued climbing to ever higher prices on
> the amazing theory that we were in a 'new era'. Therefore, in the future, year
> after year of advancing per share earnings could be taken as a matter of course.[6]

In August 1929 he wrote a report in which he predicted that the next six
months would witness the start of the greatest bear market in a quarter of
a century. Right though he was, he, like Benjamin Graham, failed to follow
through. 'I was entrapped by the lure of the market.'[7] He scraped together a few thousand dollars and bought stocks, which appeared still to be
cheap on the grounds that they had not risen yet. In choosing these companies he had not bothered to make enquiries from people who either
knew their products or were employees. By 1932, he was left with only a
tiny percentage of his original stake.

Fisher was determined to learn from his experiences: 'the chief difference between a fool and a wise man is that the wise man learns from his
mistakes, while the fool never does'.[8] One lesson was that a low price to
historic earnings ratio was no guarantor of value. What the investor needs
is a stock with a low price relative to earnings a few years ahead. He started to think of ways to predict accurately (within fairly broad limits) the
earnings of firms a few years from now.

At the age of 22, in 1930, Fisher joined a regional brokerage firm and
was asked to find stocks suitable for purchase or sale because of their
characteristics. Here he could start to develop the techniques he knew
were needed. After only eight months the firm became yet another victim
of the Depression and was suspended from the San Francisco Stock
Exchange for insolvency. Rather than take a clerical job, he started Fisher
& Co., to manage clients' investments. Unfortunately, he had no clients.

For several years he worked very hard in a tiny office with no windows.
In 1932 the net profit was $2.99 per month. There was a 1,000 per cent
improvement in 1933 – to $29! 'My hopes were high and both my purse
and my reputation in the financial community were almost non-existent.'[9]
Fisher made the most of the opportunity to hone his investment philosophy and to build up a small group of highly loyal clients.

The search was on for companies with certain key qualities: the people
were outstanding; it held a strong competitive position; operations and
long-term planning were handled well, and there were enough high
potential new product lines for growth to continue for many years. He

tried some 'in and out' investing (trading for short-term gains), but found that it was a time consuming distraction that produced small returns:

> I had seen enough of in and out trading, including some done by extremely brilliant people, that I knew that being successful three times in a row only made it much more likely that the fourth time I would end in disaster. The risks were considerably more than those involved in purchasing equal amounts of shares in companies I considered promising enough to want to hold them for many years of growth.[10]

He resolved to restrict his talent and energy solely to making major gains over the long run.

For three and half years, during World War II, the investment business was 'beached' as Fisher did a number of desk jobs in the Army Air Force. There was plenty of time to review investment successes and failures over the previous decade. It was during this period that his investment principles crystallized into an approach completely different to that of commonly accepted investment wisdom. He was keen to apply the new philosophy and started to take a very close interest in this chemical industry, which, he concluded, would experience very fast growth in the post-war period. On becoming a civilian he tried to identify the most attractive large chemical company. He would talk to anyone who had some knowledge of this industry. Distributors, chemistry professors, constructors of chemical plants and a host of others who might shed some light in the qualities of the chemical firms, were consulted. This information about the management, competitive conditions, innovation and inventions was combined with an analysis of the financial data. By the spring of 1947 he had narrowed his choice down to just one firm – Dow Chemical Company.

The reasoning that led to the purchase of Dow gives us some insight into the key features of a good company:

> As I began to know various people in the Dow organization, I found that the growth that had already occurred was in turn creating a very real sense of excitement at many levels of management. The belief that even greater growth lay ahead permeated the organization. One of my favourite questions in talking to any top business executive for the first time is what he considers to be the most important long-range problem facing his company. When I asked this of the president of Dow, I was tremendously impressed with his answer: 'It is to resist the strong pressures to become a more military-like organization as we grow very much larger, and to maintain the informal relationship whereby people at quite different levels and in various departments continue to com-

municate with each other in a completely unstructured way and, at the same time, not create administrative chaos. I found myself in complete agreement with certain other basic company policies. Dow limited its involvement to those chemical product lines where it either was or had a reasonable chance of becoming the most efficient producer in the field as the result of greater volume, better chemical engineering and deeper understanding of the product or for some other reason. Dow was deeply aware of the need for creative research not just to be in front, but also to stay in front. There was also a strong appreciation of the 'people factor' at Dow. There was in particular a sense of need to identify people of unusual ability early, to indoctrinate them into policies and procedures unique to Dow, and to make real efforts to see if seemingly bright people were not doing well at one job, they be given a reasonable chance to try something else that might be more suitable to their characteristics.[11]

The post-war world was a pessimistic one in terms of stock market outlook. Achieving good performance for clients was difficult. People were worried that war would be followed by depression, as it had been in the past. As the sense of foreboding grew, stock prices fell. And yet, business was good and corporate earnings were rising. Ah! said the pessimist, earnings rose after other wars, and then the crash came. Year after year went by, earnings continued to grow, intrinsic value continued to rise, but stock prices were held back by the Cassandras. Many companies had a higher liquidating value than their market capitalization. Fisher took advantage of this situation. By focusing on the long-term prospects for outstanding companies he was able to put into perspective the negative views of the crowd. This experience, confirmed his view (developed in the 1930s) that the market was capable of extreme and unreasonable pessimism as well as extreme and unreasonable optimism.

The maximum number of clients Fisher & Co. had at any one time through the 1950s and 1960s was twelve. His returns were good and the funds 'advanced significantly more than the market as a whole'.[12]

He held relatively few stocks and was quite prepared to put a large proportion of the fund into obscure companies. In 1955, for example, he bought two stocks that were generally regarded as highly speculative. They were small companies and were technologically oriented; they were beneath the notice of conservative investors or the big institutions. 'A number of people criticized me for risking funds in a small speculative company which they felt was bound to suffer from the competition of the corporate giants,' he said of one of the firms.[13] Both stocks turned in 'spectacular' performances. Their names? Texas Instruments and Motorola.

Even after decades of experience, in the 1960s, Fisher made the error of investing outside of those industries he really understood. He had developed a thorough knowledge of manufacturing companies serving industrial markets and companies on the leading edge of technology serving manufacturers. He knew how to evaluate their strengths, and the likely pitfalls. Analyzing say, consumer product companies, requires a different competence and knowledge set. The same applies to real estate, mining or media. Each is a difficult sector to follow; to truly understand the underlying economic forces at work. Few people have the genius qualities required to understand more than one or two sectors: 'an analyst must learn the limits of his or her competence and tend well the sheep at hand'.[14]

In reflecting on a lifetime of investment in 1980 Fisher noted that, with the possible exception of the 1960s, there has not been a decade in which the prevailing view was that common stock investment was foolhardy, because factors outside the control of corporate managers were too strong for them to control the destiny of their corporations. However, in every decade there were wonderful opportunities to buy stocks yielding returns of hundreds of per cent. On the downside, in each of these decades there were also periods in which the 'speculative darlings' of the time became disastrous traps for the unwary, 'for those who blindly follow the crowd rather than who really knew what they were doing'.[15] The next ten years will also present magnificent opportunities for those who know what to look for. They will also be littered with the same old traps for those unaware of the vital principles for good investing. Those who look for an intellectually cheap and easy way to fortune will find their path strewn with dangerous temptations. The rest of this chapter (and indeed the book) may help investors to step adeptly and avoid being caught out.

KEY ELEMENTS OF FISHER'S APPROACH

Fisher would spend a great deal of time running around in his old car talking to managers and other knowledgeable people about an industry and a company. What he was searching for were clues to indicate that the company in question is truly outstanding: that it has the probability of spectacular earnings growth for many years; that it has great management able to create opportunities and avoid dangers; that it has both a technological lead at the moment, and that it will be able to continue to innovate and maintain its lead. If a company has these qualities then an investment in its stock could be an 'investment bonanza',[16] showing a gain of several hundred per cent over a few years. 'The investor should never be interested in small gains of 10 to 20 per cent, but rather in gains which over a period of years will be closer to ten or a hundred times this amount.'[17]

To find companies of this quality requires a lot of effort and a concentration of effort. Fisher chose to devote himself to the study of technology-based companies. However, followers of Fisher do not have to confine themselves to this area. The fundamental principles are applicable in any sector. The key thing for the investor is to be knowledgeable about the chosen sector.

> ...**The key thing is to be knowledgeable about the chosen sector.**........

For Fisher an investment was to be held for many years, if not decades. A great company, with highly motivated and able managers can continue to grow way beyond the investment horizon of conventional investors.

The most important elements of Fisher's analysis are shown in Fig. 5.1. Scuttlebutt is a factor which surrounds all the others. It is through Scuttlebutt that Fisher discovered the vital facts about a firm, from the character of its managers to the effectiveness of its research.

Scuttlebutt is the use of the business grapevine to research companies. It is scavenging for information by obtaining the views and opinions of anybody associated with a company: customers, employees, ex-

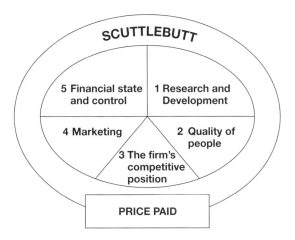

Figure 5.1   Key elements of Fisher's analysis

employees, rivals, suppliers, academics, trade association officers, industry observers, etc.

> The business 'grapevine' is a remarkable thing. It is amazing what an accurate picture of the relative points of strength and weakness of each company in an industry can be obtained from a representative cross-section of the opinions of those who in one way or another are concerned with any particular company. Most people, particularly if they feel sure there is no danger of being quoted, like to talk about the field of work in which they are engaged and will talk rather freely about their competitors. Go to five companies in an industry, ask each of them intelligent questions about the points of strengths and weaknesses of the other four, and nine times out of ten a surprisingly detailed and accurate picture of all five will emerge.[18]

Suppliers and customers can provide an opinion that is as well informed and illuminating as that of competitors. They also provide a means of cross checking. The character of the people managing the firms should emerge. The impression formed can be reinforced by talking to former employees. However, when seeking opinions here, great care is needed to ensure allowance is made for the fact that views from this source may be tainted by feelings of resentment. It is very important that the person providing the information is reassured that their identity will never be revealed. The analyst must scrupulously observe this policy. Trade association personnel, especially, will need this reassurance, as will current employees. If there is the slightest doubt as to analyst's ability to observe the rules of confidentiality he or she will simply not get to hear unfavourable opinions.

It is unlikely that each piece of data gathered through scuttlebutt will agree with every other piece of data. There is no need to worry about this:

> In the case of really outstanding companies, the preponderant information is so crystal-clear that even a moderately experienced investor who knows what he is seeking will be able to tell which companies are likely to be of enough interest to him to warrant taking the next step in his investigation. This next step is to contact the officers of the company to try to fill out some of the gaps still existing in the investor's picture of the situation being studied.[19]

Research and development

The type of company that sparked Fisher's interest was one that had a strong and well-directed research capability. It was not enough to simply observe the amount companies claim to spend on research and development. What companies include or exclude as research and development expense varies enormously, and so crude published figures are a somewhat imprecise guide. Furthermore, some programmes of research (those that are managed well) will produce twice as much ultimate gain for each dollar spent as will others. Technological advancement does not, generally, depend on dramatic break-throughs by a few isolated geniuses. Rather, new products and processes are the result of a collaborative effort of a number of highly trained individuals. Each may have a different speciality and the key to success lies both in their individual skills *and* in the quality of the leadership brought to bear on the tricky task of co-ordination. Some firms manage researchers' efforts so that they are all being directed at the common goal, others suffer confusion and low morale. Scuttlebutt may help identify the better ones.

Co-ordination is also needed between the R & D programme and both the production and sales teams. In the absence of high quality relationships it may be found that new products are not designed to be manufactured as cheaply as possible, or, the design is not appealing to customers, thus handicapping the sales effort. In highly competitive markets competitors will be looking for chinks in the armour of great research firms. They may find them in the poor co-operation between the research teams and the production and sales teams.

The final factor in effective research is the understanding of top management in their role as providers of a stable environment for innovation and creativity to take place. A long-term perspective is needed. It is not wise to expand research and development in good years and cut back in poor ones. Apart from the cost of research rising, high quality researchers do not want to join, or stay with, a company that is so capricious. Crash programmes that pull

> **A long-term perspective is needed.**

researchers away from long-term projects to work on the current pet idea of the senior managers are disruptive and demoralizing. Frequent abandonment of lines of research that do not show cashflow generating promise after only two or three years can also be damaging.

Fisher looked for companies that had produced a steady flow of profitable new products. Such a company 'will probably be equally productive in the future as long as it continues to operate under the same general methods'.[20] It has to tread the tightrope of being able to control a whole range of complex relationships at the same time as not over-controlling them and stifling researchers' drive and ingenuity.

Management has to have a programme to replace product lines once the products of the current technology have been exploited. Companies with outstanding products now, but which do not have adequate policies for further development are unlikely to provide the consistent gains expected from a bonanza investment over a ten- or 25-year investment horizon. Management must not be content with one isolated growth spurt, but be determined that there will be a continuous flow of improved old products and exciting new ones.

The best results come from investing in companies with a research and development effort directed at products with some business relationship to the existing ones. The good company will have research activities that can be viewed as a cluster of trees each growing additional branches from the trunk. A company working on a number of unrelated new products is unlikely to be as efficient at research or production or marketing as one which concentrates on products which share the resource strengths of the firms.

Quality of people

Investors should only be interested in companies under the guidance of exceptionally able management. Fisher uses the word quality to encompass four different characteristics. These are shown in Fig. 5.2.

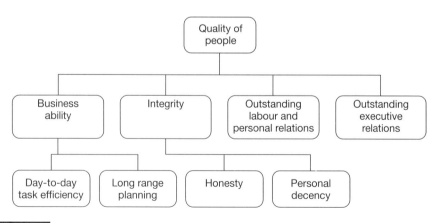

Figure 5.2 Quality of people

Business ability

Under business ability there are two different types of skills. The first is efficiency in handling day-to-day business tasks. Managers should be constantly seeking and finding superior methods to produce more efficiently. This search for continuous improvement will affect hundreds of different matters, from the layout of a factory to the negotiating stance taken with suppliers. It is vital that the managers have above average talent in handling the many things associated with regular operations.

The good manager will be prepared to accept the risks of being a pioneer. Businesses which are worth backing, are often engaged in pioneering projects in which ingenuity is combined with practicality. No matter how able the people are and no matter how good most of their ideas, there will be times when they fail, especially if they are working at the leading edge of technology. Investors and managers need the resilience and fortitude to accept the occasional failure. The excellent team of managers accepts failure as part of the process of advancement and does not chide those who give it their best and fail occasionally. If a company becomes unwilling to take chances, to merely go along with the crowd, it will, ultimately, become vulnerable to more daring competitors.

While maintaining the highest standards of efficiency in the control of day-to-day operations a good management team also has to plan effectively to keep ahead of the competition and provide for a prosperous future in the long run. Managers need the talent to look ahead and ensure the business is positioned for significant future growth without taking undue risks. Fisher said that many companies have managers that are either good at day-to-day matters or at long-range planning. For real success both are necessary.

> All corporate thinking and planning must be attuned to challenge what is now being done – to challenge it not occasionally but again and again …. Some risks must be accepted in substituting new methods to meet changing conditions. No matter how comfortable it may seem to do so, ways of doing things cannot be maintained just because they worked well in the past and are hallowed by tradition. The company that is rigid in its actions and is not constantly challenging itself has only one way to go, and that way is down.[21]

One indicator of whether managers pay sufficient attention to the long term is the extent to which they are determined to produce high profits in the current year, even if that means damaging future returns. Many companies seem to have an irresistible urge to report the highest profit possible at the end of each accounting period. The long-range perspective company will be willing to curtail current and near-term profits in order to build up goodwill, leading to higher profits over a number of years. Some companies will be forceful, even aggressive, in obtaining the finest terms from suppliers. Others will be willing to pay a little more as part of relationship building so that when trouble strikes it can be sure of a dependable supply of raw materials or components. A long-term relationship with customers is also vital. The firm that squeezes out the last nickel from a customer when the customer is in a vulnerable position may not keep them when circumstances improve. Companies that make special efforts and bear additional expense to help regular customers who find themselves in an unexpected jam may reduce the next reported profits, but may also ensure high profitability over many years. Farsighted managers will also be willing to curtail short-term profit, if by doing so, new products and processes can be developed that will build the business for the future.

Fisher said that the companies that show high growth decade after decade can be divided into two groups. The first he called the 'fortunate and able', the second the 'fortunate because they are able'.[22] Both types need a very able management team in order to defend strong competition positions from the onslaught of others. The Aluminum Company of America (Alcoa) is highlighted as an example of a fortunate and able company. The founders were people of great ability, and believed in the product. However, they were fortunate in being in an industry which showed an enormous growth over the 20th Century, as new developments increased the market beyond the wildest dreams of the pioneers. Naturally, the managers had to continue to demonstrate a high order of skill to ride the trend and not get knocked off by competitors. However, without the dramatic opening up of new markets (a development largely outside of Alcoa's control), the company would have grown at a slower rate. 'The Aluminum Company was fortunate in finding itself in an even better industry than the attractive one envisioned by its early management.'[23]

Du Pont is an example of a company which is fortunate because it is able. It was engaged in the production of blasting power. It transformed itself and developed important new industrial sectors, e.g. nylon, cellophane, Lucite. The management created the opportunity for fortune to shine upon them through innovation and repositioning. They showed ingenuity and resourcefulness in extending and adding to capabilities created in the basic business to go into related lines offering still further growth possibilities. They did this time and again.

Both the fortunate and able and the fortunate because they are able type of company can be good investments. The key factor to identify is whether the management is, and will continue to be, excellent. If not then sales growth will taper off.

Dividend policy is another indicator of managerial competence. Bad management can hoard cash far beyond the needs of the business, either now or in the future. A business with lots of cash is less likely to become bankrupt – at least, in the near term. This is a great benefit to executives looking for job security, but it may not be the best use of stockholders' money. Shareholders may be able to get a higher return on that cash by investing it in the stock of other companies.

Poor managers may also retain earnings in order to invest in projects which produce inadequate returns. They might, for example, enlarge an already inefficient operation. If managerial domains become larger, managers generally receive a higher salary. That is fine, if the money used for the enlargement achieves returns at least as high as stockholders could obtain for the same level of risk elsewhere. Too often, managers fail this test and retain too much stockholders' money.

On the other hand, it is possible for companies to return too much money to stockholders. If the firm has an array of excellent projects that will produce fine returns then the managers, by increasing dividends, are acting like a farm manager 'who rushes his magnificent livestock to market the minute he can sell them rather than raising them to the point where he can get the maximum price above his costs. He has produced a little more cash right now but at a frightful cost'.[24] For many companies the rational policy is to retain all the profits, not pay any dividend at all in the near term, and invest in all the available worthwhile projects. Because Fisher was interested only in high growth companies with a regular flow of new products he sought companies with a zero or low dividend because, by their very nature, these companies needed to plough back profits to make more profits.

Integrity

The investor needs to be reassured that those in positions of trust, holding stockholders money, possess the quality of integrity that encompasses honesty and personal decency. Academics talk about there being asymmetry of information between stockholders and executives – the management are always closer to the business and are bound to be better informed. Even without breaking the law those in control of firms can benefit themselves at the expense of the owners. The only real protection investors have against this is a management with a strong sense of trustee-ship and moral responsibility to their stockholders. If there in any doubt about the probity of the senior people then the company should not be considered for investment, even if it passes all the other tests with flying colours. It is on this issue that scuttlebutt becomes essential. How else are you to find out about the character of the CEO and the rest of the team without talking to them directly or obtaining the views of those who know them?

Intelligent and honest managers do not conceal bad news. The news may be highly embarrassing for the executive to bring to the attention of shareholders, but it is necessary that he or she be of such good character as to be able to brace himself or herself as to be able to inform outsiders of unfavourable aspects of the business, as well as the favourable develop-ments. Warren Buffett provides an excellent example of honesty in report-ing bad news in the Berkshire Hathaway Annual report for 1999:

> The numbers on the facing page show just how poor our 1999 result was. We had the worst absolute performance of my tenure and compared to the S&P, the worst relative performance as well … . Even Inspector Clouseau could find last year's guilty party: your Chairman. My performance reminds me of the quarterback whose report card showed four Fs and a D but who nonetheless had an understanding coach. 'Son,' he drawled, 'I think you're spending too much time on that one subject.' My 'one subject' is capital allocation, and my grade for 1999 is most assuredly a D. (This material is copyrighted and is repro-duced with the permission of the author.)

It is often the case that the best run companies with the greatest future prospects regularly have to report failures and set backs. Unexpected dif-ficulties, shifts in demand and new product flops are bound to happen from time to time in a dynamic business environment. Companies which are trying their damnedest to create long-term growth have to take chances. Intelligent investors know the score and do not penalize the company for temporary disappointments, if, and only if, they trust the managers to produce a stream of winners as well, and those managers are forthright about the problem cases.

Suspicion that a management has 'clammed-up' should be taken as a warning sign. It may not have a plan of action to solve the problem. It may be in a panic. It may have an arrogant attitude regarding shareholders and feel no responsibility to report more than what suits the managers at the time.

Outstanding labour and personal relations

Investors need to be reassured that the management of the company is sensitive to the needs of the employees, and that they will be treated decently, with dignity and consideration. In too many companies there are fine words about the importance of employees (for example; the 'employees are our greatest asset'), but these are merely generalizations; what managers are expected to say, not what they believe. In the da-to-day interactions between people within these organizations it becomes apparent that management have little sense of responsibility for, or interest in, their ordinary workers. They are treated as eminently dispensable, being fired at the smallest change in the sales or profit outlook. No consideration is given to the impact such off-hand decisions will have on families or communities. No serious attempt is made to make employees feel needed as part of the vision of a prosperous future for the firm.

In a good company there is a conscious and continuous effort to create a good working environment, a feeling that it is a good place to work. If the company has the loyalty of its workers then it has a massive competitive advantage; greater productivity, lower costs and a willingness to go the extra mile for the firm.

There will be additional costs associated with high quality worker relations. Time will have to be devoted to two-way communications and action taken to address grievances. Pension and profit sharing plans will be set at reasonably generous levels; wages will be above average for the area. But the cost of having poor relations is far greater. Not only is high labour turnover costly in terms of recruitment and training but it is disruptive and demoralizing for the ones who get left behind picking up the pieces, as talent seeps away (often to competitors). The cost of prolonged strikes is obvious. What is not so obvious is the hundreds of individual decisions taken by each worker not to give their best. It is this cost, which although it can't be measured in terms of lost sales and product development opportunities, that can break a company.

Scuttlebutt can be used to gauge the feelings of employees and former employers, and the reputation of the firm as a good employer in the vicinity and the industry. This can be supplemented with quantitative data, such as labour turnover rates or length of the waiting list of job applicants wanting to work for the company.

Outstanding executive relations

There must be an executive climate in which all managers have confidence in the CEO and the team at the top. These senior executives must create an environment in which co-operation, ingenuity and endeavour are respected and rewarded. Fast growing companies play for high stakes. This may result in tension, friction and occasional resentment. If this is not managed sensitively executive talent is likely to leave, or, if they do stay, they do not produce at their maximum ability.

Promotions must be based on merit and not factionalism. Family members should not be promoted ahead of others with more ability. Salaries should be reviewed regularly to ensure they are competitive and executives do not get to the point of having to demand a rise.

A well-run firm would rarely need to recruit executives from outside, except for the starting jobs. The best companies have a set of policies and ways of doing things that is particular to them. These cultural, procedural and relationship factors are often the key resource which gives the firm the competitive edge. It is difficult to retrain executives who learned a different way of doing things. A particularly damning sign of a fundamental flaw in the company is the recruitment of a CEO from outside of the firm.

It is dangerous to invest in a company in which one key person is essential for its success. A young company may have an individual with an entrepreneurial personality as its driving force. However, these companies are not suitable for bonanza growth investing. Eventually, the company will reach the stage where it will miss opportunities unless it develops executive talent in depth. The good firm has a chief executive dedicated to long-range growth and surrounded by a competent executive team, to which he has delegated considerable authority.

The groups of executives in the various strategic business units should be collaborating so as to achieve clearly defined corporate goals. One important goal is to identify and train motivated and talented junior executives to succeed seniors, where necessary:

> If from the very top on down, each level of executives is not given real authority to carry out assigned duties in an ingenious and efficient manner as each individual's ability will permit, good executive material becomes much like healthy young animals so caged in that they cannot exercise. They do not

develop their faculties because they just do not have enough opportunity to use them.[25]

If senior managers are constantly meddling in the decisions that should be taken lower down there will be two negative consequences: first, the senior executive will make errors as the detail becomes overwhelming; and second, able executives are not given the opportunity to develop, and so growth is restrained by the lack of experienced talent. A good firm creates and guides the energies of as many 'vivid spirits' as possible. It encourages suggestions for improvement from the lower echelon, often a veritable goldmine of ideas. The entrepreneurial thrust must permeate the organization.

Again, scuttlebutt is the main source of information on this issue, but a useful enlightening statistic is the gap between the salary of the top person and the next two or three. If it is very much higher that is a warning sign.

The firm's competitive position

A good company will be one with 'certain inherent characteristics that make possible an above-average profitability for as long as can be foreseen into the future'.[26] Fisher looked for companies which consistently succeeded in doing things better than others in the industry. He never forgot to apply the advice of Dr Dow to companies: 'If you can't do a thing better than others are doing it, don't do it at all'.[27] Given the inherent risks of holding stocks you should only place money with companies that have both a strong competitive spirit and a strong competitive position.

Companies with high profit margins attract attention from other companies that start to regard that market segment as an 'open jar of honey owned by the prospering company. The money will inevitably attract a swarm of hungry insects bent on devouring it'.[28] The company has to find a way of protecting its honey pot. One method is by outright monopoly. Fisher cautions against investing in this type of firm. Most monopolies are eventually curtailed by the authorities. Even those that are ignored by the regulatory bodies are liable to suddenly breakdown, and are therefore not safe to invest in.

The best way to keep the insects out is to be so efficient that present and future competition consider it futile to try to do battle. The implied threat is that they will have to commit themselves to huge expenditures, and the best they can hope for is parity in terms of output efficiency. The worst will be a damaging price war that will make their shareholders hop up and down in indignation at the irrational strategy.

Economies of scale are a potential source of competitive advantage. Fisher was very much aware of this, but said that, too often, as the organization becomes larger, the operating cost benefit is offset by the inefficiencies produced by the additional bureaucratic layers of middle management. Senior executives become increasingly isolated from the activities of subdivisions and far-flung complexes; decisions are delayed and ill informed. The greatest advantages of being the largest firm in the industry are often to be found, not on the manufacturing side of the business, but on the marketing side. Fisher was particularly enthusiastic about this. If the company is first with a new product or service and backs this up with good marketing, servicing and product improvement it may be able to establish 'an atmosphere in which new customers will turn to the leader largely because that leader has established such a reputation for performance (or sound value) that no one is likely to criticize the buyer adversely for making this particularly selection'.[29] When a company becomes the leader in its field it seldom gets displaced so long as its management remains competent. The notion that the purchasing of the stock of the number two or number three firm in the industry is a wise investment, because they have the potential to take the premier position, whereas the leader can only go down, is regarded by Fisher as not being borne out by the evidence. A well-entrenched leader with dynamic, forward-looking vigilant managers is more likely to see off a challenge than to succumb to it.

Some companies possess the advantages of low production costs and a well-recognized brand name as well as a host of other key resources to swat those pesky insects. Fisher (in the 1970s) liked to quote the case of Campbell, the soup producer. It had cost reduction through scale and backward integration, a recognized product, the most prominent position in retail outlets and one of the largest display areas, and it could spread its marketing costs over billions of cans of soup.

The competitive advantage may not come from the core activity of the firm. For example, in some retail sectors the basic business of selling goods gives the firm competitive parity and no more. What gives the edge is the skill a firm might have in handling real estate issues, for example, the quality of its leases.

Patents can provide defence against competition in the short and medium term. Fisher was cautious on this point: 'In our era of widespread technical know-how it is seldom that large companies can enjoy more than a small part of their activities in areas sheltered by patent protection. Patents are usually able to block off only a few rather than all the ways of accomplishing the same result'.[30] He believed that even technologically led firms need other forms of protection to maintain competitive positions and succeed over the long term. These include manufacturing know-how, the quality of the sales and service organization, customer goodwill and knowledge of customer problems. 'In fact, when large companies depend chiefly on patent protection for the maintenance of their profit margin, it is usually more a sign of investment weakness than strength. Patents do not run on indefinitely. When the patent protection is no longer there, the company's profit may suffer badly.'[31]

An alternative to patents is superiority in being able to bring together knowledge from more than one science. If you can find a firm that is way ahead of the field in this mastery of, not one, but two technologies and the interplay between these scientific disciplines, then you may have found a bonanza investment.

An excellent marketing team can create in its customers the habit of almost automatically specifying its product for reorder. Competitors find this position very difficult to weaken. For the dominant firm to achieve its position it has to do a number of things: first, build a reputation for quality and reliability; second, make sure the customer realizes the need for high quality and reliable inputs to its processes, so that it will not take the risk of buying an inferior product; third, ensure that competitors serve only small segments of the market so your brand becomes synonymous with the product item. To achieve maximum profits the cost of the product has to be a small part of the customer's input costs. This means that a switch to a rival product from an unknown supplier will save only a small amount, but the risk of malfunction will play on the mind of the buyer. Finally, it is best to have a market structure where there are many small customers rather than a few large ones. If these customers are very specialized then all the better, because the dominant company will attune its marketing and distribution to the needs of its customers resulting in a close relationship, personal contact and targeted marketing (e.g. salesmen spending a great deal of time with customers trying to help them find solutions). These become important attributes that potential competitors would find almost impossible to emulate. It would take a major shift in technology or a decline in the firm's efficiency to lose its hold on the honey pot.

The company in possession of a strong competitive position needs to be aware of the dangers from overexploitation in the short run. It should not aim for returns on capital many times those available in the industry generally. A spectacular profit creates an irresistible inducement for a fantastic range of companies to try and compete and carry off some of the honey. Fisher suggests that a profit margin consistently 2 or 3 per cent greater than the next best competitor is 'sufficient to ensure a quite outstanding investment'.[32]

Marketing

The investor might have identified a company with breathtaking products, being managed by some excellent people and having a strong lead over competitors, but this will not be enough to ensure success. Brilliant products are useless unless the firm is capable of convincing others of their worth. Even a strong sales team is not enough. The firm also needs the capability to appraise changing needs and desires of customers, and then to react promptly to these changes. In other words, the company must have a strong marketing capability. It should be focused on the objective of making repeat sales to satisfied customers. Fisher is amazed at the lack of attention that the majority of analysts pay to this issue. They pore over accounting data, examine research capability, and study the economic environment yet, because good marketing is difficult to quantify, it is largely ignored.

Scuttlebutt is particularly useful in this area. Competitors and customers are likely to have definite views on the relative efficiency of the sales organization – and they are likely to be very willing to share them. 'Look around you at the companies that have proven outstanding investments. Try to find some that do not have both aggressive distribution and a constantly improving sales organization.'[33]

Financial state and controls

The best returns come from companies having relatively high profit margins. Look for companies with the highest profit margins in this industry. What the analyst should be particularly interested in is the profit margins of the future rather than those of the past. Some companies have a high degree of pricing power to maintain margins. This needs to be combined with constant downward pressure on costs, for example, by the design of new equipment, new methods of production and new procedures. This will offset the rising trend of wages. 'The prospective investor should give attention to the amount of ingenuity of the work being done on new ideas for cutting costs and improving profit margins.'[34]

The investor needs to remember that some good companies may have a deliberate strategy to lower the profit margin in the short run, so as to accelerate the long-term growth rate. For example, by spending large amounts on research or sales promotion. These companies should not be shunned just because the near-term margin is low.

Fisher is careful to draw a distinction between those companies showing a rapid improvement in profit margin because of increasing competitive strength in a conducive industry environment, and those with an accelerating margin because of the stage that the industry cycle has reached. It is the marginal companies (those to be avoided) that show the fastest growth in margin when the cycle is in an upswing. The lowest cost, quality firms' profit margins do not change by such large percentages. This leads to a conclusion that seems strange to those investors with a shorter investment time horizon than Fisher: those companies that show large percentage increases in earnings in years of abnormally good business should be avoided. The truly valuable stronger companies in the same field show steady improvement with more modest margin movements. The earnings of the weaker company will decline correspondingly

> It is advisable to examine profit margins over a number of years.

more rapidly when the business tide turns. It is advisable to examine profit margins over a number of years to help establish which type of company you are dealing with.

Another major issue is the likely demand for further equity finance. 'In the foreseeable future will the growth of the company require sufficient equity financing so that the larger number of shares then outstanding will largely cancel the existing stockholders' benefit from the anticipated growth?'[35] The company's cash plus further borrowing capacity should supply the finance needed to exploit all the value creating opportunities available to the firm without a regular call to shareholders. If equity finance is required, a careful calculation weighing up the negative effect of the dilution caused by the increased number of shares with the positive effect of increased earnings is required. If a management team deliver only small earnings per share increases following equity raisings we may conclude that they have poor financial judgement or do not take their trusteeship role seriously.

Cost accounting systems are also important. All good companies are able to break down their overall costs, to show accurately, and in detail, the cost of each small step of its operation and each product line separately. A high quality cost information system will enable managers to pinpoint those areas and products needing the greatest part of their attention, and those products with the highest profit contribution potential. Inefficient parts of the production, marketing and research effort need to be identified. Managers working without good cost information are severely handicapped. For example, pricing policies that will achieve the highest profit consistent with discouraging undue competition will be virtually impossible. Managers will be ignorant of which products need additional marketing effort. Worst of all, apparently 'winning' product lines and activities may, in reality, be producing a loss.

Discovery of poor costing is very difficult because all companies have people engaged in this sort of activity. Scuttlebutt amongst the managers will get you the response that as far as they can tell the systems are adequate:

> However, it is not so much the existence of detailed figures as their relative accuracy which is important. The best that the careful investor can do in this field is to recognize both the importance of this subject and his own limitations in making a worthwhile appraisal of it. Within these limits he usually can only fall back on the general conclusion that a company well above average in most other aspects of business skill will probably be above average in this field too.[36]

Price

Stock prices move in response to appraisals by the financial community. These appraisals are subjective and heavily influenced by psychology. 'It has nothing necessarily to do with what is going on in the real world about us.'[37] Rather stock prices are influenced by the beliefs of investors as to what is going on: and these beliefs can be a long way from the actual facts. Individual stocks rise and fall not because of what is actually happening or will happen to that company, but because the financial community's consensus of what will happen gets reflected in the price, no matter how far away from the reality of future profitability that consensus might be.

As a result of the gap between the financial community's appraisal and the underlying facts, a stock may sell at considerably less than, or considerably more than, the facts warrant for a long period. Wall Street has a tendency to play 'follow the leader' in which, some lead steers take a whole herd of investors away from the track of rationality. Fads and styles dominate the market just as they do in the fashion industry. Occasionally, it is possible to identify particularly perverse behaviour. For example, when the conditions for a business or a sector remain constant, but the financial community looks at the same facts from a different viewpoint than before. In the earlier phase it could be that all the positive facts are highlighted and broadcast to all. Later, all the worries, problems and doubts, which were previously downplayed, are brought to the fore. Thus, the market shifts from irrational optimism to irrational pessimism. Many technology, media and telecommunication stocks got blown around in this way in the late 1990s.

For an investor, the wait for rationality to return to a stock's price can seem interminably long. It is possible for the gap between the market's appraisal and the true conditions to last for ages: 'Always, however – sometimes within months, sometimes only after a much longer period of time – the bubble bursts'.[38] If the stock has been overpriced, in the correction which follows, it often happens that the emotional pressure of falling prices results in the negative factors being overemphasized and, eventually, severe under-pricing occurs – the pendulum swings the other way.

The serious investor must stand back from the melée of the market and coolly analyze the facts. Then it will be possible to find a bonanza stock to buy that the financial community has rejected. Once purchased, patience and self-discipline will be needed: the stock's negative image must be supplanted with a positive one, and that takes time. 'One of the ablest investment men I have ever known told me many years ago that in the stock market a good nervous system is even more important than a good head.'[39]

The rewards for such patience and fortitude can be great. This is especially true for those investors who do not sell out as the stock starts to rise. Those that hold on, benefit from both rising earnings and a simultaneous increase in the price-earnings ratio. As the old image is revised, the rising price-earnings ratio is frequently a more important factor in giving the investor an agreeable return than the actual increase in earnings per share.

'The largest profits in the investment field go to those who are capable of correctly zigging when the financial community is zagging.'[40] By this statement Fisher is not encouraging the automatic adoption of a contrarian stance. It is vital that when the investor goes against the crowd he or she is very sure of the correctness of their analysis. If the analysis is of a high quality then huge profits are available.

It is dangerous to rely on simple comparisons of price-earnings ratios, even if the growth prospects for the next few years appear to be the same. To illustrate, consider firm X and firm Y. They have the same earnings in recent years and are both expected to double those earnings over the next four years. Both sell at a price-earnings ratio (PER) of 20. Similar companies in the same industry, but with no earnings growth prospects, are selling at ten times earnings. Now, imagine that we move forward four years and assume that investors still value no-growth stocks at PERs of ten. Company X has prospects of earnings growth for the next four years and beyond at the same level as that for the last four, therefore, it will still be selling at a PER of 20 – the share price has doubled. Company Y, on the other hand, does not have any earnings growth potential at all beyond the first period. It will now be valued at ten times earnings because it has become a no-growth stock. Even though it doubled earnings over the previous four years its stock price has not moved. The key lesson is that investors need to buy stocks in which they have confidence that earnings will continue to grow way beyond the next few years.

If the projected earnings growth is high and extends over a long period then a high historic PER can be justified. It is not always the case that the market, by placing stocks on high historic PERs, is fully discounting the further growth that might reasonably be expected. If the present growth is more than just a temporary spurt and new sources of earnings growth will be developed when the current one is exhausted, the stocks may be underpriced despite having a reported PER substantially higher than the market average. A company which has a deliberate and well-managed programme for developing new sources of earnings power is likely to have a PER in five or ten years as much above the market ratio as it does today: 'Stocks of this type will frequently be found to be discounting the future much less than many investors believe. This is why some of the stocks that at first glance appear highest priced may, upon analysis, be the biggest bargains'.[41]

Companies facing temporary trouble can turn out to be bonanza stocks. Significant price declines often occur because the market hates

uncertainty. If the management seems able to handle the short-term difficulties in a matter of months, rather than years, the investor may zig and
profit by it.

When estimating future earnings the investor needs to accept some
humility. Future profits cannot be stated with any great precision – even
by the most brilliant analyst. Often the best that
can be hoped for is that a non-mathematical conclusion can be drawn: earnings will be 'roughly
the same', 'up slightly' or 'up significantly'. The
investor must be able to judge whether sizeable
increases are likely to occur. But to try to state the
increase or to predict the year of the great surge forward is futile. If all the
ingredients are in place (quality management, excellent marketing, strong
competitive position, superb R&D, etc.) then the boost will come sooner
or later.

> **Companies facing
> temporary trouble can
> turn out to be bonanza
> stocks.**

WHAT HE AVOIDS

Rejecting companies that have made mistakes

Fisher's bonanza companies were generally engaged in pioneering technological advances. Failure, on occasion, is part and parcel of progress.
Other stock pickers gave Fisher his chance to accumulate stock in companies that had shown a good average success to average failure ratio in
the past. The less informed investors tend to dump the stock when earnings drop sharply below previous estimates: 'time and again the investment community's immediate consensus is to downgrade the quality of
the management. As a result, the immediate year's lower earnings produce a lower than historic price earnings ratio to magnify the effect of
reduced earnings. The shares often reach truly bargain prices'.[42] If these
companies are run by exceptionally capable people, and the mistakes are
only transient, the investor will do better by placing money here than if he
or she invested in a company with a management that tends to go along
with crowd, and doesn't take the risk of pioneering.

Playing the 'in and out' game

Despite Fisher's extensive experience he rejected the idea that he could
predict short-term price movements, and thereby benefit by selling a

stock when it appeared to be too high with the expectation of buying it back again after a price correction. There is:

> [a] risk to those who follow the practice of selling shares that still have unusual growth prospects simply because they have realized a good gain and the stock appears temporarily overpriced … . These investors seldom buy back at higher prices when they are wrong and lose further gains of dramatic proportions … . I do not believe it possible to play the in and out game and still make the enormous profits that have accrued again and again to the truly long-term holder of the right stocks.[43]

Fisher was equally critical of those who relied on economic forecasts to time investments, which he regarded as 'silly'. He likened the current state of our knowledge of economics (for forecasting future business trends) to the science of chemistry in the days of alchemy in the Middle Ages.

There are rare occasions when speculative enthusiasm pushes stocks to ridiculous extremes (such as 1929) when an economic analysis will predict what is likely to occur. However, such analysis would be useful in only one year in ten:

> The amount of mental effort the financial community puts into this constant attempt to guess the economic future from a random and probably incomplete series of facts makes one wonder what might have been accomplished if only a fraction of such mental effort had been applied to something with a better chance of proving useful … [the] investor should ignore guesses on the coming trend of general business or the stock markets. Instead he should invest the appropriate funds as soon as a suitable buying opportunity arises.[44]

Impatience

This is an issue which has been mentioned before in this chapter, and elsewhere in the book; however, it is so important that it receives emphasis. There is a need for 'patience if big profits are to be made from investment. Put another way, it is often easier to tell what will happen to the price of a stock than how much time will elapse before it happens'.[45]

The urge to follow

'Doing what everybody else is doing at the moment, and therefore what you have an almost irresistible urge to do, is often the wrong thing to do at all.'[46]

Trying to 'come out even' on a poor investment

The difficulty people have accepting that they made a mistake causes them to avoid taking a loss on an investment and thereby making explicit, for all the world to see, that they made a bad choice:

> More money has probably been lost by investors holding a stock they really did not want until they could 'at least come out even' than from any other single reason. If to these actual losses are added the profits that might have been made through the proper reinvestment of these funds if such reinvestment had been made when the mistake was first realized, the cost of self-indulgence becomes truly tremendous.[47]

Rejecting stocks trading on lesser markets

Generally the investor should confine buying to those stocks listed on stock markets which afford a reasonably high degree of liquidity and regulation. However, it is often the case that many stocks quoted on smaller exchanges are sufficiently liquid and regulated to be of interest to the investor. Indeed, wonderful opportunities can be missed if investors overlook these markets as potential hunting grounds.

Judging a stock on the basis of its previous pricing range

To evaluate a stock on the basis of the price ranges at which it sold in recent years puts the emphasis on 'what does not particularly matter, and diverts attention from what does matter'.[48] The crucial facts needed as an input to the appraisal are to be found in the current and future influences on the performance of the underlying business. What happened to the stock price a few months or years ago is irrelevant.

Speculators sometimes try to plead that they are being rational: they might say: 'well, the price has traded in a range for many years, it is due for a rise'. The hidden logical assumption is that stocks go up about the same amount, and it is just a matter of spotting when it is the turn of that particular stock. Equally nonsensical is the belief that because a stock has already 'risen a lot' it will not go any further. Past movements are of little relevance to the future. What does matter is the background conditions leading to growth over the next few years, and whether they are already reflected in the price or not. To understand these you must understand the business, not how to read charts.

Start ups

Start-up companies, particularly in the high technology field, are often alluring. They may have an exciting new invention or are at the forefront in an industry with great growth prospects. It is very tempting to try to 'get in on the ground floor' by buying into such companies. Fisher avoided companies that did not have an operating history of two or three years and at least one year of operating profit. His reasoning was that the investor needs to be able to evaluate the quality of the operations of the major functions of the business (production, sales, cost accounting, research, management team work, and so on) and this is very difficult to do for a very young company. The opinions of qualified observers on the matter of the company's strengths and weaknesses will not yet be properly formed. Likely future difficulties or competitive threats can only be guessed at. In short, Fisher-type analysis is simply not possible, and the stock buyer is therefore gambling, unless they have highly specialized skills and knowledge.

Over-stressing diversification

Everyone is aware of the horrors of putting too many eggs into one basket. Few people consider the 'evils' of the other extreme. 'This is the disadvantage of having eggs in so many baskets that a lot of the eggs do not end up in really attractive baskets, and it is impossible to keep watching all the baskets after the eggs get put in them.'[49] Fisher regarded it as appalling that investors were persuaded to spread their funds between 25 or more stocks. The investor, or his adviser, is highly likely to be placing money in companies of which they know little. The result is that only a small proportion of the money is left for placement in companies of which they have a thorough understanding. 'It never seems to occur to them, much less to their advisers, that buying a company without having sufficient knowledge of it may be even more dangerous than having inadequate diversification.'[50]

He draws an analogy with an infantryman stacking rifles to illustrate the degree of diversification needed. The 'stack' would be unstable with just two rifles. Five or six, properly placed, would be much firmer. 'However, he can get just as secure a stack with five as he could with fifty.'[51] The analogy is inadequate in one respect: the number needed for a stack does not depend on the type of rifles, but the number of stocks needed for adequate diversification does depend on the nature of the stock in the portfolio. For example, some chemical firms have a considerable degree of diversification within them – serving different markets, industries and consumers. Another risk reducing factor is the extent to which the companies are run by a broadly based management team rather than a one-man management. Investing in a number of cyclical industry stocks will need to be balanced by investing a reasonably large proportion of the fund in stocks less subject to fluctuation. It would be unwise to invest a high proportion of the fund in stocks belonging to one industry, say bank stocks. On the other hand an investor who splits the fund equally between ten stocks in ten different industries may be over-diversified.

Fisher suggested that if the investor was focused on large well-entrenched growth stocks (e.g. Dow, Du Pont and IBM in the 1960s) then the minimum degree of diversification should be five such stocks – with no more than 20 per cent in each. Also, there should be very little product line overlapping. If the focus is on companies that are more established than start-up technology stocks, but are not yet leading and well-entrenched growth stocks (and they meet the usual Fisher criteria, e.g. excellent management team), then the investor should not put more than 8–10 per cent of the fund in each. The final category is small companies, 'with staggering possibilities of gain for the successful, but complete or almost complete loss of investment for the unsuccessful'.[52] Never put more money into these than you can afford to lose and never put more than 5 per cent of the fund into one stock.

Investors should only add more securities to the portfolio if they can keep track of all the company events, strategic conditions, management quality and a host of other factors about each company:

> Practical investors usually learn their problem is finding enough outstanding investments, rather than choosing among too many … . Usually a very long list of securities is not a sign of the brilliant investor, but one who is unsure of himself. If the investor owns stock in so many companies that he cannot keep in touch with their management directly or indirectly, he is rather sure to end up in worse shape than if he had owned stocks in too few companies. An investor should always realize that some mistakes are going to be made and that he should have sufficient diversification so that an occasional mistake will not prove crippling. However, beyond this point he should take extreme care to own not the most, but the best. In the field of common stocks, a little bit of a great many can never be more than a poor substitute for a few of the outstanding.[53]

WHEN TO SELL

If a stock has been properly selected using the Fisher rules and it has with-stood the test of time, then the correct time for selling is 'almost never'.[54] Despite the expectations of holding a stock for the very long term, Fisher did occasionally sell. One reason for selling was when a mistake had been made in the original analysis, and the factual background is significantly less favourable than believed at the time of purchase. Honesty and self-control is needed in these circumstances to accept fallibility and to correct the error. Comfort can be taken from the fact that the process of identifying bonanza stocks is complex and requires a high degree of skill, knowledge and judgement – mistakes are bound to occur. It is important that a mistake is recognized and rectified quickly. Also, a review of the process which led to the misjudgement is advised so that lessons can be learned.

The second reason for selling was when, through the passage of time, and changes in the company and its industry, a stock no longer qualifies as a Fisher growth stock. Investors need to keep in close contact with the company's affairs throughout the time they hold the stock. There are two causes of such deterioration in growth potential. The first, a fall off in the quality of management. Perhaps key executives become smug or complacent; inertia takes the place of drive and ingenuity. Perhaps, successor managers to the ones originally backed lack the special characteristics of their predecessors. Even if the general market and industry prospects looks good, a company with deteriorating management should be sold immediately. The second adverse change is in the product markets. Perhaps market growth has reached a peak and future growth will be pedestrian. Even excellent executives cannot always manage their way out of this problem. Sometimes they can successfully develop related or allied products. However, they will not (if they are good) go into fields where they have no particular competitive edge to offer.

Fisher suggested a test to see if a company continued to qualify as a growth stock:

> This is for the investor to ask himself whether at the next peak of a business cycle, regardless of what may happen in the meantime, the comparative per-share earnings ... will probably show at least as great an increase from present levels as the present levels show from the last known peak of general business activity ... . If the answer is ... negative, it should probably be sold.[55]

A third reason for selling, which seldom arises if the investor has obeyed the Fisher buying principles, is when a better prospect is offered. Then one growth stock is sold to buy another – perhaps a 12 per cent grower is replaced by a 20 per cent grower. However, the investor has to be very sure of his ground and not be too ready to sell a growth stock for this reason. 'There is always the risk that some major element in the picture has been misjudged … . In contrast, an alert investor who has held a good stock for some time usually gets to know its less desirable as well as its more desirable characteristics.'[56] In other words, beware the fallacy of believing that the grass is greener on the other side.

Fisher also had a three-year rule. Whether a stock goes up or down in the first year after purchase is a matter of luck, and, therefore investors should not judge performance over such a short time frame. However, if it performs worse than the market over three years it should be sold even if the investor has a deep conviction about the stock.

It is not wise to sell a stock just because it appears to be selling at an unusually high price-earnings ratio:

> this is trying to measure something with a greater degree of preciseness than is possible. The investor cannot pinpoint just how much per share a particular company will earn two years from now … . How can anyone say with even moderate precision just what is overpriced for an outstanding company with an unusually rapid growth rate? Suppose that instead of selling at 25 times earnings, as usually happens, the stock is now at 35 times earnings. Perhaps there are new products in the immediate future, the real economic importance of which the financial community has not yet grasped. Perhaps there are not any such products. If the growth rate is so good that in another ten years the company might well have quadrupled, is it really of such great concern whether at the moment the stock might or might not be 35 per cent over priced?[57]

DIFFICULTIES/DRAWBACKS OF THIS APPROACH

Scuttlebutt is a very time consuming process and requires a good knowledge of strategy, finance and other managerial disciplines to be able to ask intelligent questions. Many investors do not have the time, or the background experience and training, to conduct Fisher-type scuttlebutt. Even if an investor does have the time to seek out and talk with people familiar with a company, he or she may not have the inclination or personality to make contact and converse with previously unknown people. The personality traits demanded are quite onerous: 'it is not enough just to chat with them; it is necessary to arouse their interest and their confidence to a point where they will tell what they know. The successful investor is usually an individual who is inherently interested in business problems'.[58]

Furthermore, people are likely to be more willing to grant an interview if you run a multi-million dollar portfolio. If you are investing a few thousand dollars you may have difficulty obtaining an appointment with important executives.

Fisher insisted that stock analysis must be conducted correctly and with a full commitment or it is not worth doing at all. 'When it comes to selecting growth stocks, the rewards for proper action are so huge and the penalty for poor judgement is so great that it is hard to see why anyone would want to select a growth stock on the basis of superficial knowledge.'[59] He regarded an investor's task as being so specialized and intricate that there is no more logic behind the idea that an individual should handle his own investment than be his own doctor, lawyer or automobile mechanic. He advises us to concentrate on those areas of work where we have a special interest or skill, and employ an investment expert to handle stock selection.

This is a very pessimistic viewpoint and it is one which is not shared by the other investors discussed in this book. All the approaches demand commitment, intellectual effort, and knowledge about the market, industries and companies. But, while it is taken to be a good idea to discover as much as possible through some degree of scuttlebutt, the other investors do not exclude the possibility that a diligent 'amateur' with an interest in a particular sector could learn enough about a company to make a reasoned decision to buy or leave alone, without the massive commitment to scuttlebutt that Fisher appears to have called for. The investor would have to convince himself or herself that they really do understand the company, which is likely to mean that they are aware of their circle of competence and refuse to step outside of it. Perhaps the investor is familiar with the retail sector and is able to concentrate intellectual resources here to continuously deepen knowledge of the economics of retailing, the quality of management teams, innovations, relative strategic strengths and a host of other factors. For this investor to then start investing in, say, mining stocks, would be asking for trouble, unless enormous effort is committed to developing an expertise in mining company analysis. 'Do few things well … . My mistake was to project my skill beyond the limits of experience. I began investing outside the industries which I believe I thoroughly understood, in completely different spheres of activity; situations where I did not have comparable background knowledge.'[60] I suppose there is a kind of continuum with pure Fisherian high-quality in-depth knowledge of each company in the portfolio at one end. At the other end is uninformed, intellectually lazy, speculation with investors flying from one ill-conceived stock purchase to another. The key question is whether there is any sense in putting in the effort to place oneself three-quarters of the way to the Fisher extreme. It is my view that to be halfway is unlikely to be enough to do better than the market average (point B in Fig. 5.3), but this will be a far better performance than achieved by investors that place themselves at the right hand extreme. With enough commitment, experience and knowledge (and a focusing of these qualities) it will be possible to outperform; perhaps not as impressively as one might if Fisherian perfection is achieved, but enough to make the effort rewarding (point A).

Figure 5.3 The knowledge and commitment continuum for the investor

SUMMARY OF FISHER'S APPROACH

- Scuttlebutt – the scavenging of information by obtaining the views and opinions of anybody associated with a company.
- All companies selected must have a strong and well-directed research capability. (However, Fisher said his other principles had validity for companies that are not in the high technology sector, and so this is not a requirement for investors specializing in these areas.)

- High quality of people:
  - business ability:
    - day-to-day task efficiency;
    - long-range planning;
  - integrity:
    - honesty;
    - personal decency;
  - outstanding labour and personal relations
  - outstanding executive relations.

- Strong competitive position – companies which consistently succeeded in doing things better than other companies in the industry.

- Marketing excellence – essential to convince others of the worth of the company's products and to assist the development of new product lines meeting customer needs.

- Good financial state and controls:
  - high profit margins;
  - profit margins which do not rise and fall dramatically with the business cycle;
  - constant downward pressure in costs;
  - low demands for additional equity;
  - high quality costing information system.

- Low price:
  - Investor's irrational behaviour can drive prices below the price warranted by the facts. This provides opportunities to buy bonanza stocks;
  - zig when others are zagging; but only when thorough analysis tells you to zig;
  - shares can be bought at high historic PERs, if the long-run prospects are sufficiently positive;
  - companies facing temporary trouble may turn out to be bonanza stocks.

- What to avoid:
  - rejecting companies that have made mistakes;
  - playing the 'in and out' game;
  - impatience;
  - the urge to follow;
  - trying to 'come out even' on a poor investment;
  - rejecting stocks trading on lesser markets;
  - judging a stock on the basis of its previous pricing range;
  - start ups;
  - over-stressing diversification.

- When to sell:
  - almost never;
  - when a mistake has been made;
  - the company or industry has changed and the stock no longer qualifies as a growth stock;
  - a better prospect is available;
  - after three years, if the stock underperforms the market.

- Do not sell:
  - to time the market;
  - just because a stock appears to be selling for a PER significantly above average;
  - because the stock price has risen.

Notes

1   Fisher, P. (1980), p. 204. © 1996 Philip A. Fisher. This material is used by permission of John Wiley & Sons Inc.
2   *Ibid.*, p. 205.
3   He had arranged to return to Stanford to study for the second year if things did not work out at the bank.
4   Fisher, P. (1980), p. 209.
5   Fisher, P. (1960), p. 3. © 1996 Philip A. Fisher. This material is used by permission of John Wiley & Sons Inc.
6   Fisher, P. (1980), p. 209.
7   *Ibid.*, p. 210.
8   *Ibid.*, p. 210.
9   *Ibid.*, p. 219.
10   *Ibid.*, p. 225.
11   *Ibid.*, pp. 229–30.
12   *Ibid.*, p. 233.
13   *Ibid.*, p. 222.
14   *Ibid.*, p. 236.
15   *Ibid.*, p. 244.
16   Fisher, P. (1960), p. 19.
17   *Ibid.*, p. 47.
18   *Ibid.*, p. 17.
19   *Ibid.*, p. 18.
20   *Ibid.*, p. 31.
21   Fisher, P. (1975), p. 165. © 1996 Philip A. Fisher. This material is used by permission of John Wiley & Sons Inc.
22   Fisher, P. (1960), p. 20.
23   *Ibid.*, p. 19.
24   *Ibid.*, p. 87.

25 *Ibid.*, p. 41.
26 Fisher, P. (1975), p. 172.
27 Fisher, P. (1980), p. 231.
28 Fisher, P. (1975), p. 174.
29 *Ibid.*, p. 175.
30 Fisher, P. (1960), p. 44.
31 *Ibid.*, pp. 44–5.
32 Fisher, P. (1975), p. 180.
33 Fisher, P. (1960), p. 33.
34 *Ibid.*, p. 37.
35 *Ibid.*, p. 46.
36 *Ibid.*, p. 43.
37 Fisher, P. (1975), pp. 182–3.
38 *Ibid.*, p. 183.
39 Fisher, P. (1960), p. 148.
40 Fisher, P. (1980), p. 218.
41 Fisher, P. (1960), p. 105.
42 Fisher, P. (1980), p. 231.
43 *Ibid.*, pp. 239–40.
44 Fisher, P. (1960), p. 63.
45 *Ibid.*, p. 4.
46 *Ibid.*, p. 4.
47 *Ibid.*, p. 78.
48 *Ibid.*, p. 121.
49 *Ibid.*, p. 108.
50 *Ibid.*, p. 108.
51 *Ibid.*, p. 109.
52 *Ibid.*, p. 115.
53 *Ibid.*, pp. 117–18.
54 *Ibid.*, p. 85.
55 *Ibid.*, p. 80.
56 *Ibid.*, p. 66.
57 *Ibid.*, pp. 82–3.
58 *Ibid.*, p. 53.
59 *Ibid.*, p. 143.
60 Fisher, P. (1980), p. 235.

6

Warren Buffett's and Charles Munger's business perspective investing – Part 1

Warren Buffett is the most influential investment thinker of our time; he is also the wealthiest. Charles Munger is Buffett's partner, both intellectually and in the running of one of the world's largest companies. They each started with very little capital. At first, they developed their investment philosophies independently. They were far away from each other, both in their investment approach and geographically (Munger in California and Buffett in Nebraska). Despite the different approaches to stock picking they each created highly successful fund management businesses before coming together.

In the 1970s Munger was persuaded to join Berkshire Hathaway, Buffetts' holding company, as Vice-Chairman. They make a great team. Whilst they started from different intellectual roots (Buffett used to take a predominantly quantitative approach; Munger focused on the characteristics of the business that give it a sustainable competitive edge), their ideas have converged to such an extent that they almost know what the other is thinking when it comes to stocks: 'Charlie and I can handle a four-page memo over the phone with three grunts'.[1]

Munger was always more in the Fisher school of thought rather than in Graham's. Buffett started as a Graham disciple, but began to notice the shortcomings of this approach in the late 1960s and early 1970s, as his Grahamite investments failed. Buffett had already moved a long way from his mentor when Munger's ideas started to have an impact: 'I have been shaped tremendously by Charlie. Boy, if I had listened only to Ben, would I ever be a lot poorer'.[2]

These two titans of the investment world pull each other's legs relentlessly. For example, at Berkshire Hathaway's 1992 Annual Meeting, Buffett said they would 'answer questions until around noon or until Charlie says something optimistic, whichever comes first'.[3] When Buffett acquired a fifth of the world's silver supply in 1997–8 Munger said that it had 'kept Warren amused' but would have as much impact on Berkshire's future 'as Warren's bridge playing'.[4] Hidden behind the cheerful banter they display a great respect for each other's abilities. 'Charlie is rational, very rational. He doesn't have his ego wrapped up in the business the way I do, but he understands it perfectly. Essentially, we have never had an argument, though occasional disagreements.'[5] Buffett consults Munger before any big investment decision: 'Charlie has the best 30-second mind in the world. He goes from A to Z in one move. He sees the essence of everything before you even finish the sentence'.[6] The gruff Munger is proud to call Buffett his friend. He admires his warm personality and generosity of spirit as well as his intellectual might: 'His brain is a superbly rational mechanism. And since he's articulate, you can see the damn brain working'.[7]

The relationship has been described as akin to that of elder brother (Munger) and younger brother (Buffett). They are very close friends and are fully aware of their mutual need for each other to make wise investment choices. Munger says 'everybody engaged in complicated work needs colleagues. Just the discipline of having to put your thoughts in order with somebody else is a very useful thing'.[8]

THE INVESTMENT RECORD

Buffett took managerial control of Berkshire Hathaway in 1965 when the book value per share was $19.46 (as measured at the prior year end 30 September 1964). By year end 2000, book value, with equity holdings carried at market value, was $40,442 per share. The gain in book value over 36 years came to 23.6 per cent compounded annually. At this rate of return an investment of $100 becomes worth over $200,000 over 36 years. There are people who are multi-millionaires today because in the 1960s or 1970s they invested a few thousand dollars in Berkshire Hathaway. Warren Buffett and his wife Susan own around 40 per cent of Berkshire Hathaway, a company with a GAAP net worth of $57.8 billion, the highest of any company in the United States, and a market capitalization of approximately $100 billion (it was valued at a mere $20 million in 1965). Table 6.1 shows the truly outstanding performance of Berkshire Hathaway. There have been only four years in which the rise in book value was less than the return on the S&P 500. It is even better than it looks – the S&P 500 numbers are pre-tax whereas the Berkshire numbers are after-tax!

Berkshire owns shares in publicly traded companies worth $37.6 billion. These holdings include approximately 11.4 per cent of American Express, 8.1 per cent of Coca-Cola, 9.1 per cent of Gillette, 18.3 per cent of the *Washington Post* and 3.2 per cent of Wells Fargo.

| Table 6.1 | Berkshire's corporate performance versus the S&P 500[9] |

Year	Annual percentage change		
	In per-share book value of Berkshire (1)	In S&P 500 with dividends included (2)	Relative results (1) – (2)
1965	23.8	10.0	13.8
1966	20.3	(11.7)	32.0
1967	11.0	30.9	(19.9)
1968	19.0	11.0	8.0
1969	16.2	(8.4)	24.6
1970	12.0	3.9	8.1
1971	16.4	14.6	1.8
1972	21.7	18.9	2.8
1973	4.7	(14.8)	19.5
1974	5.5	(26.4)	31.9
1975	21.9	37.2	(15.3)
1976	59.3	23.6	35.7
1977	31.9	(7.4)	39.3
1978	24.0	6.4	17.6
1979	35.7	18.2	17.5
1980	19.3	32.3	(13.0)
1981	31.4	(5.0)	36.4
1982	40.0	21.4	18.6
1983	32.3	22.4	9.9
1984	13.6	6.1	7.5
1985	48.2	31.6	16.6
1986	26.1	18.6	7.5
1987	19.5	5.1	14.4
1988	20.1	16.6	3.5
1989	44.4	31.7	12.7
1990	7.4	(3.1)	10.5
1991	39.6	30.5	9.1
1992	20.3	7.6	12.7
1993	14.3	10.1	4.2
1994	13.9	1.3	12.6
1995	43.1	37.6	5.5
1996	31.8	23.0	8.8
1997	34.1	33.4	.7
1998	48.3	28.6	19.7
1999	.5	21.0	(20.5)
2000	6.5	(9.1)	15.6

Some investors have been with Buffett long before he took control of Berkshire. An investor who placed $100 in one of his investment partnerships in the late 1950s, and placed it in Berkshire after the partnership was dissolved, would find that investment worth more than $2 million today. In the 13 years of the partnership funds (1957–69) investors made annual returns greater than that on Berkshire, at almost 30 per cent per year. The funds managed by the young Buffett outperformed the Dow Jones Industrial Average in every year and made money even when the market was sharply down. If you put the two phases of his career – first the partnership, then Berkshire – together then you have a quite remarkable performance record, one that, to my knowledge, has not been beaten.

Buffett himself has become the richest or second richest man in the world, depending on the relative performance of Microsoft and Berkshire shares in any one year. He is the only person ever to make it to the Forbes billionaire list by stock market investing.

Imagine being one of the lucky people to have trusted Buffett in the early days. It is what investors' dreams are made off. Apparently, the following conversation between two Berkshire shareholders was overheard at the annual meeting in 1996: 'What price did you buy at?' The reply: 'Nineteen'. Says the first, 'you mean nineteen hundred?' 'No, nineteen.'[10] These shares are now worth $69,000 each!

WARREN BUFFETT – THE ROAD TO BEING A BILLIONAIRE

On 30 August 1930 Warren Edward Buffett was born. Howard Buffett, his father, was a pillar of the Omaha, Nebraska Community. He was a stockbroker and a congressman, serving four terms. Warren was fascinated by numbers and the potential of using his brain to make money. He was only eight when he started to read his father's books on the stock market. When he was 11 he would mark up the board at Harris Upham, a New York Stock Exchange firm which was in the same building at his father's stock brokerage (Buffett-Falk). He would just watch the market movements. Eventually he felt confident enough to buy some shares. Together with his sister he bought three shares of Cities Service preferred stock at $38 per share.[11] He learned two lessons from this investment. First, patience and fortitude is needed if the investor is not to be panicked into selling when stock prices fall: Cities Service fell to $27. Second, if you are holding a company in which you have faith don't sell just because a short-term gain presents itself – Warren and Doris sold at $40 but the stock continued to rise, eventually reaching $200 per share.

Buffett's parents taught him more important things than stock market investment. He is one of the most gracious, honest, kind and warm people you could wish to meet. His cheerfulness combined with his folksy humour make him wonderful company. He is decisive, confident and forthright, but, at the same time charming, patient and generous. He made his money while keeping the love and respect of family and friends. Peter Buffett, his son says that his unpretentious ways account for his popularity. 'I think that's why he gets the kind of respect that he does. He really has done it honestly and quietly and with a lot of respect for other people.'[12] Warren's mother, Leila, said in 1987 that she was more proud of him 'for the kind of human being that he had become' than because of his wealth. She added, 'he's a wonderful person'.[13] Who ever said nice guys finish last is a fool.

Warren and his father were close. He taught Warren never to do anything that would make him or his family unhappy if it was blazoned on the front page of a newspaper. Buffett says that he has never known a better human being than his father. Leila said that Warren and his father were the best of friends. He never punished the children, preferring reason and persuasion. He told his son that he was never to lie under any circumstances and that while it takes 20 years to build a reputation it only takes five minutes to ruin it. 'If you think about that you'll do things differently.'[14]

After the family moved to Washington DC when Warren was 13 years old, he took a part-time job delivering newspapers. Over four years he built up five simultaneous newspaper routes. This was the humble start of a long association with the *Washington Post*. He was very enterprising: he sold Cokes to his friends (buying a six-pack for 25c and selling each bottle for 5c); he published a racetrack tip sheet; he recycled golf balls. A particularly lucrative activity was the placing of reconditioned pinball machines in barbershops. The first one cost $25 and in the first day he found customers had spent $4. With seven machines he was taking $50 per week. Buying a 1934 Rolls Royce for $350 and renting it out for $35 a day also helped to boost his fund, as did the purchase of 40 acres of Nebraska agricultural land which he rented to a farmer (when he was 14 years old!) By the time he graduated from High School he had a considerable sum of money which was to form his first investment fund. According to some reports this was $5,000; others put it at $6,000 and still others at $9,000. Whatever the true figure he was a young man with business nous who had already displayed a remarkable capacity for courage, and hard work.

At 17, Warren enrolled at Wharton's School of Finance. He soon rejected the school as he felt he was not learning much that was useful. For a 17-year-old this shows a high degree of self-confidence and a sense of purpose. It also shows an early manifestation of his distrust of the kind of finance theory taught in universities – something which he has continued to hold, in common with Charles Munger, who describes much of what is taught in modern corporate finance classes as 'twaddle'.[15]

Buffett joined the University of Nebraska. He earned a Bachelor of Science Degree in 1950, but more important than that was the reading of a single book when he was 19 – Benjamin Graham's *The Intelligent Investor*.

Buffett had been investing for some time before reading Graham's classic text, but he had made the same mistakes that millions of investors, before and, sadly, since, have made: 'I went the whole gamut. I collected charts and I read all the technical stuff. I listened to tips. And then I picked up Graham's *The Intelligent Investor*. That was like seeing the light'.[16] 'Prior to that, I had been investing with my glands instead of my head.'[17]

By serendipitous fate he failed to gain a place at Harvard (which must have been a real bruiser to his self-esteem at the time) and so applied to Columbia Graduate Business School. There he learned first hand from Graham the importance of intrinsic value and margin of safety. Graham became not only Buffett's teacher, but also his friend.

Though it seems ironic now, both his father and Graham advised Buffett not to make a career in stocks. Indeed Graham even turned down Buffett's offer of working for the Graham Newman company for nothing (Graham preferred to help young Jews who suffered from the prejudice of many gentile financial firms). With this second major knock to his pride he returned to Omaha, aged 20, to work for his father's brokerage.

GEICO

While at Columbia he had discovered that Graham was a director of a small insurance company known as GEICO. He wanted to know what it was about GEICO that had attracted Graham. In January 1951 Buffett took the train to Washington DC to see if he could talk to someone at GEICO to find out more about the company. On this Saturday morning he had to pound on the door and then persuade the surprised caretaker to open it. The caretaker said that there was one person working in the building. Mr Lorimer Davidson, assistant to the President, who was later to become CEO, was working on the sixth floor. Davidson was impressed by Buffett's intelligent interest in the company, and spent the next four hours or so graciously answering questions about GEICO, its operating methods and business prospects. Buffett was attracted by the high profit margins and its focus on low risk clients. It had an excellent market niche and good growth prospects. 'No one has ever received a better half-day course in how the insurance industry functions, nor in the factors that enable one company to excel over others. As Davy made clear, GEICO's method of selling – direct marketing – gave it an enormous cost advantage over competitors that sold through agents…. After my session with Davy, I was more excited about GEICO than I have ever been about a stock.'[18] On returning to Nebraska he focused almost exclusively on GEICO and invested $10,282, about 65 per cent of his net worth, in GEICO stock. Thus began a long association with GEICO which culminated in Berkshire Hathaway purchasing the whole company in 1995, by which time it was worth $4.6 billion.

During 1951 he tried to interest brokerage clients in GEICO, but generally failed. 'I was then a skinny, unpolished 20-year-old who looked about 17, and my best pitch usually failed.'[19] His Aunt Alice, who was always very supportive, followed his advice and bought some shares. She was handsomely rewarded in this, as she was in many future investments suggested by her nephew.

Buffett sold the GEICO shares in 1952 for $15,259. A very good return you might think, but if he had held onto those shares and gone fishing for the next 20 years he could have walked away with $1.3 million. This taught him a lesson 'about the inadvisability of selling a stake in an identifiably-wonderful company'.[20] While Buffett might kick himself for his act of 'infidelity', I think we should resist joining him as he did use the proceeds to invest in some other wonderful stocks, helping to create the billions he has today.

A 'PEASANT' AT GRAHAM-NEWMAN

While working for his father's brokerage, Buffett wrote to Graham with various investment ideas. Finally, in 1954, Graham invited him to join Graham-Newman in New York. He soaked-up his mentor's outpourings for the next two years. Graham reinforced Buffett's desire to conduct all his affairs in the most ethical manner. Both possessed high standards of integrity and discipline, and enjoyed a sophisticated dry wit.

Graham, at 61, decided to retire in 1956 and dissolve Graham-Newman. Buffett returned to Omaha which he considered a great place from which to conduct an investment business:

> I think it is a saner existence here. I used to feel, when I worked in New York, that there were more stimuli just hitting me all the time, and if you've got the normal amount of adrenaline, you start responding to them. It may lead to crazy behaviour after a while. It's much easier to think here.'[21]

THE BUFFETT PARTNERSHIPS

When he returned to Omaha at the age of 25 he owned two valuable things: first, a knowledge of investment principles that gave him confidence when talking to people many years his senior who had been investing since before he was born. Second, a substantial sum of money. By some reports this was as much as $140,000, mostly acquired from shrewd stock selection.

In 1956, he set up the first of his investment partnerships – Buffett Associates Ltd. The other seven partners contributed a total of $105,000 – the biggest investor being wise and faithful Aunt Alice, who put in $35,000.

The managing partner, Buffett, was to receive fees based on performance, and no fee would be payable if the fund did not perform well. By the end of the third year, the partners' money had doubled. Buffett's reputation grew and more investors approached him. Between 1956 and 1962 he set up nine additional partnerships. At this time his investment choices were heavily influenced by Graham's ideas, but he was prepared to take controlling interests in several public and private companies. Dempster Mill Manufacturing Company, a farm equipment manufacturer, was bought in 1961, and a substantial stake was accumulated in Berkshire Hathaway, from 1962 onward.

By 1962 there were over 90 partners. He decided to merge all the partnerships into the one fund – Buffett Partnership Ltd. The partners were to receive a return of 6 per cent before Buffett received any fees. He did not guarantee that at least 6 per cent would be returned, but he did agree this would be cumulative. That is, if less than 6 per cent is earned in one year the partnership fund would pay an additional sum the next year (or the next, and so on) to give an effective rate of 6 per cent over time. The partners also received three-quarters of any return above the 6 per cent. The extraordinary returns achieved meant that the partners were very happy, and Buffett quickly became a millionaire as he retained 25 per cent of the profits above the threshold return of 6 per cent. By 1965 the partnership's assets had grown to $26 million. Quite a large chunk of that belonged to Buffett as he had, as a matter of principle, invested his own money in the fund he managed. Even today 99 per cent of the Buffett family net worth is held in the form of Berkshire Hathaway stock (as is 90 per cent of Munger's).

Buffett started to develop his own style of investing. He could see that there were many excellent companies that could not be bought under Grahamite principles because they had so few net assets. He became increasingly interested in the potential of the firms as well as, or instead of, the asset position. GEICO was an early foray into this kind of stock, but the first big investment was in American Express.

AMEX AND DISNEY

In 1963 American Express had a very strong franchise with high brand recognition, and millions of customers. It dominated its market, but had very few tangible assets. Then disaster struck. American Express was tricked into issuing receipts certifying that its warehouses were storing huge quantities of salad-oil. In fact the containers were holding nothing more valuable than seawater. American Express became liable for millions of dollars of claims in what became known as the Salad-Oil scandal. The subsequent drop in the share price, gave Buffett his chance to purchase with a margin of safety. However, this margin of safety was different to Graham's. It was based on the value of the company's future cash generation flowing from its near monopoly position in its market – balance sheet assets were relatively unimportant in this evaluation. He put 40 per cent ($13 million) of Buffett Partnership Ltd's capital into the battered stock, giving the partnership over 5 per cent ownership in Amex. We will discuss Buffett's views on diversification later in Chapter 7, but note, for now, his willingness to have what traditionalists would call an unbalanced portfolio – 65 per cent of net worth in GEICO, 40 per cent in Amex, even when he is dealing with other people's money.

Disney caught Buffett's attention in 1966, when its market valuation was less than $90 million. This low capitalization was given by the market despite the fact that it had profits of around $21 million pre-tax in 1965 and held more cash than the value of its debt. It had a terrific franchise. Surely the film library alone was worth more than the market capitalization? 'At Disneyland, the $17 million Pirates of the Caribbean ride would soon open. Imagine my excitement – a company selling at only five times rides!'[22] The partnership bought a significant stake, which it sold in 1967 for a 55 per cent profit. In the 1995 report of Berkshire, after he had again taken a stake in Disney by exchanging Capital Cities/ABC Inc. stock for Disney shares he took a dig at himself for selling out in 1967, despite the high returns. 'That decision [to buy in 1966] may appear brilliant... but your Chairman was up to the task of nullifying it [by selling in 1967]' – he was referring to the fact that the stock price rose 138 fold between 1967 and 1995.

■■■ BULL MARKET

Ten years after starting his investment partnerships, in 1966 at the age of 35 he was controlling a fund of $44 million – of which he owned $6.5 million.[23] Naturally, the partners were over the moon at this performance and charmed by his self-deprecation when reporting the successes and failures of his adventures. However, Buffett was increasingly troubled as the 1960s wore on. Bull markets generally trouble him, and the late 1960s' one was a humdinger. Economic activity was boosted by the demand stimulus of the Vietnam War and everyone was talking about the Nifty-Fifty. Price-earnings ratios were typically between 50 and 100 for those stocks most in the public eye (e.g. Xerox, Avon and Polaroid). In the investment houses the fashion was to churn portfolios rapidly and achieve high short-term performance. Buffett seemed increasingly out of step with the new age. His long-term focus and his caution about paying high multiples made him appear to be an old fashioned stick-in-the-mud. To Buffett it was as though the world had gone mad and he felt compelled to write to the partners (in 1967) and explain his unease and unwillingness to switch from the methods that he trusts:

> Essentially I am out of step with present conditions…. I will not abandon a previous approach whose logic I understand … even though it may mean forgoing large, and apparently easy, profits to embrace an approach which I don't fully understand, have not practised successfully, and which, possibly could lead to substantial permanent loss of capital.[24]

It was another 20 months before he dissolved the partnership, during which time he managed to add even more value to the fund. In 1968 it gained 59 per cent to be worth $104 million.[25]

When he began the partnership he had set the goal of outperforming the Dow by an average of ten percentage points. Over the period 1956 to 1969 he outperformed by 22 points.[26]

When the partnership was wound up in May 1969 each partner was given a choice:

- cash, and/or
- shares in Berkshire Hathaway, and/or
- shares in Diversified Retailing.

Buffett stuck with Berkshire Hathaway and a number of other members of the partnership joined him. His share of the partnership had grown to $25 million. Initially he held 29 per cent of Berkshire Hathaway and was appointed its chairman.

BERKSHIRE HATHAWAY

Buffett was a multi-millionaire at the age of 40. He could have lived very comfortably for the rest of his life without working. But, he says that he enjoys the business of investment so much that he feels 'like tap dancing all the time'[27] and so he continued. In the 1973–4 crash he bought more stock in Berkshire Hathaway at a steep discount to book value, eventually holding 43 per cent.

Berkshire Hathaway was a Grahamite investment. It had a tendency to make losses rather than profits, but it had assets worth much more than liabilities. In 1962, when the Buffett partnership started buying stock at $8 it had current assets which exceeded all liabilities by approximately $13 per share.

Buffett and his managers put great effort into trying to turn the textile business into an enterprise that produced sufficient profits to justify the amount of capital it used. The struggle was in vain. The economics of the industry were against them. It was a commodity business, with little product differentiation, in which foreign firms, employing cheap labour, had the competitive edge. For the mills to have even the slimmest hope of competing they needed massive injections of capital. This course of action just did not make sense when Buffett could use that capital for investment in business with much brighter prospects. He decided to restrict internal investment and looked to opportunities outside of the textile business.

> ...The economics of the industry were against them. ....

The GEICO episode and Lorimer Davidson's excellent tuition had left an abiding interest in insurance companies. In March 1967, $8.6 million of Berkshire capital was used to buy two insurance companies: National Indemnity Company and National Fire and Marine Insurance Company. Insurance companies play an important role in the success of Berkshire. They have a very special element: a float of money. When policyholders pay premiums for insurance on cars, houses etc. that money is put into a pool of funds. If, at a later date, the policyholder crashes a car, say, the insurance company would take money from this pool. In the meantime the insurance company has a pot of money which it can use to generate an investment return. In the hands of a skilful investor the float can create astonishingly large amounts of money. In 1967 Berkshire, through its insurance subsidiaries, had a float of $17.3 million. This was to grow, by organic growth and acquisition, to $27,871 million by the end of 2000.

The key determinants of success in the insurance business are:

- the size of the float that the underwriting business generates;
- the cost of creating that float; and
- the returns that can be generated from the float.

For many insurers the cost of the float is high. This is measured as the extent to which the premiums fail to cover the payouts to policyholders and the cost of running the business. Thus the company makes an 'underwriting loss'. Buffett says that: 'An insurance business has value if its cost of float over time is less than the cost the company would otherwise incur to obtain funds. But the business is a lemon if its cost of float is higher than market rates for money'.[28] So, Buffett would have been prepared to accept a small underwriting loss, just so long as it was not greater than the market rates for money. In fact, he has been lucky enough over the past 33 years to have found managers for the insurance business that, on average, produced substantial underwriting profits rather than losses. He is forever grateful to these excellent managers and showers them with praise in the annual reports of Berkshire.

It can be seen in Table 6.2 that the cost of float has been generally less than zero leaving Buffett with large sums of zero-cost funds to invest. This is a wonderful way to leverage up investment gains. No wonder Buffett does not think it worthwhile leveraging up the conventional way – by borrowing money. It is paradoxical that the net float has to be recorded on the balance sheet as a liability but 'they are liabilities without covenants or due dates attached to them. In effect they give us the benefit of debt – an ability to have more assets working for us – but saddle us with none of its drawbacks'.[29]

Table 6.2 The cost of the float[30]

	(1) Underwriting loss	(2) Average float	Approximate cost of funds	Year-end yield on long-term govt. bonds
	(in $ millions)		(ratio of 1 to 2)	
1967	Profit	17.3	Less than zero	5.50%
1968	Profit	19.9	Less than zero	5.90%
1969	Profit	23.4	Less than zero	6.79%
1970	0.37	32.4	1.14%	6.25%
1971	Profit	52.5	Less than zero	5.81%
1972	Profit	69.5	Less than zero	5.82%
1973	Profit	73.3	Less than zero	7.27%
1974	7.36	79.1	9.30%	8.13%
1975	11.35	87.6	12.96%	8.03%
1976	Profit	102.6	Less than zero	7.30%
1977	Profit	139.0	Less than zero	7.97%
1978	Profit	190.4	Less than zero	8.93%

Table 6.2	continued			
1979	Profit	227.3	Less than zero	10.08%
1980	Profit	237.0	Less than zero	11.94%
1981	Profit	228.4	Less than zero	13.61%
1982	21.56	220.6	9.77%	10.64%
1983	33.87	231.3	14.64%	11.84%
1984	48.06	253.2	18.98%	11.58%
1985	44.23	390.2	11.34%	9.34%
1986	55.84	797.5	7.00%	7.60%
1987	55.43	1,266.7	4.38%	8.95%
1988	11.08	1,497.7	0.74%	9.00%
1989	24.40	1,541.3	1.58%	7.97%
1990	26.65	1,637.3	1.63%	8.24%
1991	119.59	1,895.0	6.31%	7.40%
1992	108.96	2,290.4	4.76%	7.39%
1993	Profit	2,624.7	Less than zero	6.35%
1994	Profit	3,056.6	Less than zero	7.88%
1995	Profit	3,607.2	Less than zero	5.95%
1996	Profit	6,702.0	Less than zero	6.64%
1997	Profit	7,093.1	Less than zero	5.92%
1998	Profit	22,762.0	Less than zero	4.57%
1999	1,400.0	25,298.0	5.8%	6.20%
2000	1,600.0	26,700 (approx.)	6%	5.19%

This balance sheet 'liability' has had more economic value to Berkshire than an equal amount of net worth would have had. Buffett says that in the analysis of his operations the growth of the float has 'probably never been appreciated fully'.[31] He goes on 'nor has the interplay of our having zero cost money in terms of effecting our gain in value over time. People always looked at our asset side, but they haven't paid as much attention to the liabilities side. Charlie and I pay a lot of attention to that. It's not entirely an accident that the business developed in this manner'.

Cash generated from operations and the insurance float has been invested in the following ways:

• purchases of significant minority stakes in publicly quoted large companies

- purchases of controlling interests in insurance companies
- purchases of non-quoted businesses possessing extraordinarily strong business franchises with excellent management.

THE WASHINGTON POST COMPANY

Under the first category one of Berkshire's earliest and most eye catching investments has been in the *Washington Post*. In 1973 $10.6 million bought 18.3 per cent of the company. This was a company with very strong franchises. Not only did it own the newspaper, it published *Newsweek* magazine and controlled a number of television stations. It was a consistent and dependable performer and yet Buffett could pick up a large holding for a song (or, at least, a mere $10.6 million). A newspaper with a strong brand is able to increase prices relatively easily; it also has low capital needs and so can produce high returns on equity capital invested. In short, it has excellent potential for producing high and rising cashflows long into the future. And yet, in 1973 the Washington Post Company (WPC) was unappreciated by the market. Buffett said that no unusual insights were needed to be aware of the gap between price and value.

> Most security analysts, media brokers, and media executives would have estimated WPC's intrinsic business value at $400 to $500 million just as we did. And its $100 million stock market valuation was published daily for all to see. Our advantage, rather, was attitude: we had learned from Ben Graham that the key to successful investing was the purchase of shares in good businesses when market prices were at a large discount from underlying business values. Most institutional investors in the early 1970s, on the other hand, regarded business value as of only minor relevance when they were deciding the prices at which they would buy or sell. This now seems hard to believe. However, these institutions were then under the spell of academics at prestigious business schools who were preaching a newly-fashioned theory: the stock market was totally efficient, and therefore calculations of business value – and even thought itself – were of no importance in investment activities. (We are enormously indebted to those academics: what could be more advantageous in an intellectual contest – whether it be bridge, chess, or stock selection – than to have opponents who have been taught that thinking is a waste of energy?) Through 1973 and 1974, WPC continued to do fine as a business, and intrinsic value grew. Nevertheless, by year end 1974 our WPC holding showed a loss of about 25 per cent, with market value at $8 million against our cost of $10.6 million. What we had

thought ridiculously cheap a year earlier had become a good bit cheaper as the market, in its infinite wisdom, marked WPC stock down to well below 20c on the dollar of intrinsic value. You know the happy outcome. Kay Graham, CEO of WPC, had the brains and courage to repurchase large quantities of stock for the company at those bargain prices, as well as the managerial skills necessary to dramatically increase business values. Meanwhile, investors began to recognize the exceptional economics of the business and the stock price moved closer to underlying value. Thus, we experienced a triple dip: the company's business value soared upward, per-share business value increased considerably faster because of stock repurchases and, with a narrowing of the discount, the stock price outpaced the gain in per-share business value. We hold all of the WPC shares we bought in 1973, except for those sold back to the company in 1985's proportionate redemption.[32]

By the end of 2000 Berkshire WPC holding had grown to be worth $1,066 million – see Table 6.3. It can also be seen in this table that Berkshire bought stakes in some of America's most valuable business franchises at a low cost.

Table 6.3 Berkshire Hathaway's common stock investments, 31 December 2000[33]

Shares	Company	Cost (dollars in millions)	Market value at 31.12.00 (dollars in millions)
151,610,700	American Express Company	1,470	8,329
200,000,000	The Coca-Cola Company	1,299	12,188
96,000,000	The Gillette Company	600	3,468
1,727,765	The Washington Post Company	11	1,066
55,071,380	Wells Fargo & Company	319	3,067
	Others	6,703	9,501
	Total common stocks	**10,402**	**37,619**

RETURN TO GEICO

Under the second type of use of capital generated by Berkshire – that of purchase of insurance companies – the most important company acquired was GEICO. Since Buffett's sale of his shares in 1952 Lorimer Davidson had become chairman. He led the company brilliantly until 1970, when he retired. The new management team embarked on an aggressive expansion between 1970 and 1974, in the teeth of fierce competition. As a result it managed to expand its market share; but only at the price of lowering its underwriting standards. It expanded from its niche position of insuring the safest categories of drivers to cover drivers with little experience and those falling in the higher risk categories. It also switched to a more expensive method of gaining and securing customers. GEICO made such high losses that it was touch-and-go as to whether the firms would survive 1975. The share price fell from $61 to $2 in 1976.

The appointment of 43-year-old John Byrne stopped the rot. He slashed costs, raised fresh capital to shore-up the balance sheet and reversed the strategy change so that it could compete on the basis of its traditional strengths. Buffett sought a meeting with Byrne. It was similar to the one he had had with Davison 25 years before. Buffett pumped Byrne for hours: 'He wanted to know the things I would do, what did I think of our ability to survive? I remember we talked late at night about families, other stuff. But mostly the conversation was GEICO'.[34] In 1976 GEICO was not a Grahamite stock, because it lacked the asset backing. But by this stage Buffett was being increasingly influenced by those investment philosophies that emphasized the company's strategic strengths and management competence and honesty. He was impressed by Byrne and felt that, when restructured, GEICO would beat its competitors. The franchises were still intact. The operating and financial troubles were temporary and not terminal. Buffett said of Byrne that he was like a chicken farmer who rolls an ostrich egg into the henhouse and says, 'Ladies, this is what the competition is doing'. He began to buy GEICO shares at a little over $2. He invested $4.1 million in common stock and $19.4 million in convertible preferred stocks (these were converted two years later). By the end of 1980 Berkshire held 7.2 million shares in GEICO (33 per cent of the equity) costing $47 million. Even at this early stage it was clear that this was a great investment – the market value of the holding at 31 December 1980 was $105.3 million. Buffett told his shareholders in the 1980 report that, 'GEICO represents the best of all investment worlds – the coupling of a very important and very hard to duplicate business advantage with an extraordinary management whose skills in operations are matched by

> The operating and financial troubles were temporary and not terminal.

skills in capital appreciation'. Buffett reasoned that GEICO in 1976 was like Amex at the time of the salad-oil crisis:

> Both were one-of-a-kind companies, temporarily reeling from the effects of a fiscal blow that did not destroy these exceptional underlying economics. The GEICO and American Express situations, extraordinary business franchises with a localized excisable cancer (needing, to be sure, a skilled surgeon), should be distinguished from the true 'turnaround' situation in which the managers expect – and need – to pull off a corporate Pygmalion.[35]

By the end of 1994 the GEICO stake had a market value of $1,678 million. Buffett says that before he will look at new investments he will consider adding to old ones: 'If a business is attractive enough to buy once, it may well pay to repeat the process'.[36] In 1995 he decided to purchase 100 per cent of GEICO and valued it at $4.6 billion. Lorimer Davidson at 93 years old, who continued to pay close attention to GEICO, was still Buffett's 'teacher and friend'. Buffett's enthusiasm for insurance companies is undimmed. In 1998 he acquired General Re for almost $22 billion. This will give him even more float to generate investment returns which, in turn, can be ploughed into more operations, creating more float for investment, and so on.

NON-QUOTED BUSINESSES

The third use for money thrown off by business operations and the insurance float is to buy control of unquoted companies possessing extraordinarily strong business franchises with excellent management. Berkshire Hathaway, in its guise as a holding company, owns a wide variety of businesses. These include *Buffalo News* (daily and Sunday newspapers); See's Candy Shops (chocolates and other confectionery); Scott Fetzer (diversified manufacturing and distribution); Nebraska Furniture Mart (retailers of home furnishings); as well as numerous footwear manufacturers and distributors, jewellery shops, Flight Safety International and 6,000 Dairy Queen stores.

These businesses are run in a very hands-off way. Indeed, Berkshire usually insists that they come with excellent management already in place before they are taken into the Berkshire fold. All operating decisions are pushed down to the various businesses while investment decisions and other capital allocation decisions are made by Buffett in consultation with Munger.

Berkshire's collection of managers is unusual in several important ways. As one example, a very high percentage of these men and women are independently wealthy, having made fortunes in the businesses that they run. They work neither because they need the money nor because they are contractually obligated to – we have no contracts at Berkshire. Rather, they work long and hard because they love their businesses. And I use the word 'their' advisedly, since these managers are truly in charge – there are no show-and-tell presentations in Omaha, no budgets to be approved by headquarters, no dictums issued about capital expenditures. We simply ask our managers to run their companies as if these are the sole asset of their families and will remain so far the next century.[37]

To give some idea of the type of company Buffett and Munger are interested in we will look briefly at See's Candy Shops and Nebraska Furniture Mart. Note that the same principles apply to the evaluation of companies which may be wholly owned and those in which a minority shareholding is taken.

SEE'S CANDY

The See's Candy Shops story illustrates the benefits that can flow from a company that has a powerful market position, excellent management and only a small need for additional capital as it grows sales and profits. An affiliate company of Berkshire (Blue Chip Stamps) bought control of See's, a West Coast manufacturer and retailer of boxed-chocolates, in 1972. The sellers were asking for $40 million. The company had $10 million of excess cash and so the true offering price was $30 million. Munger, who through his own investment fund had an interest in Blue Chip Stamps and therefore See's, and Buffett had not yet fully developed their investment philosophy based on the value of an economic franchise. Buffett, in particular, was still strongly influenced by Graham's ideas. This meant that they refused to offer $30 million as See's had a mere $7 million of tangible net assets. The highest they would go was $25 million. Fortunately, the sellers accepted the offer.

Over the next 20 years annual pre-tax profits increased from $4.2 million to $42.4 million. This may sound impressive, but before judgement is passed the analyst needs to know how much extra capital was needed to produce it. Take, for example, a steel producer with $4.2 million profit making use of $40 million of capital. Conventional investors may value this company more highly than See's, given the additional asset backing (assuming similar profit projections). However, Buffett would value the steel producer at much less because of its great need for additional capital as it grows. Let's imagine that both firms increase output and profit by ten-fold. The steel producer is now producing profits of $42 million while making use of $400 million of capital. See's produces the same profit, but its capital has risen from $7 million to $70 million (in this hypothetical and simplified case). The steel producer has had to come up with an additional $360 million to invest in plant machinery etc., while See's needed only $63 million. Compared with the steel company See's can distribute an extra $297 million to shareholders to invest elsewhere.

In actual fact See's has been so well managed that 20 years after purchase by Berkshire it operated comfortably with only $25 million of net worth. The starting capital base of $7 million was supplemented with only $18 million of reinvested earnings. Profits rose ten-fold to $42.4 million, but capital usage has risen less than four-fold. This allowed See's to distribute an astonishing $410 million to shareholders over those 20 years. Not bad for a $25 million investment!

See's has pricing power because of a high reputation for the quality of its product and service given to customers. This pricing power was largely untapped in 1972, but with the arrival of Chuck Huggins (put in charge 'five minutes' after Berkshire's purchase) it was exploited forcefully. At the same time Huggins bore down on costs and capital employed, producing the wonderful economics described above. Some indications of the way that Huggins delivered those returns can be seen in Table 6.4 covering the first ten years, 1973–82. He did not go for large scale store opening. Nor did he try to increase the sales figures dramatically by, say, reducing prices. The number of pounds of candy sold per store barely budged during the decade, but the price per pound rose significantly. See's stuck to its niche and grew the profit margins on a very restricted capital investment programme. If only more managers could resist the temptation to expand outside of those areas of activity (and geography) where they have competitive advantage, spending vast sums in the process and producing poor returns on capital.

> See's strengths are many and important. In our primary marketing area, the West, our candy is preferred by an enormous margin to that of any competitor. In fact, we believe most lovers of chocolate prefer it to candy costing two or three times as much. (In candy, as in stocks, price and value can differ; price is what you give, value is what you get.) The quality of customer service in our

shops – operated throughout the country by us and not by franchisees – is every bit as good as the product. Cheerful, helpful, personnel are as much a trademark of See's as is the logo on the box. That's no small achievement in a business that requires us to hire about 2,000 seasonal workers. We know of no comparably-sized organization that betters the quality of customer service delivered by Chuck Huggins and his associates.[38]

Table 6.4 See's Candy Shops data[39]

Year ended	Revenues	Profit after taxes	Number of pounds of candy sold	Number of stores open at year end
31 December 1982	$123.7m	$12.7m	24.2m	202
31 December 1973	$35.1m	$2.1m	17.8m	169

Over the 27-year period to 1999 See Candy's earned a total of $857 million pre-tax and it still requires very little capital. Chuck Huggins is still there at the age of 74. Buffett has noted a law – to be called Huggins law: when Huggins was 46 See's made approximately 10 per cent of his age expressed in millions. When he reached 74 the ratio was 100 per cent. Buffett says that after discovering this mathematical relationship 'Charlie and I now become giddy at the mere thought of Chuck's birthday'.[40]

NEBRASKA FURNITURE MART

Many retail businesses are vulnerable to competition, have little pricing power and do not possess a franchise. In too many segments of retail it is very easy for competitors to copy the leader and thus quickly erode a competitive edge. Often, suppliers are in a powerful position vis-à-vis the retailer, and entry into the industry by new players is easy. Locations are rarely unique and customer service improvements can be imitated.

For these reasons Buffett is cautious about investing in retail businesses.

[The] shooting-star phenomenon is far more common in retailing than it is in manufacturing or service businesses. In part, this is because a retailer must stay smart, day-after-day. Your competitor is always copying and then topping whatever you do. Shoppers are meanwhile beckoned in every conceivable way to try a stream of new merchants. In retailing, to coast is to fail. In contrast to this, have-to-be-smart-every-day business, there is what I call the have-to-be-smart-*once* business. For example, if you were smart enough to buy a network TV station very early in the game.[41]

Despite Buffett's caution Berkshire controls, in addition to Candy shops, shoe outlets, jewellery stores and his much loved Nebraska Furniture Mart (NFM). So, what is it that attracted Buffett to NFM? In 1983 the NFM generated $100 million of sales annually from one 200,000 square foot store in Omaha. It had no other business. The owner/managers focused all their energies in giving terrific value to its customers and growing the business on the one site. Buffett says that one of the key questions he asks himself when evaluating a business is whether he would like, assuming he had ample capital and skilled personnel, to compete with it. 'I'd rather wrestle grizzlies than compete with Mrs B [Blumkin] and her progeny.'[42] The Blumkins are the family that built the business and sold 90 per cent to Buffett in 1983 for $55 million. He regards the business as one of the most extraordinary in the country. 'They buy brilliantly, they operate at expense ratios competitors don't even dream about, and they then pass on to their customers much of the savings. It's the ideal business – one built upon exceptional value to the customer that in turn translates into exceptional economics for its owners.'[43] The reputation of the firm for giving value is so strong that customers travel hundreds of miles to buy from it. NFM deliberately operates on a gross margin of around half that of the industry generally. It is run with amazing efficiency and astute volume purchasing. All this adds up to high returns on invested capital.

Buffett puts a lot of weight on his judgement of people. He will only maintain a long-term relationship with those having the highest integrity. Once he has concluded he is dealing with someone he can trust he is prepared to put a lot of his money on the line, relying on the probity of these individuals. In the case of Mrs B and her family he never asked for an audit of NFM – indeed the firm had never had one. He did not take an inventory nor verify the receivables. He did not even check property titles. 'We gave Mrs B a cheque for $55 million and she gave us her word. That made for an even exchange.'[44] You see, Buffett is not buying a business in the sense of physical assets, brand name etc. He is buying a going concern run by people who are both honest and competent. If he can't trust them at the outset, how can he trust them in the stewardship of his money later on? The success of businesses is determined by the people running them. If you are not happy with some aspect of their character you should not be dealing with them at all. If you are happy then you have to trust them completely.

In the case of Mrs B and family, Buffett had been an admirer for years. He was aware of their high reputation and Mrs B's strategy and morality. Her motto is: 'Sell cheap and tell the truth'.

The story of Mrs B is legendary in the Omaha area – an American dream come true. Around the end of World War I, aged 23, she talked her way past a border guard to leave Russia for America. She did not speak English and had no formal education (her daughter gradually taught her, after school). She sold used clothing until she had saved $500 with which she opened a furniture store in 1937. Over the next half century she gradually built up the business that was sold to Berkshire. At the age of 90 in 1983, she refused to retire and risk as she put it, 'losing her marbles'. She remained Chairman after Berkshire took control and was on the sales floor seven days a week. She continued despite the fact that Louie Blumkin, Mrs B's son, the President of NFM and his three sons were more than up to the task of running the company. Buffett says, 'Geneticists should do handsprings over the Blumkin family'.[45] As well as being really nice people:

> they all (1) apply themselves with an enthusiasm and energy that would make Ben Franklin and Haratio Alger look like dropouts; (2) define with extraordinary realism their area of special competence and act decisively on all matters with it; (3) ignore even the most enticing propositions falling outside of that area of special competence; and, (4) unfailingly behave in a high-grade manner with everyone they deal with.[46]

> The success of businesses is determined by the people running them.

You can't get a better recipe for both managers and investors. Mrs B continued to 'outsell and out-hustle'[47] at NFM until she was 96 when she quit. However she was *still* too young to retire. She started a new business selling carpets and furniture and continued to work seven days a week. When she was 99 she agreed to sell the building and land of the new business to NFM, but insisted that she continue to run the carpet operation in her own way. Buffett, in return, half-tongue-in-cheek, made her sign a non-compete agreement having regretted not doing so when she was 89. As a centenarian she still put in seven days a week. Buffett keeps reminding his investors, now that he is over 70, that he has no intention of retiring, and great managers only just get into their stride after the normal retirement age.

CHARLES MUNGER – FROM STORE ASSISTANT TO BILLIONAIRE

Munger grew up in Omaha and worked, as a teenager, in Buffett's grandfather's grocery store. However, the two men were not to meet until much later in life (Munger is seven years older). 'The Buffett family store provided a very desirable introduction to business', Munger said, 'It required hard, accurate work over long hours, which caused many of the young workers, including me (and later Ernest's grandson Warren) to look for an easier career and to be cheerful upon finding disadvantages therein'.[48]

Following his graduation from Harvard Law School, Munger set up a law firm in Los Angeles. He and Buffett met in 1959. The conversation turned to investing and Buffett tried to persuade him that investing would be more lucrative than the law. 'I told him that law was fine as a hobby but he could do better.'[49] Buffett's arguments must have carried some weight because in 1962 Munger established an investment management firm. His portfolio was concentrated in very few securities and consequently his performance was more volatile than most funds. He looked for stocks where price was at a significant discount to value. Over the next 14 years, despite the 1973–4 bear market, he produced an average annual return of 19.8 per cent, over three times that on the market as a whole.

Throughout the 1960s and 1970s the two men would often discuss investments, and occasionally buy stock in the same firms. It was not until the late 1970s, when Munger merged some of his interests into Berkshire, that he became a shareholder.

Munger is frugal, but not a miser: he travels economy class but gives to the British anti-hunger charity Oxfam. He can be witty (in the driest form) but also blunt to the point of rudeness. He once said, 'In my whole life nobody has ever accused me of being humble. Although humility is a trait I admire, I don't think I quite got my full share'.[50] At the 1998 annual meeting of Berkshire shareholders a questioner who asked about the worth of a subsidiary company was told to work it out for himself. Buffett joked, 'Oh, Mr Nice Guy'.[51] He reserves particular opprobrium for academics who propound modern portfolio theory: 'a type of dementia I can't even classify'.[52] He does not have much more respect for the ability of investment bank analysts, as the following story, related by Buffett, in Berkshire's 1999 report shows:

In 1985, a major investment banking house undertook to sell Scott Fetzer, offering it widely – but with no success. Upon reading of this strikeout, I wrote Ralph Schey, then and now Scott Fetzer's CEO, expressing an interest in buying the business. I had never met Ralph, but within a week we had a deal. Unfortunately, Scott Fetzer's letter of engagement with the banking firm provided it a $2.5 million fee upon sale, even if it had nothing to do with finding the buyer. I guess the lead banker felt he should do something for his payment, so he graciously offered us a copy of the book of Scott Fetzer that his firm had prepared. With his customary tact, Charlie responded: 'I'll pay $2.5 million *not* to read it'.

Munger greatly respects Buffett's intellect but sees the need to restrain his enthusiasm occasionally. Buffett refers to him as 'the abominable no man'[53] and jokes about his unwillingness to give expansive answers in public meetings: 'Charlie is not paid by the word'.[54]

THE EVOLUTION OF AN INVESTMENT PHILOSOPHY

Benjamin Graham believed that the intrinsic value of a business is determined by its long-term future earning power. Given this, it seems paradoxical at first glance that he focused his attention on those firms that had high net asset values relative to stock price. He reasoned that a firm with high levels of net assets would eventually produce high earnings and the stock price would rise to reflect this. Earnings would rise, or recover from a loss position, for any one of a number of reasons: perhaps the exit of firms from the industry would correct a supply and demand imbalance, lifting prices and restoring profitability to those companies that remain; perhaps the management team would wake up, or be replaced, so that corrective action is taken by the firm to restore profitability; perhaps the firm would be sold or liquidated to release the value.

While Graham took account of some other factors to establish earning power and, therefore, intrinsic value, the primary emphasis was on net asset value. He was aware that qualitative factors were of great importance in determining earnings, but he found it difficult to trust an analysis which is fundamentally subjective and judgement based. It is not possible to obtain hard-and-fast data on elements such as the 'quality of management' or 'prospects for the business'. His search for margin of safety led him back to data that was objective, being based largely on the balance sheet. He knew this was only a proxy for what he really needed to know (future earnings) but at least it was an objectively based measure. His experience of the Crash meant that he just could not put too much weight on what might be mere conjecture influenced by enthusiasm or exuberance. And yet, knowing that the qualitative elements are important he had to include them in his analysis. With the exception of his defensive value investing approach, he did consider prospects for the business and the quality of management. However, to control the urge to substitute feel and guesswork for the objective and verifiable he insisted that companies possessed inherent stability. That is, the industry and the firm have a resistance to change and so the results displayed in the past can be taken to be a more reliable guide to future earnings. In short, Graham's cautious approach insisted that companies pass two tests, the first quantitative and the second qualitative. And, in both areas greatest weight is to be placed on objective data and stability.

Buffett gradually moved away from Graham's restrictions on what type of information was acceptable to inform the evaluation of intrinsic value and margin of safety. He concurred with Graham's view that an analysis of businesses is required (rather than treating stocks as gambling counters), but Buffett's analysis placed increasing emphasis on the subjective assessment of the future earnings and very little on the asset position. Indeed, Buffett often preferred companies with few assets as this meant fewer capital investment requirements as it expanded.

Early in his career Buffett did make a number of Grahamite investments in such businesses as Sperry and Hutchinson, Dempster Mill Manufacturing and Hochschild–Kohn, but he became increasingly disillusioned when they performed poorly. This was usually because the economics of the industry or the firms continued to be atrocious. The corrective mechanisms that Graham relied on to release the value locked up in a firm did not appear to operate sufficiently consistently to produce attractive returns.

For Graham's bargain stocks to perform well the price must rise from below its intrinsic value to reach or exceed this value. In too many cases this simply did not happen, as the industry competitive environment continued to deteriorate. In other cases the price would rise, but at a rate that was too slow to give a good compound return. For example, suppose that Buffett buys a textile company stock at $20 with a calculated (Grahamite) intrinsic value of $27 per share. The margin of safety is reasonably comfortable as the stock is 26 per cent undervalued. If the stock rises to $27 in one year the investor achieves a more than satisfactory rate of return.

The problem is that many of these investments fail to rise to their intrinsic value in the first, or even the second or third year. So, if it takes three years for the stock to reach intrinsic value, the annual rate of return falls to 10.5 per cent. After four years the rate falls to less than 7.8 per cent. If the stock continues to languish at $20 the return, of course, is zero. This is the realization-of-value problem. If value is not quickly reflected in the stock price the investor ends up with a return that is less than that available on a savings account. Buffett concluded that it is only when the stock market is going through an exceptional phase that Grahamite quantitative bargains become so undervalued that this approach should be followed.

Buffett observed that most of the 'bargain' stocks in ordinary stock market conditions were for mediocre companies in declining industries. While the history of these firms may have been stable, such enterprises really didn't have predictable future earnings. The merciless economics of the industry meant that, while they may have periods of relative success, the long-term trend was downward.

In addition, if you did hold successful Grahamite stocks your return is likely to suffer from tax payments resulting from capital gains on selling as they approached intrinsic value thus eroding profits. The most important drawback of Graham's philosophy was that all stocks bought must comply with quantitative rules. These were so tightly drawn that the majority of quoted stocks were excluded. Few, if any of the companies shown in Table 6.3, some of Buffett's most successful investees, would pass muster under Graham's restrictions. Companies like Coca-Cola, the *Washington Post* and Gillette do not have sufficient assets to qualify. 'I was taught to favour tangible assets and to shun businesses whose values depended largely upon economic Goodwill. This bias caused me to make many important business mistakes of omission.'[55]

Buffett says that his thinking has changed 'drastically'[56] but that it was not a quick or easy process:

> Keynes identified my problem: 'The difficulty lies not in the new ideas but in escaping from the old ones'. My escape was long delayed, in part because most of what I had been taught by the same teacher had been (and continues to be) so extraordinarily valuable. Ultimately, business experience, direct and vicararious, produced my present strong preference for businesses that possess

large amounts of enduring Goodwill and that utilize a minimum of tangible assets.[57]

Charles Munger assisted Buffett's evolution. He, in turn, was influenced by Fisher. The three of them advocate investing only in those businesses possessing superior economics with growing earning power, which can be purchased with a large margin of safety.

> Our goal is to find an outstanding business at a sensible price, not a mediocre business at a bargain price. Charlie and I have found that making silk purses out of silk is the best that we can do: with sow's ears, we fail. (It must be noted that your Chairman, always a quick study, required only 20 years to recognize how important it was to buy good businesses. In the interim, I searched for 'bargains' – and had the misfortune to find some. My punishment was an education in the economics of short-line farm implement manufacturers, third-place department stores, and New England textile manufacturers).[58]

INVESTMENT PRINCIPLES

Business analysis

To be a successful investor you have to be a good evaluator of businesses. There are too many so-called investors who occupy their time analyzing the stock market, and where the next fad, fashion or phase will take it; or how the momentum numbers, lines on a chart or economic forecasts divine the future:

> We have 'professional' investors, those who manage many billions, to thank for most of this turmoil [the 1987 ups and downs]. Instead of focusing on what businesses will do in the years ahead, many prestigious money managers now focus on what they expect other money managers to do in the days ahead. For them, stocks are merely tokens in a game, like the thimble and flatiron was in Monopoly.[59]

Munger and Buffett try to understand the companies they buy stocks in as living businesses. They need to know the operating realities of day-to-day management. They analyze the underlying economics of the industry and the firms to ensure that they are satisfactory. '[John Maynard] Keynes essentially said, don't try and figure out what the market is doing. Figure out a business you understand, and concentrate.'[60] Buffett says that the

> ...... To be a successful investor you have to be a good evaluator of businesses. ....

most important nine words ever written about investment were in Benjamin Graham's *The Intelligent Investor*: 'Investing is most intelligent when it is most businesslike'.[61]

Munger and Buffett approach an investment as though they were buying all of the company, even if they purchase a mere fraction of the stock. This is in order to get into the mind set of a business analyst, rather than a market analyst, or security analysts:

> If I were looking at an insurance company or a paper company, I would put myself in the frame of mind that I had just inherited that company, and it was the only asset my family was ever going to own. What would I do with it? What am I thinking about? What am I worried about? Who are my competitors? Who are my customers? Go out and talk to them. Find out the strengths and weaknesses of this particular company versus other ones. If you've done that, you may understand the business better than the management.[62]

To be a successful investor you need to employ a few simple and proven principles. Exceptionally high IQ is not required, but discipline and a capacity for hard work is. A lot of reading needs to be done: not just the annual reports of the company you are interested in, but the annual reports of its competitors. These reports are the most important source of material, but they need to be complemented with industry reports and personal original research. For example, when Buffett first discovered GEICO he would spend a lot of time in the library collecting data such as insurance industry statistics; he would read a lot of books on the subject and made the effort to talk to insurance industry experts as well as insurance company managers. When he was considering American Express he would sit behind the cash register of his favourite steakhouse, counting the number of customers using their Amex Cards. When Disney was in his sights he sat in a cinema surrounded by kids watching Mary Poppins. 'All there is to investing is picking good stocks at good times and staying with them as long as they remain good companies.'[63]

Type of business

The crucial question is: what is a good company? Well, imagine that you could only buy stocks in private companies in your county or state. What are the characteristics you would look for? First, you would, I hope, try to assess the long-term economic characteristics of each business; the second issue would be the competence and honesty of the people you would be trusting to manage the business; and third, you would be prepared to pay a sensible, but not a generous, price. What you would not do is try to have a share of every business in the locality. You would limit yourself to those that you understand and which rank highest on the above criteria. It would be a mistake to believe that risk can be reduced by spreading your fund widely between enterprises about which you know little and have no reason for special confidence.

Buffett and Munger look for the following key criteria:

- *Favourable long-term prospects*   The company must have a very hard-to-duplicate business advantage that has resulted in, and will continue to produce, consistent earnings power. The competitive advantage must be 'mouth-watering' and enduring. There must be an economic franchise castle surrounded by a very deep moat.

- *Operated by honest and competent people*   The management have to be both able and shareholder orientated. They should be of the highest integrity and you should be able to like, trust and admire them. Their extraordinary skills in operations should be matched by their skill in capital allocation.

- *A business you understand*   'Investors should remember that their scorecard is not computed using Olympic-diving methods: degree-of-difficulty doesn't count. If you are right about a business whose value is largely dependent on a single key factor that is both easy to understand and enduring, the pay-off is the same as if you had correctly analyzed an investment alternative characterized by many constantly shifting and complex variables.'[64]

- *Available at a very attractive price*   It is frequently possible to identify companies which fulfill the first three criteria. But such wonderful businesses usually sell for high prices. The price must be 'sensible' in terms of its relationship to calculated intrinsic value, leaving a large margin of safety. Fortunately, from time to time excellent companies find themselves in unusual circumstances and the stock is misappraised by the market.

For the investor to benefit from this style of analysis there has to be an enormous concentration of effort. Don't bother with any business which does not have excellent economics or management. Focus only on the minority that are clearly superior.

> Charlie and I are simply not smart enough … to get great results by adroitly buying and selling portions of far-from-great businesses. Nor do we think

many others can achieve long-term investment success by flitting from flower to flower. Indeed, we believe that according the name 'investors' to institutions that trade actively is like calling someone who repeatedly engages in one-night stands a romantic.[65]

The objective of all the hard work in analyzing business franchises and management quality is to estimate the intrinsic value. This is then compared with the current price to establish if there is an adequate margin of safety – see Fig. 6.1.

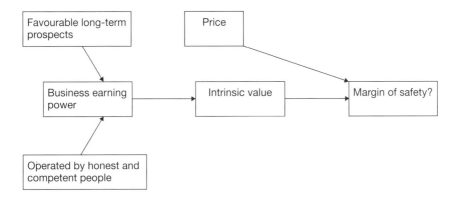

Figure 6.1 Buffett's and Munger's business perspective investing

The Inevitables

The best type of company to own is what Buffett has called an Inevitable. These are companies that will be dominating their fields for an investment lifetime. They have such enormous competitive strengths that they will be great companies 25 or 30 years from now. Inevitables are involved in businesses and industries not likely to experience major change. A fast changing industry precludes the possibility of reaching a conclusion as to the probability of a company dominating its sector three decades hence.

Imagine that you were going on a ten-year mission to Mars and while you are gone you are unable to alter your portfolio. If you could make only one investment now what would you look for? Answer: certainty. It would have to be in an industry which is on a steady growth path, and the leader was going to continue being the leader. For over a century there has been a company that has increased its business decade on decade and which, in the last 50 years has dominated its industry – Coca-Cola.

Coca-Cola started in the 1880s and went public in 1919 with a share price of $40. The following year it fell to $19. In 1938 *Fortune* carried a story on Coke which suggested that, while it was a good company, it was too late to buy the stock, as market saturation and competition now reduced the future potential. In fact, over the next five decades Coca-Cola increased its physical volume of drinks sold by over 50-fold, and the stock price rose over 600 fold. The holder of one 1919 share would today be a millionaire, many times over. The strategic and operational strengths of Coke persist to this day: 'the fundamentals of the business – the qualities that underlie Coke's competitive dominance and stunning economics – have remained constant through the years'.[66]

For companies like Coca-Cola and Gillette forecasters will differ slightly in their estimate of future demand for their products, but few would suggest they will not be around, and that their dominance will not persist. This is not to say that the management team of Inevitables can relax and become complacent. They must continue to innovate and to operate all aspects of the business to the utmost efficiency. This should not be a problem if the analysis has revealed an honest and competent team.

Market leadership does not equate to Inevitable. General Motors, Kodak and Sears enjoyed periods when they seemed invincible. 'For every Inevitable, there are dozens of Imposters, companies now riding high but vulnerable to competitive attacks.'[67]

Don't expect to come up with a long list of Inevitables. Buffett thinks that he and Munger will never be able to create a list as long as 20. The analytical tools presented in Chapters 9 and 10 may help eliminate from further consideration those companies vulnerable to competition.

When you have found an Inevitable it may still be unwise to buy stock. It is possible to overpay for even the best of businesses. A further problem is that the management may get sidetracked and end up neglecting the wonderful core business on which its success is founded. This is what happened to both Coke and Gillette before wiser management took them back to the straight and narrow:

> Would you believe that a few decades back they were growing shrimp at Coke and exploring for oil at Gillette? Loss of focus is what most worries Charlie and I when we contemplate investing in businesses that, in general, look outstanding. All too often, we've seen value stagnate in the presence of hubris or of boredom that caused the attention of managers to wander. That's not going to happen again at Coke and Gillette, however, not given their current and prospective managements.[68]

The punch card and the perfect pitch

An investor needs to be very sure that a stock is truly an outstanding one before committing money to it. Truly outstanding stocks at low prices are rare. The investor should not expect to be active on the stock market – one or two good ideas each year are more than enough. Buffett slightly exaggerates to make the point: 'Lethargy bordering on sloth remains the cornerstone of our investment style'.[69] He says that at the beginning of an investment career the investor should be given a card with 20 punches on it. This card is to last a lifetime. Every time an investment decision is made the card is punched and there is one less available for the rest of the investor's life. If the punches are saved for great ideas then the card will never be used up. 'Charlie and I decided long ago that in an investment lifetime it's just too hard to make hundreds of smart decisions…. We adopted a strategy that required our being smart – and not too smart at that – only a very few times. Indeed, we'll now settle for one good idea a year (Charlie says it's my turn).'[70] Buffett says that he made a study (when he ran the investment partnerships) of the success of the small investments compared with the larger ones. The larger investments always did better:

> There is a threshold of examination and criticism and knowledge that has to be overcome or reached in making a big decision that you can get sloppy about on small decisions. Somebody says 'I bought a hundred shares of this or that because I heard about it at a party the other night'. Well there is a tendency with small decisions to think you can do it for not very good reasons.[71]

An investor has to be more than lukewarm about a stock: he or she needs to be thoroughly convinced of its attractiveness.

The private investor has an enormous advantage over the typical professional fund manager because he or she can wait until the ideal stock comes along. It is not necessary to be investing in the market every month, or even every year. Using a baseball metaphor (as Buffett often does), the private investor (or the independent professional investor) can stand at the plate and wait a long time for the perfect pitch. Furthermore, you cannot be called out if you resist three pitches:

> we try to exert a Ted Williams kind of discipline. In his book *The Science of Hitting*, Ted explains that he carved the strike zone into 77 cells, each the size of a baseball. Swinging only at balls in his 'best' cell, he knew, would allow him to bat .400; reaching for balls in his 'worst' spot, the low outside corner of the

strike zone, would reduce him to .230. In other words, waiting for the fat pitch would mean a trip to the Hall of Fame, swinging indiscriminately would mean a ticket to the minors.[72]

Circle of competence

The investor must thoroughly understand the companies in which money is placed. It is impossible for a single investor to be knowledgeable about dozens of industries and companies. It is vital that the investor recognizes this fact and draw a circle of competence around those businesses which are understood. Those within that circle which fail to meet the investment criteria shown in Fig. 6.1 should be eliminated from further consideration. On no account should the investor contemplate investing in firms which are beyond the circle of competence:

> The most important thing in terms of your circle of competence is not how large the area is, but how well you've defined the perimeter. If you know where the edges are, you're better off than somebody that's got one that's five times as large but they get very fuzzy about the edges.[73]

By recognizing the limits of your competence you can try to tackle issues for which you have some expertise and comparative advantage. You can concentrate on the one-foot hurdles that can be stepped over rather than the seven-footers. Charles Munger puts it this way:

> try more to profit from always remembering the obvious than from grasping the esoteric. It is remarkable how much long-term advantage people like us have gotten by trying to be consistently not stupid, instead of trying to be very intelligent. There must be some wisdom in the folk saying: 'It's the strong swimmers who drown'.[74]

The Munger and Buffett principles could easily be applied to technology stocks. The reason that they choose not to be in this area is because they don't know how to do it. They have no insights into which technology companies possess truly durable competitive advantages. By avoiding not just tech companies, but most of the industrial commercial sectors they naturally miss some great opportunities, such as Intel or Microsoft. This may be regrettable, but unavoidable. They simply would not feel comfortable analyzing these companies. Investment must be rational and it cannot possibly be rational if the investor can't understand the company and its industry. Besides, there are wonderful opportunities in those areas where Munger and Buffett do have competence. 'Anybody who tells you they can value, you know, all the stocks in Value Line, and on the board, must have a very inflated idea of their own ability because it's not that easy. But if you spend your time focusing on some industries, you'll learn a lot about valuation.'[75]

If the investor does focus on a few industries he or she should develop the independence of mind and confidence that is necessary for out-performance. Intelligence is not the same as intellectual independence. Many high IQ people mindlessly imitate. Temperament and concentration are the key elements. These will enable you to think independently and avoid going along with the crowd. By really knowing the industry and the firm you can believe your own observations and conclusions, rather than someone else's. Familiarity does not breed contempt; it breeds confidence, insight and profits.

Intrinsic value and margin of safety

Intrinsic value is the discounted value of the cash that can be taken out of a business during its remaining life. The value of any financial asset, whether it be common stock, bond or some hybrid instrument is deter-mined by the cash inflows and outflows. All net inflows stretching to an infinite time horizon that are available to the financial asset holder when discounted at an appropriate rate contribute to the asset's value. With a bond the estimation of future cash flowing to the holder is relatively easy as bonds generally have regular coupons and a date at which the bond will be redeemed. Naturally complications can arise, for example there may be growing doubts about the capacity of the borrower to continue with coupon payments, in which case a reassessment of value is called for. Despite these complications, bond valuation remains relatively straight-forward.

With equities defined future 'coupons' are not given. The cash flows to the common stockholder have to be estimated by the analyst. These amounts will be determined by such factors as the quality of management and the soundness of the firm's strategic position. These qualitative factors, vital though they are to valuation, are extremely difficult to state with precision.

The analyst must conduct discounted-flows-of-cash calculations and select those stocks that show the greatest gap between current price and estimated value. This rule holds true whether the business is growing or static; whether its earnings and dividends are subject to dramatic fluctuations or are stable; whether the company currently has a low or a high historic price earnings ratio, dividend yield or market to book ratio.

Intrinsic value can never be precisely calculated, it will always be an estimate. We are dealing with future events about which it is impossible to be certain. The analysis requires a number of judgement calls. Two people examining the same company will almost inevitably arrive at different intrinsic value figures:

> Anyone calculating intrinsic value necessarily comes up with a highly subjective figure that will change both as estimates of future cashflows are revised and as interest rates move. Despite its fuzziness, however, intrinsic value is all-important and is the only logical way to evaluate the relative attractiveness of investments and businesses.[76]

Because of the subjective nature of the inputs to the intrinsic value estimate and the potential for ill-disciplined and unreasonable conjecture Munger and Buffett abide by two further rules. The first is to stick with those businesses that they understand. 'If a business is complex or subject to constant change, we're not smart enough to predict future cashflows.'[77] The second is that they insist on a margin of safety in the purchase price. 'If we calculate the value of a common stock to be only slightly higher than its price, we're not interested in buying.'[78] There should be such a large margin of safety that calculations to three decimal places are simply not needed.

There is a strong divergence of views between most financial economists on the one hand and Buffett and Munger on the other, on a range of crucial financial questions, e.g. is the stock market efficient at pricing shares? Yet, on the issue of share valuation there is a high degree of convergence. Both sides agree that discounted future cashflow is what gives a share its value. However, Buffett is determined to think for himself and not to follow textbook practice automatically. The academics would like to see finely detailed mathematical calculations, preferably running to several pages, before they would judge the result to have plausibility. They would also expect the discount rate used to be carefully crafted to take account of systematic risk, as measured by beta (in other words, a higher discount rate is used for more risky company stocks, with risk being defined by the capital asset pricing model).

Complex and lengthy cashflow estimates and detailed mathematical analysis on paper is not Buffett's and Munger's style. Munger said at the 1996 meeting of Berkshire shareholders, 'we have such a fingers and toes style about Berkshire Hathaway. Warren always talks about those discounted cashflows – I've never seen him do one', and Buffett replied, 'There are some things you only do in private'.[79] Buffett has always been interested in mathematics and the explanation could lie in the possibility that he could just click the calculations off in his head. A more likely explanation is that it is not necessary to be all that precise – a ball park figure is all that is required. To go into a morass of detailed mathematics can have you stuck in the detail and unable to see the bigger picture. 'If [the value of a company] does not scream out at you, it's too close.'[80]

It would appear that Buffett uses the current risk free rate of return (US government long-term bond rate) without any upward adjustment to allow for the additional risk in buying common stocks rather than lending to the US government. He has justified this by pointing out that he has reduced the risk of investing in the common stocks of particular companies because he thoroughly understands those companies – and so, by implication there is no need for a risk premium: 'I put a heavy weight on certainty … If you do that, the whole idea of a risk factor doesn't make any sense to me. Risk comes from not knowing what you are doing'.[81]

The 'cashflow' that Buffett discounts is the owner earnings. These are defined as:

(a) reported earnings; plus,
(b) depreciation, depletion, amortization and certain other non-cash charges; less,
(c) the amount of capitalized expenditures for plant and machinery, etc. that a business requires to fully maintain its long-term competitive position and its unit volume; less,
(d) any extra amount for working capital that is needed to maintain the firm's long-term competitive position and unit volume.[82]

The last two elements are guesses and therefore the owner earnings figure is bound to be imprecise. Buffett says that he agrees with Keynes: 'I would rather be vaguely right than precisely wrong'.[83]

Many businesses produce poor owner earnings because they are obliged to spend more than (b) over the long run just to maintain unit volume and competitive position. That is, (c) + (d) is greater than (b).

Buffett's owner earnings numbers are significantly different from many published 'cashflow' figures. Typically these include (a) and (b), but fail to subtract (c) and (d). 'These imply that the business being offered is the commercial counterpart of the Pyramids – forever state-of-the-art, never needing to be replaced, improved or refurbished.'[84] Such 'cashflow' numbers are meaningless for most manufacturing and service companies because (c) and (d) are always significant – if they don't invest the business decays.

The case of Scott Fetzer illustrates the use of owner earnings in the calculation of intrinsic value. Scott Fetzer was acquired in 1986. It was a collection of 22 businesses, including World Books and Kirby. Berkshire paid $315.2 million for the company, which had $172.6 million of book value.

Table 6.5   Scott Fetzer's owner earnings, 1986

		$000s
(a)	1986 GAAP earnings, plus:	40,231
(b)	depreciation, depletion, amortization and other non-cash charges	
		8,301
		48,532
	less:	
(c) and (d)	expenditures on plant, equipment, working capital etc. needed	
	to maintain long-term competitive position and unit volume[85]	8,301
		40,231

In the case of Scott Fetzer, Buffett and Munger judged that items under (b) are equal to those for (c) and (d) combined. This is the case for most of the companies owned by Berkshire. However, it does not always apply. For See's in the late 1980s Buffett estimated that annual expenditure on (c) and (d) exceeded depreciation etc. by between $500,000 and $1 million. This was so that the company could hold its competitive position.

We are unable to obtain Buffett's projections of owner earnings at the time that he and Munger made the decision to buy Scott Fetzer, but we do have the actual earnings for the following nine years (they were published in the 1994 Berkshire report). These may not be the same as Buffett projected, but they give us some idea of the figures that could have been fed into a discounted cashflow calculation – whether roughly done in Buffett's head or on a piece of paper. When examining Table 6.6 it should be borne in mind that the value of owner earnings after 1994 should be included. Of course, these will be heavily discounted and so won't add a great deal to the total, but they might be important and need to be considered. If it is safe to assume that the reported earnings are the same as the owner earnings for Scott Fetzer because (b) is equal to (c) + (d) then we may discount the figures shown in column 2 (plus an estimate of earnings after 1994) to calculate the value of the company. It is plain that Scott Fetzer was a bargain purchase whether the earnings figures are discounted at 10 per cent, 15 per cent or even 20 per cent. Furthermore, Scott Fetzer had excess cash when it was purchased. It was able to pay Berkshire a dividend of $125 million in 1986 even though it earned only $40.3 million, so you could say that the net investment made by Berkshire was much less than the $315.2 million handed over. At the same time as producing this growing pattern of earnings and dividends, Scott Fetzer reduced capital employed and went from a position of very modest debt to one of virtually no debt at all. Nor did the company enter into any artificial cash boosting exercises such as sale and leaseback, or selling receivables. It has been operated as a conservatively financed and liquid enterprise. By 1994, return on capital employed had reached such extraordinary heights that had it been in the Fortune 500 list in 1993 it would have had the highest return on equity (except for three companies emerging from bankruptcy).

Table 6.6   Scott Fetzer's performance figures (1986–94)[86]

Year	(1) Beginning book value	(2) Earnings ($ million)	(3) Dividends ($ millions)	(4) Ending book value (1) + (2) – (3)
1986	172.6	40.3	125.0	87.9
1987	87.9	48.6	41.0	95.5
1988	95.5	58.0	35.0	118.5
1989	118.5	58.5	71.5	105.5
1990	105.5	61.3	33.5	133.3
1991	133.3	61.4	74.0	120.7
1992	120.7	70.5	80.0	111.2
1993	111.2	77.5	98.0	90.7
1994	90.7	79.3	76.0	94.0

The magnetic attraction of companies with low requirements for additional capital expenditure and which produce high owner earnings have brought Buffett and Munger some rich rewards. For example, the three businesses Nebraska Furniture Mart, See's Candy Shops and Buffalo Evening News earned an aggregate of $72 million pre-tax in 1985. This compares with $8 million pre-tax in 1970. This $64 million improvement was achieved despite the fact that the businesses used only about $40 million more invested capital in 1985 than 1970. 'The financial characteristics of these businesses have allowed us to use a very large portion of the earnings they generate elsewhere.'[87] American companies generally need about $5 of additional capital to increase annual pre-tax earnings by $1. On this basis these Berkshire subsidiaries would have required $320 million in additional capital from the owners, rather than a mere $40 million. 'Leaving the question of price aside, the best business to own is one that over an extended period can employ large amounts of incremental capital at very high rates of return. The worse business to own is one that must, or *will*, do the opposite – that is, consistently employ ever-greater amounts of capital at very low rates of return. Unfortunately, the first type of business is very hard to find: most high-returns businesses need relatively little capital. Shareholders of such a business usually will benefit if it pays out most of its earnings in dividends or makes significant stocks repurchases.'[88]

Notes

1   Train, J. (1987), *The Midas Touch* – New York: Harper & Row, p. 70.
2   Loomis, Carol J. 'The Inside Story of Warren Buffett' *Fortune*, 11 April 1988, p. 26.
3   Berkshire Hathaway's Annual Meeting, Omaha, 27 April 1992. Quoted in Lowe (1997). © 1997 Janet C. Lowe. This material is used by permission of John Wiley & Sons Inc.
4   Lewis, W. (1988).
5   Lenzner, Robert (1993) 'Warren Buffett's Idea of Heaven: I Don't Have to Work With People I Don't Like' Forbes 400, 18 October, 1993.
6   Lenzner, Robert and Fondiller, David S. (1996) 'Meet Charlie Munger' Forbes, 22 January 1996, p. 78.
7   Fromson, Brett Duval (1990) 'And Now, A Look at the Old One' *Fortune* (1990) Investor's Guide, p. 98.
8   Lenzner, Robert, and Fondiller, David S. 'The Not-So-Silent Partner' *Forbes*, 22 January 1996, p. 78.
9   Taken from Berkshire Hathaway's Annual Report, 2000 (www.berkshirehathaway.com). This material is copyrighted and is reproduced with the permission of the author.

10   Urry, M. (1996) *Financial Times*, 11/12 May, p. 1 of Weekend Money.

11   Lowe (1999), p. 66.

12   Ineck, Tom (1991) 'A Little "Dance" Music Lifts Son of Omaha Billionaire'. The Lincoln Journal and Star, 8 August, p. 11. Reproduced in Lowe (1997).

13   McMorris, Robert (1987) 'Leila Buffett Basks in Value of Son's Life, Not Fortune'. Omaha World – Herald, 16 May, p. 17. Reproduced in Lowe (1997).

14   Buffett quoted in Roger Lowenstein (1995) *Buffett: The Making of an American Capitalist*, New York: Random House, p. 111.

15   Munger quoted in Urry, M. (1996) *Financial Times Weekend*, 11/12 May.

16   Quoted in Smith, Adam (1972) *Super Money*, New York: Random House, p. 181.

17   Warren Buffett Correspondence to Benjamin Graham, 17 July 1970. Reproduced in Lowe (1997), p. 88.

18   Buffett, W. (1995). This material is copyrighted and is reproduced with the permission of the author.

19   *Ibid*.

20   *Ibid*.

21   Quoted in Davis, L. J. (1990), 'Buffett Takes Stock'. The *New York Times Magazine*, April, p. 16. Reproduced in Lowe (1997).

22   Buffett, W. (1995). This material is copyrighted and is reproduced with the permission of the author.

23   Lowenstein, R. (1996).

24   Letter to Partners, 9 October 1967. This material is copyrighted and is reproduced with the permission of the author.

25   Lowestein, R. (1996).

26   Hagstrom (1995), p. 4.

27   Linda Grant (1991), 'The $4 Billion Regular Guy' the *Los Angeles Times Magazine*, 7 April, p. 34.

28   Buffett, W. (1998). This material is copyrighted and is reproduced with the permission of the author.

29   Buffett, W. (1996). This material is copyrighted and is reproduced with the permission of the author.

30   Figures taken from: Buffett, W. (1996, 1997, 1998, 1999, 2000). This material is copyrighted and is reproduced with the permission of the author.

31   Quoted in the *Financial Times*, 11/12 May 1996. Weekend Money, p.1.

32   Buffett, W. (1985). This material is copyrighted and is reproduced with the permission of the author.

33   Buffett, W. (2000). This material is copyrighted and is reproduced with the permission of the author.

34   Quoted in Dickson, M. (1995) *Financial Times*, 28 August.

35   Buffett, W. (1980). This material is copyrighted and is reproduced with the permission of the author.

36   Buffett, W. (1994). This material is copyrighted and is reproduced with the permission of the author.

37 Buffett, W. (1999). This material is copyrighted and is reproduced with the permission of the author.

38 Buffett, W. (1983). This material is copyrighted and is reproduced with the permission of the author.

39 Munger, C.T. and Koeppel, D.A. (1982), Annual Report of Blue Chip Stamps.

40 Buffett, W. (1999). This material is copyrighted and is reproduced with the permission of the author.

41 Buffett, W. (1995). This material is copyrighted and is reproduced with the permission of the author.

42 Buffett, W. (1983). This material is copyrighted and is reproduced with the permission of the author.

43 *Ibid.*

44 Buffett, W. (1984). This material is copyrighted and is reproduced with the permission of the author.

45 Buffett, W. (1983). This material is copyrighted and is reproduced with the permission of the author.

46 Buffett, W. (1984). This material is copyrighted and is reproduced with the permission of the author.

47 Buffett, W. (1986). This material is copyrighted and is reproduced with the permission of the author.

48 Quoted in Dorr, Robert (1977) 'Ex-Omahan Traded Law for Board Room'. *Omaha World-Herald*, 3 August, p. B1. Reproduced in Lowe (1997).

49 Buffett, W. (1984a). This material is copyrighted and is reproduced with the permission of the author.

50 Quoted by Loomis, Carol J. (1988) 'The Inside Story of Warren Buffett' Fortune, 11 April, p. 26.

51 Lewis, W. (1998).

52 Quoted by Lowe (1997). Spoken at Berkshire Hathaway's Annual Meeting, Omaha, 6 May 1996. © 1997 Janet C. Lowe. This material is used by permission of John Wiley & Sons Inc.

53 Spoken at the Berkshire Hathaway Annual Meeting, Omaha, 1996. Quoted by Lowe (1997). © 1997 Janet C. Lowe. This material is used by permission of John Wiley & Sons Inc.

54 *Ibid.*

55 Buffett, W. (1983). This material is copyrighted and is reproduced with the permission of the author.

56 *Ibid.*

57 *Ibid.*

58 Buffett, W. (1987). This material is copyrighted and is reproduced with the permission of the author.

59 *Ibid.*

60 Buffett, W. quoted in Lenzner, Robert,, 'Warren Buffett's Idea of Heaven: I Don't Have To Work With People I Don't Like', Forbes 400, 18 October 1993 p. 40.

61   Graham, B. (1973), p. 286.
62   Rasmussen, J. (1994)'Billionnaire talks Strategy with Students', *Omaha World Herald*, 2 January, p. 17S. Quoted in Lowe (1997).
63   'Warren Buffett Triples Profits', *New York Post*, 14 May 1994, p. D1.
64   Buffett, W. (1994). This material is copyrighted and is reproduced with the permission of the author.
65   Buffett, W. (1991). This material is copyrighted and is reproduced with the permission of the author.
66   Buffett, W. (1996). This material is copyrighted and is reproduced with the permission of the author.
67   *Ibid*. (1996).
68   *Ibid*.
69   Buffett, W. (1990). This material is copyrighted and is reproduced with the permission of the author.
70   Buffett, W. (1993). This material is copyrighted and is reproduced with the permission of the author.
71   'Warren Buffett Talks Business', The University of North Carolina, Center for Public Television, Chapel Hill, 1995. Quoted in Lowe (1997).
72   Buffett, W. (1997). This material is copyrighted and is reproduced with the permission of the author.
73   'Warren Buffett Talks Business', The University of North Carolina, Center for Public Television, Chapel Hill, 1995. Quoted in Lowe (1997).
74   Munger, C. (1989) Wesco Financial Corporation Annual Report (1989).
75   Buffett, W. (1985a) 'Investing in Equity Markets', quoted in Columbia University Business School, Transcript of a Seminar held 13 March, pp. 28–9. Quoted in Lowe (1997). This material is copyrighted and is reproduced with the permission of the author.
76   Buffett, W. (1994). This material is copyrighted and is reproduced with the permission of the author.
77   Buffett, W. (1992). This material is copyrighted and is reproduced with the permission of the author.
78   *Ibid*.
79   Quoted in Urry, M. (1996) *Financial Times*, 11/12 May, Weekend Money, p. 1.
80   Buffett at Berkshire Hathaway's Annual Meeting, Omaha (1996). Quoted in Lowe (1997). © 1997 Janet C. Lowe. This material is used by permission of John Wiley & Sons, Inc..
81   Quoted by Jim Rasmussen. 'Buffett Talks Strategy with Students. Omaha World Herald, 2 January, 1994, p. 26.
82   Buffett, W. (1986). This material is copyrighted and is reproduced with the permission of the author.
83   Buffett quoting Keynes, Buffett, W. (1986). This material is copyrighted and is reproduced with the permission of the author.
84   Buffett, W. (1986). This material is copyrighted and is reproduced with the permission of the author.

85 As estimated by Buffett in the Appendix to the 1986 Letter to Shareholders that accompanied the Berkshire Annual Report. This material is copyrighted and is reproduced with the permission of the author.

86 Taken from Buffett, W. (1994). This material is copyrighted and is reproduced with the permission of the author.

87 Buffett, W. (1985). This material is copyrighted and is reproduced with the permission of the author.

88 Buffett, W. (1992). This material is copyrighted and is reproduced with the permission of the author.

7

Warren Buffett's and Charles Munger's business perspective investing – Part 2

This chapter examines the following:

- a strong economic franchise
- indications of honest and competent management
- what to avoid in investment
- when to sell.

ECONOMIC FRANCHISE

Pricing power

Coca-Cola is the most valuable franchise in the world. It has the strongest brand the world has ever seen, and, just as important, a high degree of control over the distribution chain. Buffett and Munger look for two characteristics in business, and Coca-Cola has them in spades: first, an ability to increase prices even when product demand is flat without the danger of losing significant volume or market share; second, an ability to achieve large volume increases with only small requirements for additional investment of capital.

For the retention of pricing power the company's product/service should have no close substitute. This may be merely a perception in the mind of the consumer rather than a reality. The producers of branded products, from jean manufacturers to chocolate bars and soft drinks, rely on such perceptions. Vast quantities of dollars are spent reinforcing the message that a brand is worth a premium payment. The second element needed for long-term pricing power is a strong moat preventing other companies entering the territory of the franchise. This may be achieved in a wide variety of ways from possessing economies of scale to sending out messages that any entry will result in severe retaliation. Third, the product/service must not be subject to price regulation.

Walt Disney is a company with a very strong franchise. The name itself is one recognizable throughout the world. The rights to the film library and characters will produce profits for generations to come. Snow White will be watched by our grandchildren and great-grandchildren and Disney can collect revenue without having to spend a cent more to produce the product. Buffett says that the nice thing about Mickey Mouse is that he does not have an agent. The cost of his creation was written off long ago and Disney can use him year after year and not pay anything more.

See's Candy has terrific pricing power: 'If you own See's Candy, and you look in the mirror and say "mirror, mirror on the wall, how much do I charge for candy this fall", and it says "more", that's a good business'.[1]

Buffett points out that Hershey has the ability to charge a little more than others in its industry: 'If [you go into a store and] they say "I don't have Hershey bar; but I have this unmarked chocolate bar that the owner of the place recommends", if you'll walk across the street to buy a Hershey bar or if you'll pay a nickel more for the [Hershey] bar than the unmarked bar or something like that, that's franchise value'.[2]

Berkshire never invested in Hershey – perhaps the stock did not pass another of Buffett's and Munger's tests: the price did not give a margin or safety. However, a company that they did invest in is a favourite for illustrating pricing power.

> There are 20 to 21 billion razor blades used in the world a year: Thirty per cent of those are Gillette's, but 60 per cent by value are Gillette's. They have 90 per cent market shares in some countries – in Scandinavia and Mexico. Now, when something has been around as long as shaving and you find a company that has both that kind of innovation, in terms of developing better razors all the time, plus the distribution power, and the position in people's minds … You know, here's something you do every day – I hope you do it everyday – for $20 bucks (per year) you get a terrific shaving experience. Now men are not inclined to shift around when they get that kind of situation.[3]

Dominant newspapers also have excellent pricing power. A paper that is dominant within its community, whether that is a geographic community such as a small town, or a group of people with similar interests, will be able to sell well, even if the price is raised, not least because of its value as a bulletin board for that group of people.

Deep and dangerous moat

In 1999 Berkshire purchased Executive Jet Aviation (EJA). EJA sells and manages the fractional ownership of jet aircraft. The fractional-ownership industry is at an early stage of development and EJA is in a dominant position, it is larger than its next two competitors combined. It intends to maintain this dominance and is currently taking delivery of 8 per cent of all business jets produced worldwide: $4.2 billion of planes are on order. Buffett and Munger acknowledge that it is very expensive to establish dominance of this young industry but they say it is well worth it. The company that operates on the greatest scale will be the most attractive to customers. 'The company with the most planes in the air worldwide will be able to offer its customers the best service. "Buy a fraction, get a fleet", has real meaning at EJA.'[4] So EJA will be able to set a very high hurdle for any other firm thinking about entering this industry. An entrant would have to spend billions of dollars, and even then is not assured of success, because the incumbent, with an established presence and brand, will take retaliatory action. EJA has another important advantage: its two largest competitors are both subsidiaries of aircraft manufacturers and sell only the aircraft made by their parents. EJA can offer a much wider array of planes, cabin styles and mission capabilities. Would you prefer to compete with EJA or wrestle Grizzlies?

The defensive moat can be created by nothing more than excellent day-to-day management that current competitors and potential entrants find impossible to emulate. In furniture retailing it is very difficult to establish a barrier to entry in the conventional way. Patent rights don't apply, nor does high capital commitment cost, nor are locational advantages decisive. The industry itself does not have attractive economies, and yet, some companies within the industry do have economic franchises.

Following Berkshire's pleasant experience with the acquisition of Nebraska Furniture Mart in 1983 it has gone on to purchase other dominant firms in this sector: R C Willey in 1995, Star Furniture in 1997 and Jordan's in 1999. Jordan's is a family firm run by the Tatelman brothers, Barry and Elliot. Under their leadership it became the largest furniture retailer in New Hampshire and Massachusetts. Jordan's differentiates itself from its competitors by presenting customers with a dazzling entertainment experience, called 'shoppertainment', while they view the exceptionally wide selection of merchandise. It now has the highest sales per square foot of any major furniture operation in the US.

Another example of a deep and dangerous moat dug by the excellence of the management team is GEICO. In insurance it is easy for actual and potential competitors to copy innovations. Policies are standardized and it is not difficult to obtain a licence. Control of raw materials, patents, copyrights or location will not deliver any important advantage to insulate the firm from competition. Because of the general absence of barriers to entry and the often intense competition between those already in the insurance industry, returns are frequently very poor. However, GEICO is different. It has exceptionally low costs. The team at GEICO are continually deepening and widening the moat by driving down the cost of acquiring new policyholders and the cost of retaining the old ones through the renewal business to way below that of other auto insurers. 'Both of these major competitive advantages are sustainable. Others may copy our model, but they will be unable to replicate our economies.'[5] GEICO also benefits from its long-standing image as a company that gives good prices and service. Its best source of new business is word-of-mouth. It has built up long-term relationships with millions of families that are difficult for a competitor to disrupt.

An any fool business

There are some businesses that require excellent management all the time. The slightest slip and they will be trampled on by the competition, or by customers, or by suppliers. There are other businesses that have such strong franchises that incompetent managers could be put in charge for a while and still it would not suffer too badly – it could be run by any fool. 'It is comforting to be in a business where some mistakes can be made and yet a quite satisfactory overall performance can be achieved.'[6] The classic example of a business that could not afford one managerial error is the original Berkshire textile operation. Here even a team of very good managers produced only modest results. It is very important to be in a business 'where tailwinds prevail rather than headwinds',[7] such as is the case with Coca-Cola or the *Washington Post*.

The achievements and performance record of managers is more determined by the quality of the business boat they get into than by their skill and efforts at rowing. 'Should you find yourself in a chronically-leaking boat, energy devoted to changing vessels is likely to be more productive than energy devoted to patching leaks.'[8] One of the most atrocious industries to invest in has been airline transportation. This seems odd at first glance. Ever since Kitty Hawk, demand for air travel has grown by large percentages each year. As an investor you may say that an industry with billions of dollars in turnover and terrific growth in sales must be a sound investment. In the absence of war or a major energy crisis there seems to be no reason why airline passenger numbers and freight would not continue to take a larger and larger share of world GDP. This is true, and yet Buffett says that if a capitalist had been at Kitty Hawk he should have shot down Wilbur: 'Despite the huge amounts of equity capital that have been injected into it, the industry, in aggregate, has posted a net loss since its birth'.[9] The airline business is generally selling a service that is undifferentiated into a market with over-capacity. If new demand does appear it is more than matched by new supply, either from the existing players or by new entrants.

> Businesses in industries with both substantial over-capacity and a 'commodity' product (undifferentiated in any customer-important way by factors such as performance, appearance, service support etc.) are prime candidates for profit troubles … If … costs and prices are determined by full-bore competition, there is more than ample capacity, and the buyer cares little about whose product or distribution services he uses, industry economics are almost certain to be unexciting. They may well be disastrous. Hence the constant struggle of every vendor to establish and emphasize special qualities of product or service. This works with candy bars (customers buy by brand name, not by asking for a 'two ounce candy bar') but doesn't work with sugar. (How often do you hear, 'I'll have a cup of coffee with cream and C & H sugar, please'?) In many industries, differentiation simply can't be made meaningful. A few producers in such industries may consistently do well if they have a cost advantage that is both wide and sustainable. By definition such exceptions are few, and, in many industries, are non-existent. For the great majority of companies selling 'commodity' products, a depressing equation of business economics prevails: persistent over-capacity without administered prices (or costs) equals poor profitability. Of course, over-capacity may eventually self-correct, either as capacity shrinks or demand expands. Unfortunately for the participants, such corrections often are long delayed. When they finally occur, the rebound to prosperity frequently produces a pervasive enthusiasm for expansion that, within a few years, again creates over-capacity and a new profitless environment. In other words, nothing fails like success. What finally determines levels of long-term profitability in such industries is the ratio of supply-tight to supply-ample years. Frequently that ratio is dismal. (It seems as if the most recent supply-tight period in our textile business – it occurred some years back – lasted the better part of a morning.)[10]

At the time that Buffett decided to reallocate capital away from the textile operations of Berkshire in 1964 the largest competitor was Burlington Industries. It had 1964 sales of $1.2 billion compared with Berkshire's $50 million. It was far better than Berkshire in both production and distribution and had a far superior earnings record.

At the end of 1964 its stock sold for $60, whereas Berkshire sold for $13. Burlington decided to invest heavily in the textile business and by 1985 its sales had risen to $2.8 billion. Between 1964 and 1985 it made capital expenditure of about $3 billion, equivalent to $200-per-share on a $60 stock. The Burlington managers were perhaps the best jockeys in the business; unfortunately they tried to ride a poor horse. Over the 1964–85 period Burlington lost sales volume in real dollars and reduced the return on sales and equity significantly. The stock traded only slightly above its 1964 level in 1985 at $68 (if adjusted for a stock split). Over that same period inflation reduced the purchasing power of money by about two-thirds. Burlington may have been a remarkable textile company but it is not a remarkable business. 'When a management with a reputation for brilliance tackles a business with a reputation for poor fundamental economics, it is the reputation of the business that remains intact.'[11]

INDICATIONS OF HONEST AND COMPETENT MANAGERS

Buffett and Munger look for managers that love the game and like to excel. If managers are passionate about their work, and relish the thrill of outstanding performance, it is a pleasure to be partners with them (by being shareholders). As well as being enthusiastic experts on the subject of the businesses they are running, managers should think in the same way as owners about the company. To say that a manager thinks like an owner is the 'highest compliment we can pay'.[12] In all business decisions they will have an instinctive and unerring capacity to look at issues from the shareholders' perspective, and to take the option which is best for the owners: 'Directors should behave as if there is a single absentee owner, whose long-term interest they should try to further in all proper ways'.[13] The managers that run Berkshire's subsidiaries are given a simple mission. They are to run their businesses as if they owned all of it and it is the only asset in the world that they own, or will ever own. Furthermore, they will never to be able to sell or merge it for at least a century.[14]

One way in which Berkshire achieves a convergence of goals between managers and shareholders, apart from the more important way of selecting only managers who have the natural desire to perform well for their employers, is to make sure that managerial incomes are closely tied to those aspects of value creation that they have some control over. For example, at the shoe business, H H Brown managers receive a low basic salary, but are paid a bonus based on a percentage of the profits after these are reduced by a charge for capital employed. These managers can earn a lot if they perform well. On the other hand they will earn very little if they do badly for the owners: 'In contrast, most managers talk the talk but don't walk the walk, choosing instead to employ compensation systems that are long on carrots but short on sticks (and that almost invariably treat equity capital as if it is were cost-free)'.[15]

The institutional imperative

Buffett refers to an insidious and dangerous unseen force at work in companies that must be avoided, or, at least, kept under control. The institutional imperative is the tendency of organizations to stray from the path of rationality, decency and intelligence.

For example:
1. as if governed by Newton's First Law of Motion, an institution will resist any change in its current direction;
2. just as work expands to fill available time, corporate projects or acquisitions will materialize to soak up available funds;
3. any business craving of the leader, however foolish, will be quickly supported by detailed rate-of-return and strategic studies prepared by his troops; and
4. the behaviour of peer companies, whether they are expanding, acquiring, setting executive compensation or whatever, will be mindlessly imitated.[16]

It is not always venality, or even stupidity, which leads companies down the wrong path. It is often simply the institutional dynamics.

It is the job of the outside board members to both set standards for the CEO and his team, and then to periodically judge their performance. These non-executive directors should have business savvy and an owner-orientation. Unfortunately, many boards are stuffed with people who lack key qualities. They were hired for other reasons: they have the right connections; they add diversity to the board; they are simply prominent. These attributes are not enough for them to fulfill their primary duty of goal setting and performance monitoring. This results in numerous CEOs

> **Non-executive directors should have business savvy and an owner-orientation.**

keeping their jobs despite manifest incompetence. One of the problems is that the board do not lay down a clearly specified performance standard that they expect. Even repeated poor performance is waived or explained away. There is a tendency for the CEO, to shoot the arrow of managerial performance, and then to quickly paint a bulls-eye around the place where it lands. Lazy, sycophantic or substandard non-executive directors go along with this for year after year. 'Relations between the Board and the CEO are expected to be congenial. At board meetings, criticism of the CEOs performance is often viewed as the social equivalent of belching. No such inhibitions restrain the office manager from critically evaluating the substandard typist.'[17]

Because the institutional imperative is difficult to correct once it is well established Buffett and Munger will not go into business with people unless they are likeable, trusted and admired. 'We've never succeeded in making a good deal with a bad person.'[18]

Candid managers

The Berkshire annual reports are noted for the candour of the chairman. Buffett regularly reports failures as well as successes. He wants the shareholders to understand the business facts that he would want to know if he was in their position. Buffett and Munger look for the same degree of honesty from their managers. They believe that the owners are entitled to hear a pluses and minuses evaluation of how the business has performed, is performing, and is expected to perform in the future. If you hold shares in a private company you would demand such an honest assessment. So you should demand it of a company quoted on the stock exchange. Always beware of those CEOs who rely on specialist staff or public relations people to communicate with the owners. These hired hands are unlikely to be able to talk frankly and with full knowledge.

Managers who willingly tell shareholders the bad as well as the good news are less likely to squander the shareholders' assets. Business errors are bound to occur and managers need to learn the proper lessons from them: 'the CEO who misleads others in public may eventually mislead himself in private'.[19]

It is, of course, difficult for CEOs to publicly announce their mistakes. But they must remember that they demand the same of the managers that report to them, and should believe in practising what they preach.[20] Munger has a dictum: 'Just tell me the bad news; the good news will take care of itself'.[21] It would seem that few managers are able to live up to the high standards of honesty Buffett and Munger demand: 'Managers who put their trust in capitalism seem in no hurry to put their trust in capitalists'.[22]

Decent behaviour

Buffett and Munger put great store by people who are 'nice', 'of high character' or 'the greatest integrity'. When describing Colman Mockler Jr, the CEO of Gillette, Buffett used the word 'gentleman' by which he meant that he admired his integrity, courage and modesty.[23] He not only describes Tom Murphy and Dan Burke, of Capital Cities, as great managers, they are also 'precisely the sort of fellows that you would want your daughter to marry'.[24]

You can run a business the size of Berkshire and 'still have time for an afternoon nap'[25] if you have able managers of high character. However, if you have one person reporting to you who is deceitful, inept or uninterested you will not be able to handle it:

> Somebody once said that in looking for people to hire, you look for three qualities: integrity, intelligence, and energy. And if they don't have the first, the other two will kill you. You think about it; it's true. If you hire somebody without the first, you really want them to be dumb and lazy.[26]

The senior manager sets the tone for the whole organization. It is vital that the CEO exhibit exemplary behaviour. Buffett asks managers to think about their behaviour in the same way that his father taught him: when contemplating any business act, ask yourself whether you would be willing to have it explained on the front page of a newspaper to be read by family and friends. This should restrain you from committing offensive acts and encourage the performance of commendable ones.

Buffett agreed to purchase the Star Furniture business in 1997 after a single, two-hour meeting with Melvyn Wolff, the controlling shareholder and CEO. As has been so often the case Buffett felt no need to check leases, work out employment contracts, etc. 'I knew I was dealing with a man of integrity and that's what counted.'[27] The character of Melvyn Wolff and his sister, Shirley, was clear after the sale was agreed. They announced that they would make special payments to those that helped them succeed – they defined that group as everyone in the business. This money came from their own pockets not from Berkshire.

No accounting gimmickry

Investors need accurate and unbiased accounting data to be able to answer three key questions:[28]

1. How much is the company worth?
2. What is the probability of its failing to meet its future obligations?
3. Are the managers doing a good job, given the hand that they have been dealt?

The executives of many corporations try to provide trustworthy information. Unfortunately, too many regard the accounting rules 'not as a standard to be met, but as an obstacle to overcome'.[29] Buffett says that many decent CEOs – ones you would be happy to have as spouses for your children – have succumbed to temptation to manipulate earnings to satisfy what they see as Wall Street desires. 'Earnings can be as pliable as putty.'[30] Buffett believes that it is a disgrace that the accounting profession is so willing to help in the subterfuge and obfuscation. In his view auditors 'tend to kowtow?'[31] to the managers who write their cheques, rather than regard the investing public's interest as their primary responsibility. 'Whose bread I eat, his song I sing.'[32] The old joke about accountants seems to have as true a ring to it as it ever did: 'How much does two and two equal' asks the CEO. The co-operative accountant replies: 'what figure did you have in mind'.

Many otherwise honest CEOs are persuaded to think that earnings manipulation is okay. They are told that it is their duty to encourage the market to rate the company's stock as highly as possible. To push up the price they, commendably, begin with striving for operational excellence. But if this is not enough, they will resort to less admirable accounting manipulation. They will say that shareholders want a high stock price, not least so that the company can use highly priced stock as a currency for acquisitions. And anyway, they will argue, everyone else is doing it.

Then there are managers who set out actively to deceive and defraud who:

> interpret the rules 'imaginatively' and record business transactions in ways that technically comply with GAAP but actually display an economic illusion to the world…. Over the years Charlie and I have observed many accounting-based frauds of staggering size. Few of the perpetrators have been punished; many have not even been censored. It has been safer to steal large sums with a pen than small sums with a gun.[33]

Investors have to be vigilant in keeping up their guard against biased or manipulated accounting numbers. They should regard the accounts presented as merely a starting point in the calculation of true economic earnings.

One of the most popular accounting tricks is the misuse of the restructuring charge. If managers predict that there are going to be large unusual annual costs stretching over many years related to a business operation (say, a newly acquired subsidiary) they are permitted to make a large charge for all of these costs in the current quarter. So, instead of the costs being properly spread out over the relevant years a massive hit is taken now. Managers seem to prefer to 'suffer' this apparent severe drop in earnings when they were likely to be reporting poor results anyway. This gets all the bad news out of the way and shareholders can look forward to steadily rising earnings for the next few years. It is remarkable how often restructuring charges are introduced shortly after a CEO is appointed from outside the firm. Presumably in the honeymoon period a large loss will be attributed to old management and the new management then have lower costs to apportion to each of the future years, making their performance figures look much better.

This dump-everything-into-one-quarter behaviour suggests a corresponding 'bold, imaginative' approach to – golf scores. In his first round of the season, a golfer should ignore his actual performance and simply fill his card with atrocious numbers – double, triple, quadruple bogeys – and then turn in a score of, say, 140. Having established this 'reserve', he should go to the golf shop and tell his pro that he wishes to 'restructure' his imperfect swing. Next, as he takes his new swing onto the course, he should count his good holes, but not the bad ones. These remnants from his old swing should be charged instead to the reserve established earlier. At the end of five rounds, then, his record will be 140, 80, 80, 80, 80 rather than 91, 94, 89, 94, 92. On Wall Street, they will ignore the 140 – which, after all, came from a 'discontinued' swing – and will classify our hero as an 80 shooter (and one who *never* disappoints). For those who prefer to cheat up front, there would be a variant of this strategy. The golfer, playing alone with a co-operative caddy-auditor, should defer the recording of bad holes, take four 80s, accept the plaudits he gets for such athleticism and consistency, and then turn in a fifth card carrying a 140 score. After rectifying his earlier scorekeeping sins with this 'big bath', he may mumble a few apologies but will refrain from returning the sums he was previously collected from comparing scorecards in the clubhouse. (The caddy, need we add, will have acquired a loyal patron.) Unfortunately, CEOs who use variations of these scoring schemes in real life tend to become addicted to the games they're playing – after all, it's easier to fiddle with the scorecard than to spend hours on the practice tee – and never muster the will to give them up. Their behaviour brings to mind Voltaire's comment on sexual experimentation: 'Once a philosopher, twice a pervert'.[34]

There are hundreds of ways in which accounts can be manipulated, but we can't go into this here. Suffice to say, if the accounts are difficult to understand then be very suspicious – they probably don't want you to understand. Also, any management that stresses accounting appearance rather than economic substance 'usually achieve little of either'[35] in the long run.

Perform the ordinary extraordinarily well

In both investment and business management it is not necessary to do extraordinary things to get extraordinary results. In both fields of endeavour it is necessary only to 'handle the basics well and not get diverted'.[36] Buffett looks for managers who do ordinary things with such a focus and skill that they do them extraordinarily well. They work hard, protect the franchise and control costs. All basic humdrum tasks but, when done with a zeal, extraordinary things happen. They will not become distracted by trying to stretch their talent, skills and experience into unrelated areas of business. They always build on existing strengths, concentrating on the detail of what they can do well rather than trying to be jacks of all trades and masters of none.

Buffett described some of the qualities of a good management team when referring to Carl Reichardt and Paul Hazen of Wells Fargo, and to Tom Murphy and Dan Burke at Capital Cities/ABC:

> First, each pair is stronger than the sum of its parts because each partner understands trusts and admires the other. Second, both managerial teams pay able people well, but abhor having a bigger head count than is needed. Third, both attack costs as vigorously when profits are at record levels as when they are under pressure. Finally, both stick with what they understand and let their abilities, not their egos, determine what they attempt.[37]

Roberto Goizueta of Coca-Cola was praised as a manager possessing a good blend of marketing and financial skills. He did not permit the business to be dominated by one at the expense of the other, and thus achieved both a marketing triumph and terrific rewards for shareholders. He concentrated on the details of the core business and refused to be distracted. Managers need to know their limitations and not to boldly step outside of them. Thomas J. Watson Jr of IBM said that he was no genius 'I'm smart in spots – but I stay around those spots'.[38]

Managers need experience and business nous to be aware of where they should concentrate their efforts and what is merely a distraction. He says his experience with newly graduated MBAs is that they tend to lack personal commitment to the company and general business savvy: 'It's difficult to teach a new dog old tricks'.[39]

Focused on the long term

A management team worth backing is one that manages for maximum long-term shareholder value – rather than for next year's earnings. Near-term earnings are important but they should never be achieved at the expense of 'building ever-greater competitive strengths'.[40] Roberto Goizueta had a clever and clear strategic vision for Coke – one that was focused on advancing the wellbeing of shareholders. He knew exactly where he was leading the company and how it was going to get there: 'equally important, he had a burning sense of urgency about reaching his goals. An excerpt from one handwritten note he sent to me illustrates his mind-set: "By the way, I have told Olguita that what she refers to as an obsession, you call focus. I like your term much better".'[41] Bill Anders at General Dynamics was backed by Berkshire in 1992 when much of the rest of the stock market had given up on a company suffering from post cold war restructuring. 'Bill had a clearly articulated and rational strategy.'[42] In contrast, many company managers focus their thinking on short-term results and the short-term stock market consequences of their actions and announcements. This is often despite knowing that damage is being done to long-term welfare of shareholders. Such destructive acts need to be detected by investors; and companies that are prone to short-termism must be avoided.

Other companies are run by managers with a long-term focus, but they lack the necessary skills to make intelligent capital allocation decisions and so are frustrated in the achievement of their admirable goal. Usually CEOs rise to the top because they have proven skills in marketing, production or, sometimes, institutional politics. But once in place at the top, they have to deal with a very demanding new responsibility, the allocation of the capital that the firm is generating. This requires skills which are difficult to master. Furthermore, the consequences of a lack of ability in this area can have severe consequences. Buffett reckons that a company that retains earnings equivalent to 10 per cent of net worth will, over a ten-year period have deployed over 60 per cent of all the capital being used in the business. The CEO must have a sound grasp of both the techniques assisting the rational allocation of capital and an instinctive desire to use shareholders' money in a way that is most beneficial to their long-term interests. Unfortunately, too many firms are run by people who have neither the knowledge nor the inclination to direct capital to its best uses: 'In the end plenty of unintelligent capital allocation takes place in corporate America (that's why you hear so much about "restructuring")'.[43]

High earnings on equity capital

Good managers concentrate on improving the earnings of their businesses while utilizing little additional capital. The best way to measure operating performance is the ratio of operating earnings to shareholders' equity. Buffett reported in 1989 that Berkshire's non-insurance businesses produced after-tax earnings at 57 per cent of average equity capital:[44] for every $1 of shareholders' money held in the business, managers produced a profit of 57 cents in one year! This is an astonishingly good performance, especially when the fact that these companies had no net debt is taken into account.

Most companies give a higher priority to the earnings per share record than to the profit per dollar of equity capital. This is misguided, as it is easy to increase earnings per share simply by adding more to the equity base. So a management that added 10 per cent to the equity base and produced a 5 per cent increase in earnings per share should not be regarded as praiseworthy. It is possible to produce an increase in 'earnings per share' in a savings account simply by ploughing back the 'earnings' (interest) adding to the capital base. Just so long as the payout of income is low, a significant rise in 'earnings' can be achieved. If you trebled the amount of capital deposited in the savings account (or in the business) you will treble earnings. It is vital to assess whether any increase in earnings is attributable to the policy of retaining income and the workings of compound interest, or it is due to a superior return on capital employed.

Distributable earnings that have been withheld from the owners must earn their keep. Each dollar of retained earnings must result in at least one dollar of market value, preferably two or three dollars. In many companies the money that comes from the core business is sunk into operations that earn low returns. The core business, with its strong economic franchise, will dominate the earnings per unit of equity figure to start with, but over time there will be a decline as the low return business takes a greater portion of the equity capital. The decline is often camouflaged for many years, but eventually the poor capital allocation is plain for all to see. By then it is too late for the shareholders. On the downhill road, 'the managers at fault periodically report on the lessons they have learned from the latest disappointment. They then usually seek out future lessons (failure seems to go to their heads)'.[45]

Tight cost control

Look out for managers who are frugal with the owners' money. Those that run a tight operation generally continue to search for and to find new ways of reducing costs even when they are already the low cost producer in the industry. On the other hand 'our experience has been that the manager of an already high-cost operation frequently is uncommonly resourceful in finding new ways to add to overhead'.[46]

> **Look out for managers who are frugal with the owners' money.**

Be wary of those companies that make grand announcements that they are to engage in a major cost cutting exercise. This is an indication that they do not really know what cost cutting is about. A good manager is continually examining the business for ways of cutting costs. He or she does not wake up one morning and say that, 'This is the time for some cost cutting' any more than they decide this is the time for breathing. When Munger heard that Carl Reichardt, CEO of Wells Fargo, had told a manager who wanted to purchase a Christmas tree for the office, that he should do so out of his own money, he knew it was time to buy some more stock.

Berkshire itself is determined not to have any head office bloat – the ruin of many companies. It runs a $100 billion, 112,000 employee company with a total staff of 13.8 people. The total expense of the head office is less than 1 per cent of reported earnings. This contrasts with other companies that spend over 10 per cent of operating earnings on their headquarters. If a company with 1 per cent of its profits devoted to central costs achieves the same earnings at the operating level as the firm that devotes 10 per cent of profits to central costs, shares in the first business will have a value 9 per cent higher than in the second simply because of corporate overhead:

Charlie and I have observed no correlation between high corporate costs and good corporate performance. In fact, we see the simpler, low-cost operations as more likely to operate effectively than its bureaucratic brethren. We're admirers of the Wal-Mart, Nucor, Dover, GEICO, Golden West Financial and Price Co. models.[47]

Repurchasing stock

If a stock is selling below intrinsic value, when conservatively calculated, then shareholders can benefit if the company repurchases its shares. There are caveats to this. First, the company must have funds available (cash plus sensible borrowing capacity) that are not needed for investment within the business. This type of internal investment comes in two forms:

- investment to maintain competitive position; and
- investment aimed at business growth; growth that management are convinced will produce more than one dollar of value for every dollar spent.

Second, shareholders should have been supplied with all the facts needed to assess the value of the stock. In the absence of such information it is conceivable that insiders could take advantage of the uninformed partners (shareholders) and buy their interests at less than the true worth.

If these conditions prevail then shareholders will be rewarded by repurchasing for two reasons. The first is based on simple arithmetic. Buying shares at less than per share intrinsic value will raise the value of the remaining stock – often significantly. Companies may be able to buy $2 of present value for $1 – the stock that remains will have a higher per share intrinsic value immediately.

Second, a management team that chooses to repurchase shares when they are trading below intrinsic value send a very strong message that they take actions that enhance the wealth of shareholders, rather than actions that expand their power, prestige and domain. This gives shareholders and potential shareholders greater confidence in the company. They will raise their estimates of future returns and increase the price of the stock. Investors, quite rationally, are willing to pay more for a business being run by managers with 'demonstated pro-shareholder leanings'[48] rather than one that is run in the interests of managers. A manager that, over a period of time, refuses to buy back shares despite clear evidence that it would be in the owner's interest to do so, 'reveals more than he knows about his motivations. No matter how often or how eloquently he mouths some public relations-inspired phrase such as 'maximizing share-holder wealth' (this season's favourite), the market correctly discounts assets lodged with him. His heart is not listening to his mouth – and, after a while, neither will the market'.[49]

In the mid 1970s, the logic of carrying out repurchases was 'virtually screaming at managements'[50] but few responded. Buffett and Munger searched for those companies that were sufficiently aware of shareholder interests to engage in the repurchase of shares because it was an important indicator that the company was run by managers with the correct goals and was undervalued. However, during the 1980s and 1990s buy backs became fashionable and managers started to lose sight of owner-orientated rationales for doing them. Increasingly the motivation became to pump or support the stock price. This benefits the shareholder who will sell in the near-term but the continuing shareholder suffers a loss in value if the shares are repurchased at a price above intrinsic value. 'Buying dollar bills for $1.10 is not good business for those who stick around.'[51] Buffett and Munger believe that many companies are now overpaying when they repurchase thus damaging the interests of the owners who stay with the firm: 'I can't help but feel that too often today's repurchases are dictated by management's desire to "show confidence" or be in fashion rather than by a desire to enhance per-share value'.[52]

Mergers

Always look for management that makes rational decisions when it comes to mergers.[53] Such decisions should be justified on the basis of maximizing real economic benefits and not driven by a desire to maxi-mize the managerial domain or to boost short-term accounting numbers. A merger should raise the per share intrinsic value of the acquirers' stock. A company should never issue common stocks unless it receives as much in business value as it gives. Shareholders will lose if managers sell assets (stock in the firm) for 70 cents that in fact are worth $1. There seems to be a lack of clarity of thought on the subject of mergers. When a company that agrees to issue shares to merge with another makes an announcement in the Press it is usually described as 'Company A to acquire Company B', or 'B sells to A'. A clearer way of looking at it is to say, 'Part of A sold to acquire B', or 'Owners of B to receive part of A in exchange for their properties'.[54] It is crucially important to examine what is being given as well as what is being acquired. Buffett suggests that managers of acquirers might ponder the question: would I sell 100 per cent of the business on the same basis that I am offering part of it? If the answer is no, then why is it smart to sell a portion at that price? The basic rule must be that shares will not be issued in exchange for the shares in a target firm unless at least as much intrinsic business value is received as is given.

That leaves two possible options open to the owner-orientated manager. The first is what Buffett calls a business-value-for-business-value merger. Here the two groups of shareholders give just as much as they receive in terms of intrinsic value. The second is only possible when the acquirer's stock sells at, or above, its intrinsic value. The use of stock as currency may then enhance the wealth of the acquirer's shareholders. Logically, the acquirer should not offer its stock when it is undervalued if it is buying a fully valued property, and yet this appears to happen with shocking regularity. Some of the reasons for irrational (from the shareholders' perspective) deals are given below:

- *Animal spirits* Leaders often relish activity and challenge. The pulse beats faster and you can be the centre of press attention.

  The acquisition problem is often compounded by a biological bias: Many CEOs attain their positions in part because they possess an abundance of animal spirits and ego. If an executive is heavily endowed with these qualities – which, it should be acknowledged, sometimes have their advantages – they won't disappear when he reaches the top. When such a CEO is encouraged by his advisers to make deals, he responds much, as would a teenage boy who is encouraged by his father to have a normal sex life. It's not a push he needs.[55]

- *Size is everything* Managers measure themselves and are measured by others, by the size of the organization that they control. Increasing the span of control leads to higher compensation and status. Managers may try to justify growth; 'we have to grow,' they might say. Buffett condemns this attitude:

  Who, it might be asked, is the 'we'? For present shareholders, the reality is that all existing businesses shrink when shares are issued. Were Berkshire to issue shares tomorrow for an acquisition, Berkshire would own everything that it now owns plus the new business, but *your* interest in such hard-to-match businesses as See's Candy Shops, National Indemnity, etc. would automatically be reduced. If:
  1. your family owns a 120-acre farm; and
  2. you invite a neighbour with 60 acres of comparable land to merge his farm

into an equal partnership – with you to be managing partner; then

3. your managerial domain will have grown to 180 acres but you will have permanently shrunk by 25 per cent your family's ownership interest in both acreage and crops.[56]

- *Hubris*

Many managements apparently were overexposed in impressionable childhood years to the story in which the imprisoned handsome prince is released from a toad's body by a kiss from a beautiful princess. Consequently, they are certain their managerial kiss will do wonders for the profitability of Company T(arget).

Such optimism is essential. Absent that rosy view, why else should the shareholders of Company A(cquisitor) want to own an interest in T at the 2X takeover cost rather than at the X market price they would pay if they made direct purchases on their own? In other words, investors can always buy toads at the going price for toads. If investors instead bankroll princesses who wish to pay double for the right to kiss the toad, those kisses had better pack some real dynamite. We've observed many kisses but very few miracles. Nevertheless, many managerial princesses remain serenely confident about the future potency of their kisses – even after their corporate backyards are knee-deep in unresponsive toads.[57]

Buffett has tried the toad kissing approach to mergers. He says his kisses fell flat despite the low prices paid. However, Berkshire did well with princes – but they were princes before they were bought. The best performing category has been the purchase of 'fractional interests in easily-identifiable princes at toad-like prices'.[58]

- *A focus on short-term earnings* Whenever a merger is announced one of the first reassurances that the CEO gives is that it will not be dilutive. This means that current earnings per share of the acquirer will not decline. Current earnings per share, and earnings per share for the next few years, are important, but are not all-powerful. An excessive emphasis on near-term earnings per share can be dangerous. Many value-destroying (in the long run) mergers have been non-dilutive. On the other hand, many mergers that have depressed current and near-term earnings per share have been value creating when a long-term perspective is taken. The dilution that really counts is the dilution of intrinsic value per share, not earnings per share. To highlight the stupidity of focusing on near-term earnings per share Buffett asks us to imagine that a 25-year-old first year MBA is considering merging his future economic interests with those of a 25-year-old day labourer. The non-earning MBA student would receive an immediate boost to his near-term earnings in this 'share-for-share' merger of equity interests. But who would be stupid enough to value near-term income so much as to sacrifice long-term economic value?

WHAT TO AVOID

Macro economic forecasts, charts and predicting tops and bottoms

Economic forecasts for the economy as a whole are 'an expensive distraction for many investors and businessmen'.[59] Buffett and Munger spend no time thinking about macro economic factors. Even if the most revered expert on the subjects of interest rates, unemployment, GDP growth, exchange rates and so on were to give them the latest projections for the next two years, they would pay absolutely no attention to them. They focus on businesses, company by company. If they understand the business economics, and the management, and they like the price, why would they want highly fallible macro economic predictions? Besides, none of the great economic events of the second half of the 20th Century (e.g. the late 1960s expansion, the oil shocks of the 1970s) made any difference to the application of sound investment principles. Buy fine businesses at sensible prices regardless of the latest scare on the macro economic scene. 'Indeed, we have usually made our best purchases when apprehensions about some macro event were at a peak. Fear is the foe of the faddist, but the friend of the fundamentalist.'[60]

Investors must never respond to price movements of stocks *per se*, rather than the relationship between price and value. Trying to estimate when the market has reached a peak or a trough is equally futile: 'we make no attempt to predict how security markets will behave; successfully forecasting short-term stock price movements is something we think neither we nor anyone else can do'.[61] Buffett believes that the only value of stock forecaster is to make fortune tellers look good. People who do believe in these forecasts are being child-like. If a stock is priced low relative to its conservatively estimated intrinsic value then the investor would be a fool to defer purchase just because of short-term worries about the direction of the stock market: 'Why scrap an informed decision because of an uninformed guess?'[62] Fear and greed will produce strange prices in stocks from time to time. The problem is that the arrival or departure of market wide anomalies is unpredictable and therefore you cannot forecast the short-run direction of market indices. You can, however, aim to be 'fearful when others are greedy and to be greedy only when others are fearful'.[63]

Impatience

Don't be impatient to place your money in stocks. There could be long periods when you are unable to find a stock that meets sound investment criteria. Don't compromise those standards. Stand on the plate and let those pitches pass you by until the pitcher throws a ball right down the middle. 'Masterly inactivity'[64] is to be commended not frowned upon. 'You can't produce a baby in one month by getting nine women pregnant.'[65] If all the stocks you examine are over-priced then be content to stockpile funds. When it is your turn to bat again you'll be ready. Buffett and Munger have had many years when they made no major investment decisions at all; there were no attractive securities available.

Patience is needed also once you have purchased a stock. Market prices can remain below business values for what seems like an age and prices can gyrate capriciously. However, over the long run if the business does well the stock will follow. If you have concluded that the company is sound on the basis of the key quantitative and qualitative criteria then you should be in no hurry to sell. You will have examined the long-term prospects of the business and should have bought only if these were outstanding. Buffett and Munger declared that they would be quite content, once they hold good stocks, for the stock market to close for five years. The availability of a daily price quote and the opportunity to sell is an irrelevance to shareholders interested in buying shares of truly powerful businesses. When Buffett says he intends to hold stock for the very long term, he means it – some have now been in the portfolio for over 30 years. He says his intention is that some of these will never be sold.

> Patience is needed once you have purchased a stock.

Going along with the crowd

The investor must think independently. You must gather the relevant facts and go with your own reasoning. If you don't know enough to make sound investment decisions then don't put yourself up for the game. The crowd, that is the Wall Street consensus, composed of the financial Press, the professional investors, analysts etc., in setting market prices provide ample rational sounding arguments as to why they are all so cheery, or alternatively, so downbeat. Their rationales can be beguiling, but you must stand strong and turn your head away from the siren voices enticing you on to the rocks. Examine the facts within a rational framework. Apply tests and standards which have proved themselves reliable over decades. Don't swap these for new measures of values (e.g. Internet firms were valued as the basis of turnover rather than the universally applicable criteria discussed in this book). Remember always that 'prices are set by participants with behaviour patterns that sometimes resemble those of an army of manic-depressive lemmings'.[66] For an experienced investor one of the great paradoxes of our time is that most people become interested in stocks when everyone else does, and prices have been bid up to unsustainable levels. The best time to get interested is when everyone else is shunning stocks. If a stock is popular you are unlikely to do well. Buffett and Munger are so independently minded that they will not pay attention to brokers' recommendations, nor even to the assessments of credit quality made by Moody's or Standard and Poors. You must have the confidence in a stock that only comes from having conducted your own detailed analysis.

Gambling and derivatives

People seem attracted to gamble when there is a large prize and a small entry fee, no matter how poor the odds may be (Las Vegas has been built on such psychology). It is possible to take these long-shot chances when investing in common stocks (such as when you buy stock in a company that is on the verge of bankruptcy in the hope of a rescue bid), but in modern times the way to really leverage up returns is to make use of derivatives. Buffett and Munger are quite scathing about derivative traders and ordinary investors who participate in the derivative markets. As for the professional traders they wonder what would happen if a couple of dozen were shipwrecked and had to organize production on a deserted island. Would they agree that five of them should not actually produce food, but would concentrate on trading options and futures on the output of the others? As for the ordinary investor using the derivative markets: here you often get the fatal mix of ignorance and high leverage.

As far as serious investors are concerned the derivative markets should be seen as casinos where the owners are only too willing to take a big skim. The brokers do fine, but the investor, on balance, loses. Investors must concentrate on the long-term prospects for an enterprise and not enter into leveraged market wagers.

Trusting Wall Street fund managers

Buffett has strongly attacked professional money managers as people who, in aggregate, bring nothing to society. They fail in a number of ways:

- *They cause market instability and loss of Reason* 'You might think that institutions, with their large staffs of highly paid and experienced investment professionals, would be a force for stability and reason in financial markets. They are not: stocks heavily owned and constantly monitored by institutions have often been among the most inappropriately valued.'[67] In February 1987, eight months before the sharp market decline Buffett said that fear had been replaced by euphoria on Wall Street. Investment managers had lost touch with the fundamentals of what shares represent, that is, a portion of a real business with real business constraints.

  What could be more exhilarating than to participate in a bull market in which the rewards to owners of businesses became gloriously uncoupled from the plodding performances of the businesses themselves. Unfortunately, however, stocks can't outperform businesses indefinitely. ... Bull markets can obscure mathematical laws, but they can't repeal them.[68]

- *They waste investors' money with their hyperkinetic activity* Fund managers generally regard all their holdings as candidates for a quick sale when they are swayed by the latest Wall Street preference, craze or concept. If the operating conditions of a business worsen they won't do something about the officers and directors of the company of which they own a part. Rather, they will dump the stock. So much buying and selling takes place that Buffett says their behaviour during trading hours makes whirling dervishes appear sedate by comparison. 'Indeed the term "institutional investor" is becoming one of those self-contradictions called an oxymoron, comparable to "jumbo shrimp", "lady mud wrestler" and 'inexpensive lawyer"'.[69]

- *They are absurdly risk averse* 'Most managers have very little incentive to make the intelligent-but-with-some-chance-of-looking-like-an-idiot decision. Their personal gain/loss ratio is all too obvious: If an unconventional decision works out well, they get a pat on the back and, if it works out poorly, they get a pink slip. (Failing conventionally is the route to go; as a group, lemmings may have a rotten image, but no individual lemming has ever received bad press.)'[70]

Equations with Greek letters

Keep investment as simple as possible. Don't be over active: 'Charlie and I ... do very little except allocate capital. And, even then, we are not all that energetic. We have one excuse though: in allocating capital, activity does not correlate with achievement. Indeed, in the fields of investments and acquisitions, frenetic behaviour is often counter productive'.[71] One area where you can save energy is working out investment values using complex mathematic formulae. Buffett said to the New York Society of Analysts: 'If calculus were required, I'd have to go back to delivering news-papers'.[72] Buffett says he sees no need for mathematics beyond the ability to divide the value of a business by the number of shares outstanding. (This is a slight exaggeration; discounting calculations can be challenging, but even these are not beyond the average person with a little coaching and practice.)

> **Keep investment as simple as possible.**

When Buffett and Munger tell us not to do equations with Greek letters in them they are usually referring to modern portfolio theory, popular in business schools. Volatility is measured by sigma, σ, and systematic risk is measured by beta, β. Buffett and Munger regard these as irrelevant to an investor analyzing a business and buying for the long term.

> Most professionals and academicians talk of efficient markets, dynamic hedging and betas. Their interest in such matters is understandable, since techniques shrouded in mystery clearly have value to the purveyor of investment advice. After all, what witch doctor has ever achieved fame and fortune by simply advising, 'Take two aspirins'? ... In my opinion, investment success will not be produced by arcane formulae, computer programs or signals flashed by the price behaviour of stocks and markets. Rather an investor will succeed by coupling good business judgement with an ability to insulate his thoughts and behaviour from the super-contagious emotions that swirl about the market place.[73]

At the May 1996 Berkshire Hathaway annual meeting in Omaha, Buffett said that current financial classes can help you do averagely.

Being too ambitious

Even Buffett and Munger aim for no more than 15 per cent return per year. By trying to achieve more you may accept too much risk and lower your standards.

In the 1999 Berkshire letter to shareholders Buffett makes plain that expectation of high growth in market values is irrational even if GDP grows at a reasonable rate:

> Equity investors currently seem wildly optimistic in their expectations about future returns. We see the growth in corporate profits as being largely tied to the business done in the country (GDP), and we see GDP growing at a real rate of about 3 per cent. In addition, we have hypothesized 2 per cent inflation. … If profits do indeed grow along with GDP, at about a 5 per cent rate, the valuation placed on American business is unlikely to climb by much more than that. Add in something for dividends, and you emerge with returns from equities that are dramatically less than most investors have either experienced in the past or expect in the future. If investor expectations become more realistic – and they almost certainly will – the market adjustment is apt to be severe, particularly in sectors in which speculation has been concentrated.[74]

Diversifying to mediocrity

Diversification is a protection against the ill-informed investor's ignorance. For the investor who knows what he or she is doing, diversification beyond a handful of stocks makes very little sense.

> We continue to concentrate our investments in a very few companies that we try to understand well. There are only a handful of businesses about which we have long-term convictions. Therefore, when we find such a business, we want to participate in a meaningful way. We agree with Mae West: 'Too much of a good thing can be wonderful'.[75]

Buffett likens a portfolio of 40 or more stocks as a Noah's Ark way of investing – you end up with a zoo. Another metaphor is attributed to Billy Rose, the Broadway impresario, 'If you have a harem of 40 women, you never get to know any of them very well'.[76] At the end of 1999 and 2000 Berkshire had 70 per cent of its investment fund in just four companies. Buffett and Munger concentrate their attention, skills and experienced judgement because it is 'too hard to make hundreds of smart decisions'.[77]

This attitude flies in the face of standard portfolio theory dogma. Critics say that this will lead to a very risky portfolio. Buffett disagrees:

'We believe that a policy of portfolio concentration may well *decrease* risk if it raises, as it should, both the intensity with which an investor thinks about a business and the comfort-level he must feel with its economic characteristics before buying into it.'[78]

Buffett's and Munger's notion of risk differs from that of standard finance textbooks, because they focus on the possibility of loss and injury. In contrast, academic finance courses focus on the relative volatility of a stock or portfolio of stocks (compared to a large universe of stocks). The two are related, but not identical:

> For owners of a business – and that's the way we think of shareholders – the academics' definition of risk is far off the mark, so much so that it produces absurdities. For example, under beta-based theory, a stock that has dropped very sharply compared to the market – as had *Washington Post* when we bought it in 1973 – became 'riskier' at the lower price than at the higher price. Would that description have then made *any* sense to someone who was offered the entire company at a vastly-reduced price?[79]

The following quotation is long but gets right to the core of the Buffett and Munger philosophy and also ridicules the measuring of risk using beta and therefore is quoted in full:

> In our opinion, the real risk that an investor must assess is whether his aggregate after-tax receipts from an investment (including those he receives on sale) will, over his prospective holding period, give him at least as much purchasing power as he had to begin with, plus a modest rate of interest on that initial stake. Though this risk cannot be calculated with engineering precision, it can in some cases be judged with a degree of accuracy that is useful.
>
> The primary factors bearing upon this evaluation are:
>
> 1. the certainty with which the long-term economic characteristics of the business can be evaluated;
> 2. the certainty with which management can be evaluated, both as to its ability to realize the full potential of the business and to wisely employ its cashflows;
> 3. the certainty with which management can be counted on to channel the rewards from the business to the shareholders rather than to itself;
> 4. the purchase price of the business; and
> 5. the levels of taxation and inflation that will be experienced and that will determine the degree by which an investor's purchasing-power return is reduced from his gross return.

These factors will probably strike many analysts as unbearably fuzzy, since they cannot be extracted from a data base of any kind. But the difficulty of precisely quantifying these matters does not negate their importance nor is it insuperable. Just as Justice Stewart found it impossible to formulate a test for obscenity but nevertheless asserted, 'I know it when I see it', so also can investors – in an inexact but useful way – 'see' the risks inherent in certain investments without reference to complex equations or price histories.

Is it really so difficult to conclude that Coca-Cola and Gillette possess far less business risk over the long term than, say, *any* computer company or retailer? Worldwide, Coke sells about 44 per cent of all soft drinks, and Gillette has more than a 60 per cent share (in value) of the blade market. Leaving aside chewing gum, in which Wrigley is dominant, I know of no other significant businesses in which the leading company has long enjoyed such global power.

Moreover, both Coke and Gillette have actually increased their worldwide shares of market in recent years. The might of their brand names, the attributes of their products, and the strength of their distribution systems give them an enormous competitive advantage, setting up a protective moat around their economic castles. The average company, in contrast, does battle daily without any such means of protection. As Peter Lynch says, stocks of companies selling commodity-like products should come with a warning label: 'Competition may prove hazardous to human wealth'.

The competitive strengths of a Coke or Gillette are obvious to even to the casual observer of business. Yet the beta of their stocks is similar to that of a great many run-of-the-mill companies who possess little or no competitive advantage. Should we conclude from this similarity that the competitive strength of Coke and Gillette gains them nothing when business risk is being measured? Or should we conclude that the risk in owning a piece of a company – its stock – is somehow divorced from the long-term risk inherent in its business operations? We believe neither conclusion makes sense and that equating beta with investment risk also makes no sense.

The theoretician bred on beta has no mechanism for differentiating the risk inherent in, say, a single-product toy company selling pet rocks or hula hoops from that of another toy company whose sole product is Monopoly or Barbie. But it's quite possible for ordinary investors to make such distinctions if they have a reasonable understanding of consumer behaviour and the factors that create long-term competitive strength or weakness. Obviously, every investor will make mistakes. But by confining himself to a relatively few, easy-to-understand cases, a reasonably intelligent, informed and diligent person can judge investment risks with a useful degree of accuracy.[80]

Being an active trader

'Marketability' and 'liquidity' of stocks are commonly regarded as blessings for investors. Brokers sing the praises of companies with high share turnover, 'but investors should understand that what is good for the croupier is not good for the customer. A hyperactive stock market is the pickpocket of enterprise'.[81] Consider the case of a company earning 12 per cent on equity capital. If its shares have a turnover rate on the stock market of 100 per cent per year and each purchase and sale incurred commissions and other costs of 1 per cent and the stock trades at book value, then the shareholders will pay, in aggregate, 2 per cent of the company's net worth per year just to transfer ownership.

Thus the equivalent of 16.7 per cent (1/6th) earnings are swallowed up by market activity. A year of trading on the NYSE or NASDAQ costs investors billions of dollars each year. These charges for 'financial flip-flopping'[82] do not enlarge the pie, they merely decide who eats a diminished pie.

> We are aware of the pie-expanding argument that says that such activities improve the rationality of the capital allocation process. We think that this argument is specious and that, on balance, hyperactive equity markets subvert rational capital allocation and act as pie shrinkers … Casino-type markets and hair-trigger investment management act as an invisible foot that trips up and slows down a forward moving economy.[83]

It doesn't make sense to fiddle continually with a portfolio. If you have selected businesses that you understand and which have wonderful and durable economic franchises it would be foolish to part with them, because, say, the Federal Reserve moves the discount rates by 25 basis points, or you have been given a hot tip. A portion of a truly great business is simply too difficult to replace. And yet, so many investors impetuously move money from one stock to another when presented with nothing more than a superficial argument in a newspaper or by their broker. 'An investor should ordinarily hold a small piece of an outstanding business with the same tenacity that an owner would exhibit if he owned all of that business.'[84]

While it is illogical that investors would frequently trade shares, it is equally irrational that managers should be proud that there is a high level of activity in their stock. In effect, what is happening is that a high proportion of their existing clientele are continually deserting them.

> At what other organization – school, club, church, etc. – do leaders cheer when members leave? (However, if there were a broker whose livelihood depended upon the membership turnover in such organizations, you could be sure that there would be at least one proponent of activity, as in: 'There hasn't been much going on in Christianity for a while; maybe we should switch to Buddhism next week'.)[85]

Turnarounds

Buffett and Munger have learned from bitter experience that businesses on the ropes which are bought on the expectation that they will be turned around usually produce nothing but disappointment. Don't waste time and energy in this area. Concentrate on good businesses. '"Turn-arounds" seldom turn.'[86]

Ignoring your errors

Every year Buffett owns up to his blunders in the letter he sends to shareholders. For example, in 1998 he declared, 'my decision to sell McDonald's was a very big mistake'. He advises us all to examine our mistakes and learn from them. The secret is not to become despondent when mistakes occur. Don't take it personally. After all: 'A stock doesn't know that you own it'.[87]

> ....The secret is not to become despondent when mistakes occur. ....

On the other hand, don't be too self-congratulatory when your returns are high in a booming market: 'a rising tide lifts all yachts'.[88]

Glamorous companies you don't understand

It is very difficult to achieve high returns on businesses subject to rapid change. Many investors seem to search for companies where the industry is in a constant state of flux. They are willing to pay high price-earnings ratios for exotic-sounding businesses that promise lots, but are currently delivering little. Investors seem to have a capacity to fantasize about what might be rather than facing up to the reality of what is plain today. 'For such investor-dreamers, any blind date is preferable to one with the girl next door, no matter how desirable she may be.'[89] They should bear in mind that a business subject to major change is also exposed to a high chance of major error. How many investors that piled into the Internet boom stopped to consider the likelihood of a particular company being able to build a fortress-like business franchise? Even if they were aware of the necessity of analyzing the potential for barriers to entry and pricing power could they have drawn conclusions in which they had confidence, when the terrain shifted from one week to the next?

Worrying if prices fall

Investors have a tendency to become euphoric when stock prices are rising and depressed when they fall. This does not make sense: 'selling fine businesses on "scary" news is usually a bad decision'.[90] Buffett asks us to consider whether we are to be net investors or disinvestors over the next few years. If the answer is investors then stock price falls should be welcomed. Consider the analogy with food. People expect to be purchasers of food in the future. This being so they would welcome falling prices and dislike rising prices. For investors who expect to add attractive companies to their portfolio, lower stock prices provide the opportunity to take a larger portion of the company for the same amount of money. 'Declining prices for businesses benefits us and rising prices hurt us.'[91] The key factor is the amount of intrinsic value that is being purchased. If this remains constant as a wave of pessimism sweeps the market it becomes possible to acquire X amount of intrinsic value for ½ X. 'We look to business performance, not market performance. If we are correct in expectations regarding the business, the market eventually will follow along.'[92] Market pessimism is the friend of the investor. It is widespread optimism that is the enemy.

The new issue market

The primary equity market, where companies sell shares to investors, is controlled by current stockholders and corporations. They are able to select the timing of offerings until they are reassured that the shares will fetch a full price. Bargains are unlikely to be available 'in the case of common-stock offerings, selling shareholders are often motivated to unload *only* when they feel the market is overpaying'.[93] In contrast, the mass folly that frequently reigns in the secondary market will occasionally set clearing prices that are foolishly low.

WHEN TO SELL

When Buffett and Munger buy a stock they do not have in mind any time or price for sale. They are willing to hold the stock indefinitely 'so long as we expect the business to increase in intrinsic value at a satisfactory rate'.[94] So, we can deduce from this that one reason for selling is that the growth of business intrinsic value falls below the 'satisfactory' threshold. If the prospective return on equity capital of the underlying business is satisfactory (and expected to remain so) and the management is competent and honest there is no reason to sell. Even if the market appears to be temporarily overpricing a stock relative to its intrinsic value, Buffett and Munger are reluctant to sell. One reason for this is that experts have frequently said in the past that a remarkable company, despite all its good qualities should nevertheless be sold because the market has got ahead of itself, and is being over optimistic in its pricing, to then discover that they have missed out on the greatest period of returns, e.g. Coca-Cola. A second reason is that Buffett and Munger have personally experienced the embarrassment of selling a stock only to find that a few years later, when they wanted to buy in again, that a much higher price had to be paid, e.g. Disney. A third reason is that if you follow a policy of selling when a stock rises above intrinsic value you are likely to incur capital gains tax, which will negate any benefit of regularly switching between stocks slightly above intrinsic value to those below intrinsic value.

Occasionally, Buffett and Munger will sell a stock because there is an even better opportunity. But these are rare events because they have to be absolutely sure that the investment is truly superior to the old one, and such confidence is difficult to come by, especially when you regard the existing holding as a good investment.

Another reason for selling is when a mistake in the original analysis becomes apparent as familiarity with the company grows. The error could be in any one of the following categories:

1. the assessment of the quality of the management;
2. estimation of the future economics of the business;
3. the price paid.

Buffett says that category (2) is the most common:

> of course, it is necessary to dig deep into our history to find illustrations of such mistakes – sometimes as deep as two or three months back. For example, last year your Chairman volunteered his expert opinion on the rosy future of the aluminium business. Several minor adjustments to that opinion – now aggregating approximately 180 degrees – have since been required.[95]

What Buffett and Munger will not do is sell for the silly reasons many other investors do. They will not sell simply because a stock has appreciated or because it has been held for a long time ('of Wall Street maxims the most foolish may be, "you can't go broke taking a profit"'[96]). They will definitely not sell because market volatility has irrationally forced the market down. Just because everyone else is infected with pessimism does not mean Buffett and Munger will buckle under the same psychological pressures.

They have one attitude to selling which they admit seems 'highly eccentric'.[97] They will not sell any core stock holdings (including Coca-Cola, *Washington Post* and GEICO) even if they become far overpriced in the market. 'In effect, we view these investments exactly like our successful controlled businesses – a permanent part of Berkshire rather than merchandise to be disposed of once Mr Market offers us a sufficiently high price.'[98] This attitude is influenced by 'personal',[99] considerations and the 'way we want to live our lives'.[100] It simply fits their personalities, 'we would rather achieve a return of X while associating with people whom are strongly like and admire than realize 110 per cent of X by exchanging these relationships for uninteresting or unpleasant ones'.[101] Even if these companies run into problems they will not be abandoned. Buffett says that you don't get rid of a kid with problems so why should you dump a partner in business? Buffett and Munger expect the relationships they have with the people running the firms they have taken an interest in to last a lifetime. This does not mean that the CEOs have free reign: when Coca-Cola wanted to spend what Buffett thought was an unreasonable amount to acquire Quaker Oats in 2000, he put his foot down because he believed more intrinsic value was being given than would be received.

A high level of loyalty is also extended to the subsidiary companies, even those that are sub-par businesses. Buffett and Munger are very reluctant to sell these: 'as long as we expect them to generate at least some cash and as long as we feel good about their managers and labour relations'.[102] These businesses will not be treated as though they are cards disposed of in a game of gin rummy – discarding your least promising business at each turn – because this 'is not our style. We would rather have our overall results penalized a bit than engage in that kind of behaviour … . We focus hard on curing the problems'.[103]

This attitude may seem irrational to many fund managers but consider the point of view of the managers running other Berkshire companies. How secure and loyal would you feel if you witnessed regular sales of the wholly owned businesses and the minority shareholdings? If you were talented and wanted to build a business for the long-term would you hang around? or would you move to an employer that helped you through the bad times and encouraged you to grow through the good, that is, an employer that gave you the room to create and then backed you to the hilt? Maybe Berkshire does lose a little on those businesses which don't perform as expected, but they gain a tremendous amount in terms of loyalty and commitment from the dozens of talented multi-millionaires (and their lieutenants) put in charge of the Berkshire businesses. In corporate life having people around you that you like and trust, and with whom you can build a long-term relationship is far more important than having people that you merely respect for their managerial skill.

DIFFICULTIES/DRAWBACKS OF THIS APPROACH

Time and knowledge are the two limitations most people will have when trying to emulate Buffett and Munger. Understanding a business and its competitive environment requires a significant amount of work and a firm grasp of strategic management principles. Getting to know the character of a manager is likely to be difficult for the average small investor.

Buffett can pick up the telephone and CEOs will talk to him – the rest of us will often have to resort to less direct and less reliable methods. Clearly the followers of Buffett and Munger will have to narrow down the range of companies and industries that they try to understand so that they can develop the depth of knowledge required to create a circle of competence that has some real meaning.

Most investors possess the intellectual capacity to understand the principles described by Buffett and Munger, but few have the dedication, strength of character, capacity for hard work and patience to put the principles into practice successfully. If an investor is prepared to put in the effort to develop these personality traits and to learn the keys to business analysis then a rich reward awaits: 'the market, like the Lord, helps those who help themselves. But, unlike the Lord, the market does not forgive those who know not what they do'.[104]

KEY PRINCIPLES OF BUFFETT'S AND MUNGER'S APPROACH

- Analyze businesses not stocks:
  - investing is most intelligent when it is most business-like.
- What is a good company?
  - good long-term economic franchise
  - competent and honest management.
- Only buy shares in a business you understand – stay within your circle of competence:
  - degree of difficulty doesn't count.
- Calculate intrinsic value:
  - the discounted value of cash that can be taken out of a business during its remaining life.
- Allow for a large margin of safety:
  - the shares must be available at a very attractive price.
- Try to find 'Inevitables':
  - companies dominating their fields for an investment lifetime due to their competitive strengths.
- Don't expect to be active in the stock market:
  - wait for the perfect pitch
  - imagine you have a punch card with 20 punches on it.
- Estimate current and future owner earnings:
  - (a) reported earnings; plus,
  - (b) depreciation, depletion, amortization and certain other non-cash changes; less,
  - (c) the amount of capitalized expenditure for plant and machinery, etc. that a business requires to fully maintain its long-term competitive position and its unit volume; less,
  - (d) any extra amount for working capital that is needed to maintain the firm's long-term competitive position and unit volume.
- Look for a strong economic franchise:
  - long-term pricing power
  - deep and dangerous moat
  - an any fool business.
- Look for honest and competent managers. These managers:
  - love the game and like to excel
  - are passionate about their work
  - relish the thrill of outstanding performance

- think like an owner
- are not consumed by the institutional imperative
- are candid: failures as well as successes are reported, and lessons are learned
- are decent
- do not use accounting gimmickry
- perform the ordinary extraordinarily well
- focus on the long term
- have tight cost control all the time
- repurchase stock when it is priced below intrinsic value
- make rational (from the shareholders' perspective) merger decisions.

- What to avoid:
  - macro economic forecasts
  - price charts
  - predicting tops and bottoms
  - impatience:
    - in looking for a stock to buy
    - in waiting for the market to reprice a stock after you have bought
    - in holding on to a good stock
  - going along with the crowd
  - gambling and derivatives
  - trusting Wall Street fund managers:
    - they cause market instability
    - their hyperkinetic activity wastes investors' money
    - they are absurdly risk averse
  - equations with Greek letters
  - being too ambitious
  - diversifying to mediocrity
  - being an active trader
  - turnarounds
  - ignoring your errors
  - glamorous companies you don't understand
  - worrying if prices fall
  - the new issue market

- When to sell:
  - if the business continues to increase intrinsic value at a satisfactory rate then never sell;
  - if the intrinsic value growth is expected to fall below a satisfactory rate then sell;
  - don't sell if the current price is temporarily above intrinsic value;
  - very occasionally it may be wise to sell if a superior investment presents itself;
  - long-term relationships bring understanding, loyalty and a higher

calibre team of managers. This factor may override some of the reasons for selling listed above.

Notes

1   Buffett quoted in Jim Rasmussen (1994) 'Billionaire Talks Strategy with Students', *Omaha World-Herald*, 2 January, p. 17S.
2   Buffett, W. (1995a) 'Warren Buffett Talks Business', The University of North Carolina, Center for Public Television, Chapel Hill.
3   *Ibid.*
4   Buffett, W. (1999). This material is copyrighted and is reproduced with the permission of the author.
5   *Ibid.*
6   Buffett, W. (1977). This material is copyrighted and is reproduced with the permission of the author.
7   *Ibid.*
8   Buffett, W. (1985). This material is copyrighted and is reproduced with the permission of the author.
9   Buffett, W. (1991). This material is copyrighted and is reproduced with the permission of the author.
10 Buffett, W. (1982). This material is copyrighted and is reproduced with the permission of the author.
11 Buffett, W. (1985). This material is copyrighted and is reproduced with the permission of the author.
12 Buffett, W. (1986). This material is copyrighted and is reproduced with the permission of the author.
13 Buffett, W. (1993). This material is copyrighted and is reproduced with the permission of the author.
14 Buffett, W. (1998). This material is copyrighted and is reproduced with the permission of the author.
15 Buffett, W. (1991). This material is copyrighted and is reproduced with the permission of the author.
16 Buffett, W. (1989). This material is copyrighted and is reproduced with the permission of the author.
17 Buffett, W. (1988). This material is copyrighted and is reproduced with the permission of the author.
18 Buffett, W. (1989). This material is copyrighted and is reproduced with the permission of the author.
19 Buffett, W. (1983). This material is copyrighted and is reproduced with the permission of the author.
20 Munger, C. T. and Koeppel, D. A. (1981), Annual Report of Blue Chip Stamps.
21 Buffett, W. (1995). This material is copyrighted and is reproduced with the permission of the author.

22 Buffett, W. (1984). This material is copyrighted and is reproduced with the permission of the author.

23 Buffett, W. (1990). This material is copyrighted and is reproduced with the permission of the author.

24 Buffett, W. (1985). This material is copyrighted and is reproduced with the permission of the author.

25 Buffett, W. (1986). This material is copyrighted and is reproduced with the permission of the author.

26 Rasmussen, J. (1994) 'Billionaire Talks Strategy with Students', *Omaha World-Herald*, 2 January, p. 17S.

27 Buffett, W. (1997). This material is copyrighted and is reproduced with the permission of the author.

28 Buffett, W. (1988). This material is copyrighted and is reproduced with the permission of the author.

29 *Ibid.*

30 Buffett, W. (1990). This material is copyrighted and is reproduced with the permission of the author.

31 Buffett, W. (1998). This material is copyrighted and is reproduced with the permission of the author.

32 *Ibid.*

33 Buffett, W. (1988). This material is copyrighted and is reproduced with the permission of the author.

34 Buffett, W. (1998). This material is copyrighted and is reproduced with the permission of the author.

35 Buffett, W. (1981). This material is copyrighted and is reproduced with the permission of the author.

36 Buffett, W. (1994). This material is copyrighted and is reproduced with the permission of the author.

37 Buffett, W. (1990). This material is copyrighted and is reproduced with the permission of the author.

38 Quoted in Buffett, W. (1990). This material is copyrighted and is reproduced with the permission of the author.

39 Buffett, W. (1988). This material is copyrighted and is reproduced with the permission of the author.

40 Buffett, W. (1998). This material is copyrighted and is reproduced with the permission of the author.

41 Buffett, W. (1997). This material is copyrighted and is reproduced with the permission of the author.

42 Buffett, W. (1992). This material is copyrighted and is reproduced with the permission of the author.

43 Buffett, W. (1987). This material is copyrighted and is reproduced with the permission of the author.

44 Buffett, W. (1989). This material is copyrighted and is reproduced with the permission of the author.

45 Buffett, W. (1984). This material is copyrighted and is reproduced with the permission of the author.

46 Buffett, W. (1978). This material is copyrighted and is reproduced with the permission of the author.

47 Buffett, W (1992). This material is copyrighted and is reproduced with the permission of the author.

48 Buffett, W. (1984). This material is copyrighted and is reproduced with the permission of the author.

49 Ibid.

50 Buffett, W. (1999). This material is copyrighted and is reproduced with the permission of the author.

51 Ibid.

52 Ibid.

53 A term which covers acquisitions and takeovers.

54 Buffett, W. (1982). This material is copyrighted and is reproduced with the permission of the author.

55 Buffett, W. (1994). This material is copyrighted and is reproduced with the permission of the author.

56 Buffett, W. (1982). This material is copyrighted and is reproduced with the permission of the author.

57 Buffett, W. (1981). This material is copyrighted and is reproduced with the permission of the author.

58 Ibid.

59 Buffett, W. (1994). This material is copyrighted and is reproduced with the permission of the author.

60 Ibid.

61 Buffett, W. (1978). This material is copyrighted and is reproduced with the permission of the author.

62 Buffett, W. (1994). This material is copyrighted and is reproduced with the permission of the author.

63 Buffett, W. (1986). This material is copyrighted and is reproduced with the permission of the author.

64 Buffett, W. (1984). This material is copyrighted and is reproduced with the permission of the author.

65 Buffett, W. (1985). This material is copyrighted and is reproduced with the permission of the author.

66 Buffett, W. (1982). This material is copyrighted and is reproduced with the permission of the author.

67 Buffett, W. (1985). This material is copyrighted and is reproduced with the permission of the author.

68 Buffett, W. (1986). This material is copyrighted and is reproduced with the permission of the author.

69 Ibid.

70 Buffett, W. (1984). This material is copyrighted and is reproduced with the

permission of the author.

71 Buffett, W. (1994). This material is copyrighted and is reproduced with the permission of the author.

72 Buffett, W. (1994b) Speech to the New York Society of Security Analysts, 6 December. Quoted in Lowe (1997). This material is copyrighted and is reproduced with the permission of the author.

73 Buffett, W. (1987). This material is copyrighted and is reproduced with the permission of the author.

74 Buffett, W. (1999). This material is copyrighted and is reproduced with the permission of the author.

75 Buffett, W. (1988). This material is copyrighted and is reproduced with the permission of the author.

76 Buffett, W. (1984). This material is copyrighted and is reproduced with the permission of the author.

77 Buffett, W. (1993). This material is copyrighted and is reproduced with the permission of the author.

78 *Ibid.*

79 *Ibid.*

80 *Ibid.*

81 Buffett, W. (1983). This material is copyrighted and is reproduced with the permission of the author.

82 *Ibid.*

83 *Ibid.*

84 Buffett, W. (1993). This material is copyrighted and is reproduced with the permission of the author.

85 Buffett, W. (1988). This material is copyrighted and is reproduced with the permission of the author.

86 Buffett, W. (1979). This material is copyrighted and is reproduced with the permission of the author.

87 Buffett speaking at Berkshire Hathaway Annual Meeting, Omaha (1994) . Quoted in Lowe (1997). © 1997 Janet C. Lowe. This material is used by permission of John Wiley & Sons, Inc.

88 Buffett, W. (1995). This material is copyrighted and is reproduced with the permission of the author.

89 Buffett, W. (1987). This material is copyrighted and is reproduced with the permission of the author.

90 Buffett, W. (1996). This material is copyrighted and is reproduced with the permission of the author.

91 Buffett, W. (1990). This material is copyrighted and is reproduced with the permission of the author.

92 Buffett, W. (1984). This material is copyrighted and is reproduced with the permission of the author.

93 Buffett, W. (1992). This material is copyrighted and is reproduced with the permission of the author.

94   Buffett, W. (1987). This material is copyrighted and is reproduced with the permission of the author.
95   Buffett, W. (1981). This material is copyrighted and is reproduced with the permission of the author.
96   Buffett, W. (1987). This material is copyrighted and is reproduced with the permission of the author.
97   *Ibid.*
98   *Ibid.*
99   *Ibid.*
100 *Ibid.*
101 *Ibid.*
102 Buffett, W. (1996b) An Owner's Manual. This material is copyrighted and is reproduced with the permission of the author.
103 *Ibid.*
104 Buffett, W. (1982). This material is copyrighted and is reproduced with the permission of the author.

PART TWO

The Valuegrowth
►method

8

The Valuegrowth investor

This book is a synthesis of ideas developed in a range of different fields of intellectual endeavour. Its main claim to originality is the way it brings together investment theory, strategic business analysis and the practical experience of the key thinkers on investment. The first part of the book described the investment philosophies of the world's most influential investors. The next stage is to fuse the main elements of these approaches to develop a philosophy and set of guidelines for the Valuegrowth investor.

The degree of overlap between the investment styles described in Part One is remarkable. This is especially interesting when we consider that the investors developed their approaches, for most part, independently (with the possible exception of Buffett who was initially strongly influenced by Graham, and later by Fisher and Munger). Their styles differed in some elements because they were each developed largely through heuristic learning (trial and error) and astute observation of market practice over many years. And yet, most of the investment principles formulated individually have great commonality with the principles formulated by all the other great investors. These thinkers did not all study the same university courses, live in the same city, read the same books or have the same mentor. And still, their philosophies are 70–80 per cent the same.

In contrast, when we compare this group with other stock pickers, such as momentum investors, technical analysts or day traders we see a high degree of difference. The percentage of style-features in common ranges from around 20 per cent to zero.

In pulling together the key elements of the great investment philosophies and adding the insights of modern strategic analysis we need to create a simple workable framework. It must be within the grasp of the ordinary investor and not for the exclusive use of those with a PhD in rocket science and access to a bank of computers. It will not, however, be a tool that can be mechanically employed. There will not be a set of simple rules requiring the user to simply plug in, say, price-earnings ratios, dividend yields, book-to-market ratios, etc., to obtain a buy or sell signal. No, all the great investors have said that while the concepts of intelligent investing are easy to take on board, the skill lies in the interpretation of data obtained, whether it is quantitative or qualitative. It is that skill of interpretation together with a focus on the really important elements creating value within a firm that are the keys to successes. No simple formula will ever be provided which will allow investors to outperform – if it was, the potential for out-performance would quickly disappear.

To have an edge we must develop relevant capabilities that the main body of the investing public either do not have or choose to ignore the importance of. All six of the investors discussed in this book bring up time and again how amazed they are that most investors follow the latest fad or pursue a strategy that has a track record of failure, even when the lessons of history and the observations of wiser counsels show a better way. The superior approach is not too complex, and yet most investors do not follow it despite the widespread availability of knowledge of the key elements.

Why don't they switch from the illusory glittering path being followed by the crowd? This largely remains a mystery. Perhaps it is a case of memories being so short that the lessons of more than three or four years ago are forgotten. Perhaps people are easily persuaded by 'expert' opinion, which is usually merely crude extrapolation. Perhaps it is groupthink on a vast scale. Or maybe it is because the investment philosophies discussed in this book require deep thought and hard work for successful implementation and most investors do not have the time, inclination or background knowledge to put in this effort. Professional fund managers may be working under strict rules of diversification that force them to hold hundreds of stocks. How can we expect them to spend the necessary time to thoroughly understand each company they buy into? Even if they acknowledge the importance of studying strategy and managerial quality they are unable to follow their better judgement. Moreover, for most fund managers there is little incentive to be different from the generality of managers. To stick your neck out and attempt a 'radical' investment strategy (such a Valuegrowth, with its low diversification and other non-conventional features) risks, first, ridicule, and second, the dire possibility of underperformance against a quarterly benchmark.

> ...The foolishness of the majority creates conditions that throw up bargains. ....

The foolishness of the majority creates conditions that throw up bargains. The irony is that if this book is a success, more investors will come over and join us on this side of the fence, and, in ceasing their foolish ways, make the stock market more efficient, thus reducing the opportunity to buy mispriced shares. But, on further reflection, this is no great problem. After all, Graham and Dodd published their book in 1934, Fisher first published in 1958, Lynch in 1990. Buffett has been making sagacious comments in his letters to shareholders since the 1960s, and still the opportunities abound. Long may it remain the case that we play poker with people who refuse to look at their hands or to think.

There are three parts to the Valuegrowth framework:

1. *Release time by avoiding expensive distractions*
   Valuegrowth investing is a demanding discipline requiring significant amounts of time. Many investors do not have this time available because they have allocated what time they do have to studying irrelevancies. The newspapers are full of such distractions, e.g. GDP and inflation predictions, stock tips and chart signals. By ignoring all those elements that do not contribute to an understanding of a business and its future owner earnings we release time and mental energy.

   There are many things the investor should avoid doing. These 'don'ts' fall under four categories:
   - don't trust the crystal-ball gazers
   - don't touch certain types of company
   - don't manage your portfolio conventionally
   - don't make investment too difficult.

2. *The Valuegrowth model*
   The Valuegrowth model is focused on the underlying business rather than the stock market. You should only invest in a business you understand. The business should have a strong economic franchise, be operated by honest and competent managers and have financial strength. The analysis of the strength of the franchise, the management and the finances should permit the estimation of owner earnings. The discounted value of all the future owner earnings is the intrinsic value of the firm. If this calculated value is significantly above the current price then there is a margin of safety and the stock should be bought. Note that this approach pays no attention to whether the stock is classified by conventional investors into 'a growth stock' or 'a value stock'. The Valuegrowth investor could one month be buying a stock with a low PER and high dividend yield, and the next month be purchasing a stock in a different company with a high PER, low yield, but with

strong growth of earnings potential. It doesn't matter, just as long as the value of the estimated discounted future owner earnings is greater by a large margin than the price being currently asked for by Mr Market.

There are two other crucial elements for successful Valuegrowth investing. The first is to restrict the size of the portfolio to a mere handful of stocks. To go beyond this would be to invite disaster because you are unlikely to be able to understand and monitor more than a few companies. Also, you would be moving too far down the diminishing marginal attractiveness curve. The second is to invest for the very long term. If you have the intention of staying with a company through numerous economic cycles and stock market fads and fashions you will have a different attitude when buying a stock than somebody buying for short-term gain. You will be looking for different attributes, and you won't invest unless you are sure that the company will still be dominating its market decades from now. Once purchased, you will have a different attitude to that of the investor who is concerned about short-term market vicissitudes. You won't be panicked, and you will avoid high transaction costs and taxes.

3. *Character traits and personal qualities*

A Valuegrowth investor has to develop a frame of mind that sets him or her apart from other investors. The qualities needed fall into six categories:

- independence of mind
- capacity for hard work
- the ability to make decisions with incomplete information
- resistance against the temptation to speculate
- patience, perseverance, fortitude and consistency
- willingness to admit and learn from mistakes.

EXPENSIVE DISTRACTIONS

There are dozens of distractions for investors. The most important are discussed below in four categories:

1. *Don't trust the crystal ball gazers*

The Valuegrowth investor pays little or no attention to the following:

- *Macro economic forecasts* A tremendous amount of time and energy can be saved by not trying to forecast GDP growth, unemployment statistics, purchasing managers' confidence levels and so on. Every day the newspapers are full of discussions on the next move in inflation, interest rates or currencies – much of it contradictory. The Valuegrowth investor should read the headline and move on. The latest statement from the Federal reserve or a report from an economic forecaster at a prestigious investment bank should be given less than ten seconds of your time. Guesses about the future of the economy are largely irrelevant to the investor who is focused on company analysis. Intrinsic value is determined by the owner earnings generated over a number of economic cycles. Whether GDP rises by 3 per cent or falls by 1 per cent in the next year has little impact on this calculation. And besides, forecasts are notoriously unreliable.

  As Table 8.1 shows the great investors have explicitly rejected the notion that there is any value to be had from trying to estimate the movement of economic aggregates. I suspect Neff agrees with the others; there is, however, no reference to the issue in his writing. It is clear that he certainly does not promote the use of macro economic data to determine stock buying and selling decisions.

Table 8.1 Crystal ball gazing don'ts

Investors explicitly advising us to avoid doing the following:	Lynch	Neff	Graham	Fisher	Buffett and Munger
Forecasting the economy	✔		✔	✔	✔
Engage in market timing	✔	✔	✔	✔	✔
Use chartism or technical analysis	✔	✔	✔	✔	✔
Engage in short-term selectivity	✔		✔	✔	✔

- *Market timing* Attempting to time purchases and sales to coincide with market highs and lows is wasteful. Unless you are exceptionally clever, and most Valuegrowth investors are not, you will not be able to call market tops and bottoms with any consistency. You are likely to be pessimistic and optimistic at precisely the wrong times.

Furthermore, buying and selling on the basis of a prediction of short-term market trends can be very expensive in terms of brokers' fees and tax. The great investors, with scores of years of experience insist that they cannot predict short-term movements. Why do people with a fraction of the experience of Buffett and Neff believe they can tell you where the market is headed next? These people are everywhere: on the television, at brokerage houses, in the newspapers. Ignore them all. They display a dangerous combination of supreme confidence and profound ignorance. They are people who don't have a clue but are paid to have a view.

- *Chartism and technical analysis* Do not look to price wiggles and other trend data to guide you. The great investors and academic researchers agree that you cannot, with any useful degree of regularity, outperform the stock market indexes by exploiting a perceived pattern in the statistical record. Past movements are of little relevance to the future.

- *Short-term selectivity* Buying shares on the strength of the corporation's or the industry's near-term business prospects – say, earnings over the next 6–12 months – is a pointless exercise and does not deserve to be termed security analysis. There are three potential problems:
  - analysts' fallibility means that the forecast can be wrong, and frequently are – the expected improvement does not take place;
  - even if the forecast is correct, the good prospects may already be reflected in the price;
  - the market behaves in strange ways and the price may not move the way it should.

2. *Don't touch these types of companies*
   It would save a lot of time if the Valuegrowth investor ignored certain types of company.

- *Hot stocks receiving lots of publicity* The hottest stocks in the hottest industry receive vast amounts of favourable publicity. The result is sky-high share prices often supported by nothing more than hope and thin air.

Table 8.2 Types of company don'ts

Investors explicitly advising us to avoid doing the following:	Lynch	Neff	Graham	Fisher	Buffett and Munger
Buy hot stocks receiving lots of publicity	✔	✔	✔	✔	✔
Buy technology stocks		✔			✔
Buy companies lacking a profit history or start up stocks	✔	✔	✔	✔	✔
Buy turnaround stocks					✔
Buy new issues					✔

- *Technology stocks* This is an optional don't. If you have particular knowledge of a technology and think you could analyze the strength of a business franchise in a rapidly changing technological environment, and assess the ability of a hi-tech managerial team to lead the company to long-term success, then you are entitled to ignore this don't. For those of us that don't know our DNA from our Megabyte Ram, it is best if we don't try to pretend we can understand a technological industry. Analyzing companies riding on the coat tails of science is especially difficult: avoid it if you have no discernible edge.

- *Companies lacking a profit history or start ups* Companies that are full of promises of future profits but lack solid evidence of actual profits should be shunned. It is impossible to assess the durability of the competitive advantage or the strength of the management of such firms. Often these are companies in industries in a constant state of flux. Investors are being enticed to fantasize about what might be. This is not a rational basis for investment with the principle of margin of safety at its heart. There are too many imponderables and the chance of error too great. Why take unreasoned risks when you could devote this energy to the analysis of stocks that do meet the criteria of a Valuegrowth investor?

- *Turnaround stocks* For many years Buffett tried buying companies that had fallen on hard times in the hope that they could be turned around. After repeated failure he concluded that the struggle was generally in vain as turnarounds seldom turn.

- *New issue stocks* Initial public offering stocks are generally fully priced. Bargains are few and far between in the primary market; richer pickings are available in the secondary market.

3. *Don't manage your portfolio conventionally*
   There are a number of approaches to stock selection and portfolio management that are inimical to investor wealth:

   - *Playing the 'in-and-out' game* Many investors have a tendency to churn their portfolio in a belief that they can take advantage of short-term price movements. Investors simply cannot profit from financial flip-flopping over the long run. Continually fiddling with the portfolio means that the investor (or, more properly entitled, speculator) does not become acquainted with the underlying businesses. In addition, he or she faces high transaction costs. Thousands of day traders have discovered that even if they were lucky enough to throw four sixes in a row the fifth throw of the dice brought disaster.

   - *Pulling the flowers and watering the weeds* Some investors seem to believe that it makes sense to automatically sell stocks that have risen in price, but hold on to those that have fallen. The maxim that 'you can't go broke taking a profit' is a foolish premise on which to sell a good company's stock. By selling when it has doubled you may miss out on the greatest part of its capital appreciation. A good stock can rise 10- or 20-fold in value.

     Equally silly is the tendency to hold on to a poor stock because you are afraid of crystallizing a loss. If the company fails to meet the Valuegrowth investor's criteria after purchase then the mistake should be admitted and the attempt to 'at least come out even' be abandoned. Money, thus released, can be invested in a good company.

Table 8.3 Portfolio management don'ts

Investors explicitly advising us to avoid doing the following:	Lynch	Neff	Graham	Fisher	Buffett and Munger
Playing the in-and-out game	✔	✔	✔	✔	✔
Pulling the flowers and watering the weeds	✔			✔	✔
Operate stop-loss orders	✔		✔		✔
Naïve contrarianism	✔	✔	✔	✔	✔
Accept consensus optimism or pessimism	✔	✔	✔	✔	✔

- *Stop-loss orders* Stop-loss orders are illogical. Just because the market, in its manic-depressive way, has caused your stock to fall from your buying price you should not automatically sell. If your analysis is sound then you should be a *buyer*, not a seller, at the lower price.

- *Simple contrarianism* Naïve contrarians are always zigging when the market is zagging. Such knee-jerk contrarians, who seem to bask in the warmth of just being different, are being as foolish as those that always follow the crowd. The true contrarian may take a different view to the generality of investors based on thorough analysis. Often, however, the Valuegrowth investor's conclusions will agree with the market consensus, or, at least, not disagree sufficiently to provide a margin of safety.

- *Accepting consensus optimism or pessimism* Periodically the market gets carried away with optimism or pessimism. The herd of investors over-react, pushing up the price of a favoured stock to irrational levels, while selling or ignoring stocks with intrinsic value much higher than the current price. At the top of bull markets vast numbers of stocks become the object of over-excitement. Speculation runs riot and people who, in normal circumstances behave as investors morph into speculators. Even Graham and Fisher seemed unable to resist the temptation to play the market for short-term gains in 1928–9. At times of market exuberance stock pickers seem to have an infinite capacity to believe in something good. On the other hand there are times when bad news becomes over represented in stock prices. The mood of investors can become so downbeat that even good news is ignored or spun into bad news.

The Valuegrowth investor must not get caught-up in these psychological traumas. Concentrate on analyzing a company and its long run owner earnings. Exploit the market madness and do not participate in it.

4. *Don't make investment too difficult*

The principles of good investment are straightforward – do not complicate the issue. Therefore, remember the following list of 'Don'ts':

- *Don't use equations with Greek letters in them* None of the investors studied in this book make use of modern financial theory constructs such as the capital asset pricing model with its β or portfolio theory with its focus on σ. And these are the relatively simple models being produced by business schools. Financial academic journals are full of complex mathematics that attempt to explain market behaviour, provide tools for valuation, or to understand and reduce risk. All of this is rejected as ephemera by the practitioners who rely on much simpler methods. And yet, these investors are highly successful.

  That's all very well, say the financial economists 'perhaps it does work in practice, but it'll never work in theory!' Could it be that the investors studied here are merely 'lucky', rather than that the stock market is inefficient in pricing shares, and this inefficiency is exploitable by those with superior techniques and judgement? Is it that the complex models will prove, in the end, to possess the truly valuable insights while the personal experiences and accumulated knowledge of the practitioners turns out to be of limited applicability? Perhaps. But I know whose judgement I trust, especially having discussed with university students over many years the difficulties of many of these academic models.

  It would seem that modern complex financial models sometimes allow you to perform average. To outperform, it is necessary to invest in under-priced businesses that you understand rather than in shares with particular correlation coefficients and covariances. Complex behaviour is not rewarded more than simple behaviour.

Table 8.4   Investment technique don'ts

Investors explicitly advising us to avoid doing the following:	Lynch	Neff	Graham	Fisher	Buffett and Munger
Using equations with Greek letters in them	✔	✔	✔	✔	✔
Use derivatives	✔				✔
Continually go for home runs	✔	✔	✔	✔	✔
Confine yourself to high liquidity stocks	✔			✔	✔

- *Don't use derivatives* Derivatives are an expensive way of reducing risk. The Valuegrowth investor knows that risk is reduced through a thorough understanding of the business, not by using hedging instruments. As for the use of derivatives for leveraging-up returns; this is gambling and should not be considered by an investor in businesses.

- *Don't continually try to go for home runs* Most of us are not brilliant at baseball. We have to add to the score by going for a series of base hits. Don't expect to find a series of spectacular winning stocks. Be consistent, persistent and patient. Stretching yourself to try and make extraordinary high gains can result in disaster. Be reasonable in your goals.

- *Don't confine yourself to high liquidity stocks* There are many bargains to be had in stocks that have a low market turnover. Many institutions ignore these stocks and thereby prepare the ground for bargains to be found by the Valuegrowth investor. Ease of divorce is no sound basis for a relationship.

THE VALUEGROWTH MODEL

The framework for Valuegrowth investing is shown in Fig. 8.1. We will take each factor in turn.

A business you understand

A very important distinction between a Valuegrowth investor and other stock pickers is that the former undertakes research to understand the business lying behind the stock. The vast majority of stock pickers either regard stocks as trading counters in a game, hardly aware that there is an underlying business, or buy and sell on the basis of the most superficial knowledge of the determinants of the company's long-term prosperity.

A successful investor is a successful evaluator of businesses. A favourite trick of the outstanding investors to get them into the frame of mind needed for business analysis rather than stock analysis is to imagine the purchase of 100 per cent of the company (or that they had inherited it). Furthermore, they imagine it is their only business asset. This helps them to focus on the key business questions, such as: how is the firm going to compete? What are its strengths and weaknesses? Who are the customers and how are they best served? How good are the managers? Will the firm be well positioned in 20 or 30 years' time? To find answers to these questions requires considerable work:

> ... **A successful investor is a successful evaluator of businesses.** ....

- talking to customers, employees, suppliers, competitors, etc., may reveal important clues (Scuttlebutt);

- a lot of reading needs to be done – e.g. annual reports of the company and its competitors, industry reports, trade magazines, newspapers, company announcements, competitor announcements;

- experiencing the company at first hand – trying the product, attending meetings of shareholders, quizzing the managers and directors; going to trade shows.

In developing knowledge about a company intelligent investors play to their strengths. If you already have some knowledge of an industry or particular firm, perhaps it would be wise to build on that foundation rather than try to analyze the unfamiliar and esoteric. Remember: investors do not get extra points for taking in a difficult analysis. (Olympic diving method of scoring degree-of-difficulty does not apply.) Easy to understand companies can have strong and enduring competitive advantages and the other important attributes that the Valuegrowth investor is looking for – the pay-off is the same as if you had correctly analyzed a company with many shifting and complex variables.

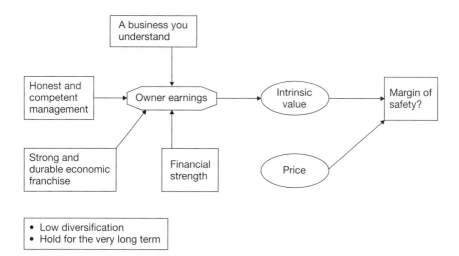

Figure 8.1 The Valuegrowth framework

The Valuegrowth investor does not step outside of his or her circle of competence. He or she takes care in drawing the circle of competence around those businesses that are understood so that there is no fuzziness at the edges. The perimeter must be clearly defined. This reduces the need for extraordinary cleverness; it allows concentration on avoiding acting stupidly. Familiarity with a company breeds confidence, insight and profit.

Honest and competent managers

There are many important indicators of good managers. The checklist below covers most of the elements a Valuegrowth investor looks for in managers:

- They are owner-orientated. The maximization of long-term shareholder wealth is their objective.
- They love the game and like to excel. Passionate about their work and relish the thrill of out-performance. Their enthusiasm and energy are infectious.
- They fight against the institutional imperative.
- Excellent in both day-to-day operational management and long-term planning.

- Highest integrity.
- Follow a rational (from the shareholder's perspective) dividend and share buy-back policy.
- Constantly bearing down on costs.
- Realistic in defining their area of special competence and act decisively on all matters within it. Perform the ordinary extraordinarily well.
- Ignore even the most enticing propositions falling outside of their area of special competence.
- They do not 'diworsify' the firm or allow shareholder wealth destroying mergers.
- Report bad news as well as good news.
- Treat staff with respect and fairness.
- Penny pinchers in the executive suite.
- No accounting gimmickry.
- Excellent marketing.
- Executive relations are characterized by a high degree of co-operation, mutual support, ingenuity, endeavour and respect.
- The management team has depth and breadth. Executive talent is nurtured so there are numerous vivid spirits.
- Decent behaviour.
- Non-executive directors who set standards and monitor performance.
- Confidence to take risks.
- Strong and well directed research capability. High quality of leadership in the co-ordination of researchers, and between the research team and the sales and production teams.

Strong and durable economic franchise

Valuegrowth investors look for a business that has a superior competitive position in an industry with excellent economics surrounded by a deep and dangerous moat, ensuring durability of its above average earning power. Analysis of the industry is needed to establish the average owner earnings within that industry. Analysis of the company's resources that give it competitive advantage within that industry will indicate the degree to which the firm can achieve higher than average owner earnings.

The combination of industry analysis and company resource analysis will shed light on the strength and durability of the economic franchise. Frameworks to assist these two types of analysis are presented in Chapters 9 and 10.

Financial strength

These are the standards required by a Valuegrowth investor:

- earnings can be increased while utilizing little additional capital (high return on equity);
- a large margin of safety on the issue of solvency – low debt to equity ratio, a good spread of debt maturity dates;
- excellent cost accounting systems.

Owner earnings and intrinsic value

We've managed to reach Chapter 8 without any mathematics. For a professor of finance this shows remarkable restraint – I hope you agree! More importantly, it demonstrates the lowly place of formulae and calculations in the evaluation of stocks. Most time should be spent assessing the qualities of the business – substantially a qualitative exercise. However, at some point we must calculate an intrinsic value that can then be compared with the current price to see if there is a margin of safety between the two to allow us to invest.

The following mathematical explanation is kept as simple as possible. However, to keep the discussion short it is assumed that the reader has some familiarity with basic financial calculations.[1]

The value of any financial asset is the discounted value of the future net cashflows. For common stock, intrinsic value is the discounted value of the owner earnings that can be taken out of a business during its remaining life. We discount because $1 received next year, or the year after, etc., does not have the same value to an investor as $1 received now.

Future owner earnings are determined by the strength and durability of the economic franchise, the quality of management and the financial strength of the business. Valuegrowth investing makes use of Buffett's definition of owner earnings, but with the additional factor in (c) and (d) of 'investment in all new value creating projects'. Owner earnings are defined as:

(a) reported earnings after tax; plus
(b) depreciation, depletion, amortization and certain other non-cash charges; less,
(c) the amount of capitalized expenditures for plant and machinery, etc. that a business requires to fully maintain its long-term competitive position, its unit volume and make investment in all new value creating projects; less,
(d) any extra amount for working capital that is needed to maintain the firm's long-term competitive position, unit volume and make investment in all new value creating projects.

Thus, there are two types of investment. First, that which is needed to permit the firm to continue to maintain its existing competitive position at the current level of output. Second, investment in value creating growth opportunities beyond the current position.

So, for example, Cotillo Inc. has reported earnings after tax for the most recent year of $16.3 million. In drawing up the income (profit and loss) account deductions of $7.4 million were made for depreciation, $152,000 for the amortization of intangible assets and $713,000 of Goodwill was written off. It is estimated that an annual expenditure of $8.6 million on plant, machinery, etc., will be required for the company to maintain its long-term competitive position and unit volume. For the sake of simplicity we will assume that no further monies will be needed for extra working capital to maintain long-term competitive position and unit volume. Also, Cotillo has no new value creating projects.

The trading record of Cotillo Inc. has been remarkably stable in the past and is unlikely to alter in the future. It is therefore reasonable to use the above figures for all the future years. This would result in an estimated annual owner earnings of $15.965 million (see Table 8.5).

Table 8.5   Cotillo Inc. owner earnings

		$000s
(a)	Reported earnings after tax	16,300
	plus	
(b)	Depreciation, depletion, amortization and other non-cash	
	charges (7,400 + 152 + 713)	8,265
		24,565
	less	
(c) and (d)	Expenditure on plant, equipment, working capital etc. required to maintain long-term competitive position, unit volume and investment in new projects	8,600
		15,965

The discounted value of all the annual owner earnings stretching to an infinite horizon is the annual owner earnings divided by the appropriate discount rate, when each year's owner earnings are identical to all the other year's and the first is to be received a year from now:

$$\text{Intrinsic value} = \frac{\text{Annual owner earnings}}{\text{Discount rate}}$$

The discount rate is set as the required rate of return for an asset in this risk class. It is equal to the opportunity cost of placing funds in this stock rather than another one with equal risk. In other words, if the next best alternative use for the money shareholders put into Cotillo pays a return of 10 per cent, and that alternative has the same level of risk as Cotillo's shares, then the discount rate for Cotillo's shares is 10 per cent.

In the case of Cotillo the intrinsic value = $159.65 million, if we take the discount rate to be 10 per cent (the derivation of the discount rate is discussed below):

$$\text{Intrinsic value} = \frac{\$15.965m}{0.10} = \$159.65m$$

It was stated earlier that intrinsic value is determined by the owner earnings that can be *taken out* of the business during its remaining life. Logically the management of Cotillo should pay out the full $15.956 million each year to shareholders if the managers do not have investment projects within the firm that will generate returns of 10 per cent or more because shareholders can get 10 per cent return elsewhere for the same level of risk as holding a share in Cotillo. If the managers come across another project that promises a return of exactly 10 per cent shareholder wealth ($159.65 million) will be unchanged whether the company invests in this or chooses to ignore the project and continues with the payment of all owner earnings each year. If the management discover, in a future year, a value creating project that will produce, say, a 15 per cent rate of return (for the same level of risk as the existing projects) then shareholders will welcome a reduction in dividends during the years of additional investment. The total value of discounted future owner earnings will rise and intrinsic value will be greater than $159.65 million if such a project is undertaken.

GROWTH OF OWNER EARNINGS

So, let's assume that Cotillo now has a series of new value creating (i.e. generating returns greater than 10 per cent) projects it can invest in. By investing in these projects owner earnings will rise by 5 per cent in each future year (owner earnings are on the one hand decreased by the need for additional investment under (c) and (d), but, on the other hand, reported earnings are boosted under (a) to produce a net 5 per cent growth). Thus:

		$m
Most recent owner earnings		15.965
Next year's owner earnings:		
$15.965 (1 + 0.5)$	=	16.763
In two years:		
$15.965 (1 + 0.05)^2$	=	17.601
In three years :		
$15.965 (1 + 0.05)^3$	=	18.481
and so on…		

Each of these future owner earnings is then discounted at the appropriate rate:

$$\text{Intrinsic value} \; = \; \frac{\$16.763\text{m}}{1 + 0.10} \; + \; \frac{\$17.601\text{m}}{(1 + 0.10)^2} \; + \; \frac{\$18.481\text{m}}{(1 + 0.10)^3} \; +...+...+...$$

$$\text{Intrinsic value} \; = \; \$15.239\text{m} \; + \; \$14.564\text{m} \; + \; \$13.885\text{m} \; +...+...+...$$

This method of calculating intrinsic value could take a long time because owner earnings received decades into the future contribute to intrinsic value and therefore need to be discounted and included in the formula. Don't be disheartened though. The long (infinite) formula with a constant growth of owner earnings from one year to the next can be simplified and the whole calculation completed in under 30 seconds. The formula below is equivalent to the one above – but much more simple to use:

$$\text{Intrinsic value} \; = \; \frac{\text{Owner earnings next year}}{\text{Discount rate} - \text{Growth rate}}$$

Don't be misled: This formula explicitly includes only next year's owner earnings, but the formula as a whole represents the discounting of *all* the future annual owner earnings growing at a constant rate.

So, if we apply it to our example, Cotillo, the intrinsic value becomes $335.26 million, *viz*:

$$\text{Intrinsic value} \; = \; \frac{\$16.763\text{m}}{0.10 - 0.05} \; = \; \$335.26\text{m}$$

Note that even a relatively modest rate of growth in owner earnings makes a large difference to the intrinsic value. A growth rate of 5 per cent more than doubles intrinsic value (in the case where the discount rate is 10 per cent) compared with the situation where no growth is expected to occur.

The discount rate

The discount rate to use is the rate of return available on investments of the same risk class. If an investment is made in US government bonds there is virtually no risk of default and those instruments may, for practical purposes, be considered risk free. Investors in 20-year US bonds are currently (early 2001) demanding a rate of return of 5.5 per cent. If we

were to lend money by buying a financial instrument from another organization that has a similarly tiny risk of default we would need a return of
5.5 per cent because we have an opportunity cost of this amount. That is,
the next best use of the funds (investing in US government bonds) yields
5.5 per cent. Why would we accept anything less?

Warren Buffett has stated that he uses the rate of return offered on US
government bonds when he discounts owner earnings. He justifies this on
the grounds that the companies in which he invests are very safe. He has
so thoroughly analyzed the management, the strategic position and the
finances that he is convinced there is little chance of default (or, in the case
of common stocks, of non-payment of dividends and liquidation).

On this point I have to disagree with Buffett. When a share is purchased, the buyer is accepting a higher level of risk than would be the case
if a US government bond is bought. Even great companies like Coca-Cola,
Disney and the *Washington Post* are subject to risk. Perhaps a new technology will wipe out their competitive advantage, perhaps a war will destroy
their global growth strategy. Whatever it is, there is a reasonable expectation that things can go wrong. When profits do plunge and companies are
in trouble the common stockholders are at the back of the queue to receive
payouts (annual dividend or liquidation payments), behind a long list of
interested parties, from bondholders to the tax authorities.

Because the equity investors are exposed to loss of capital (or merely
poor returns for long periods) they demand whatever rate of return is
available if they invest in a risk free investment (e.g. US government
bonds) *plus* an extra annual rate called the equity risk premium. That is,
the required rate of return on a share is the risk free rate of return (r_f) plus
the equity risk premium (RP):

Required rate of return, $k_e = r_f + RP$

Investors will not take an investment risk unless they are compensated for
their risk exposure.

It is impossible for us to measure the risk premium investors will
require for the future. What we can do is observe the historical risk
premium on the average share and use this as a proxy for the future
orientated equity risk premium, if we assume that currently and in the
future investors demand the same additional return to compensate them
for accepting the additional risk of investing in shares that they received
in the past. We need to measure the extra returns that investors receive on

shares compared with a risk free investment over a long period of time. It is no use observing the return on equity compared with government bonds over a year or two because this could vary from one year to the next depending on stock market and bond market vicissitudes (in some years, e.g. 2000, the returns on equities will be less than that on bonds!). However, over many decades we can observe the additional return investors have received for holding an average share.

Elroy Dimson, Paul Marsh and Mike Staunton, of the London Business School in association with ABN Amro,[2] published a study of equity risk premiums for a number of countries for periods of up to 101 years (start of 1900 to end of 2000). For US quoted equities they discovered that investors received an average annual premium of 5.0 per cent over the long-term US government bond return. That is, for an average year in the 20th Century the average share gave an additional 5.0 per cent return compared with long-term government bonds.

Another study was conducted by Fred Cleary based on data compiled by The University of Chicago, Graduate School of Business' Center for Research into Security Prices and published in Barclays Capital's Equity – Gilt Study 2001.[3] He examined returns over the 75 years to December 2000. He estimated an equity risk premium of 5.3 per cent per annum (over 20-year US government bonds).

So, on the one hand we have Buffett saying that a risk premium of zero should be applied and on the other we have evidence that the average share has given investors a risk premium of 5.0 or 5.3 per cent. What are we to do? In early 2001 should we discount the future owner earnings by the returns offered on a 20-year US government bond, i.e. 5.5 per cent? That is, $k_e = r_f + RP = 0.055 + 0 = 0.055$, or, should we add the risk premium displayed on an average share over a long period of time? That is (taking the Barclays Capital equity risk premium) the discount rate is,

$r_f + RP = 0.055 + 0.053 = 0.108$, 10.8%?

The answer lies, as usual in finance, in judgement. In other words there is no hard and fast rule that we can use mechanically. We have to judge whether the share we are evaluating is more risky or less risky than the average. If more risky then the risk premium should be more than 5.3 (or 5.0) per cent and the required rate is greater than 10.8 per cent. If less risky the discount rate will be less than 10.8 (or 10.5) per cent.

Here are a few thoughts to guide that judgement: To reach the stage of an intrinsic value calculation a stock has passed a number of tests. The underlying business is sound and stable with a high degree of predictability (at least, compared with most firm's). It has a strong and durable competitive advantage in an industry with good economic characteristics. The management is honest and capable, and the finances are strong. Such businesses are, arguably, subject to less risk than average. Therefore we can justify making use of a risk premium that is smaller than that for the average stock over the last 100 years. The size of the reduction is very difficult to pinpoint. Financial economic theory is virtually useless for this (despite mountains of academic papers on the subject) and we have to admit that we are guessing. My guess is that the risk premium is not zero, nor is it as high as 5 per cent for shares that have passed all the other tests of Valuegrowth investing. To err on the side of caution in calculating intrinsic value I suggest that the premium to be used should be closer to 5 per cent than to zero. I will use 4.5 per cent, but would not argue against anyone who chose a different figure within the parameters of 0–5 per cent.

Thus, with some humility I will plump for a discount rate that happens (purely by chance, you understand) to be a nice round 10 per cent for US stock evaluation in early 2001:

$$k_e = r_f + RP = 0.055 + 0.045 = 0.10$$

Finance, as a discipline, continually strives towards being a scientific and quantitative subject, but at the higher level we are often kidding ourselves. We find that it is fundamentally qualitative and artistic. At least, that is the case if we want to apply it to real world problems. Whew! That statement will upset a lot of academic colleagues, many of whom would, with great confidence, provide you with a value for the discount rate to two decimal points. Trust such a number at your peril.

The discount rate will vary depending on the changing rate of return on government long-term bonds. If we imagine that in 2003, 20-year US government bonds are offering 7.5 per cent, then the discount rate would move to 12 per cent:

$$r_f + RP = 0.075 + 0.045 = 0.12$$

The risk premium changes very slowly over time, if at all, but the discount rate can move significantly as risk free rates alter.

Risk premiums have been calculated for stocks in other countries. These are shown in Table 8.6. For the UK in early 2001 the rate of return offered on a 20-year UK government bond was 4.7 per cent. If a risk premium of 4.4 per cent is added then the required rate of return on an average share (the discount rate) will be:

$k_e = r_f + RP$
$k_e = 0.047 + 0.044 = 0.091$, or 9.1%

If the company under evaluation passes all the other Valuegrowth tests then a discount rate lying between 4.7 per cent and 9.1 per cent (but with a bias toward the upper limit) would seem appropriate.

Eurozone long-term government bond rates are about 5.2 per cent in early 2001. So, for example, if an average German company was being studied the discount rate would be about 11.9 per cent:

$k_e = r_f + RP = 0.052 + 0.067 = 0.119$, or 11.9%

A German firm that passed the Valuegrowth tests would have a lower discount rate.

For Japan long-term government bond interest rates were exceptionally low at 2 per cent in 2001. Thus for the average stock a discount rate of 2 + 6.3 = 8.3% would seem appropriate, with the rate for a Valuegrowth stock being less than this, but above 2 per cent.

Table 8.6   **Equity risk premiums**

	% Per annum	Source
Australia 101 years 1900–2000	6.3	Dimson et al.
Belgium 100 years 1900–2000	3.0	Dimson et al.
Canada 101 years 1900–2000	4.5	Dimson et al.
Denmark 85 years 1915–2000	2.2	Dimson et al.
France 101 years 1900–2000	5.0	Dimson et al.
Germany 99 years 1900–2000 (ex. 1922/23)	6.7	Dimson et al.
Ireland 101 years 1900–2000	4.0	Dimson et al.
Italy 101 years 1900–2000	5.0	Dimson et al.
Japan 101 years 1900–2000	6.3	Dimson et al.
Netherlands 101 years 1900–2000	4.7	Dimson et al.

Table 8.6   continued

	% Per annum	Source
Spain 101 years 1900–2000	3.2	Dimson et al.
Sweden 101 years 1900–2000	5.5	Dimson et al.
Switzerland 89 years 1911–2000	2.7	Dimson et al.
UK 101 years 1900–2000	4.4	Barclays
UK 101 years 1900–2000	4.4	Dimson et al.
US 101 years 1900–2000	5.0	Dimson et al.
US 75 years 1926–2000	5.3	Barclays
US 50 years 1951–2000	6.5	Barclays

Sources: Barclays Equity-Gilt Study 2001, Barclays Capital (2001); and Elroy Dimson, Paul Marsh and Mike Staunton (2001), Millennium Book II: 101 years of Investment Returns, ABN Amro/LBS, copyright © Dimson, Marsh and Staunton – ABN Amro/LBS.

MARGIN OF SAFETY

Valuegrowth analysis is subject to uncertainty. Not only are we dealing with estimation of future events with a variety of possible outcomes, but there is large room for doubt about some of the variables used in the calculation of intrinsic value. We could be wrong about many things, for example:

- *Economic franchise evaluation* Perhaps the strength or durability of the competitive advantage and the characteristics of the industry are not as good as we think they are.
- *Management evaluation* Judging people, especially if you don't work with them day-in-day-out, can be extremely difficult.
- *Financial strength* Outsiders may not be in possession of the full facts.
- *Discount rate* There is ample scope for different views on the most appropriate discount rate.

Because there is so much potential for getting it wrong it is necessary to build-in a large margin of safety. It is only when the difference between intrinsic value and current stock price is screaming at you that you should buy.

LOW DIVERSIFICATION

The Valuegrowth method requires a detailed knowledge of each stock purchased. Such depth of understanding is impossible if there are more than a dozen companies in the portfolio. Indeed, most of us could only cope with three to seven stocks before losing track. Investors that can devote a great deal of time to stock selection may be able to follow the fortunes of 12 companies. The rest of us have to make a judgement as to the appropriate number of stocks that we can deal with taking into account the time and energy we can spend on the exercise.

Remember risk is related to the amount of high quality intellectual effort put into the analysis of a security. This effort must be concentrated. Beyond the first four or five securities in a portfolio risk is not reduced much by further diversification on the principles of portfolio theory. But further diversification does *increase* the chance of failure to understand the businesses underlying the stocks, and therefore *increases* risk – this increased risk factor quickly outweighs the benefits of greater diversification. Diversification is frequently undertaken because it is a protection against ignorance. Conventional stock pickers do not take the time to become knowledgeable about their companies and so, in their fear of the unknown, grasp for the safety of spreading the fund far and wide. This Noah's Ark method of investing results in mediocre performance at best – you cannot watch all the eggs in all your baskets.

Valuegrowth investors must increase the intensity of analysis of particular businesses to reduce risk. They must not move too far down the diminishing marginal attractiveness curve. It is too difficult to be smart about investment choices day after day. Expect to make only a few key investment decisions in a lifetime (remember Buffett's imaginary punch card with a maximum of 20 punches on it) and to concentrate on being clever a few times.

HOLDING FOR THE VERY LONG TERM

Expect to hold stocks for a very long time. The Valuegrowth investor almost never sells. This expectation helps to focus the mind when analyzing a stock for purchase – you will concentrate on the durability of the firm's advantages rather than on short-term stock market movements.

You will ask questions such as will the company still be the strongest in its sector in 30 years? Rather than questions such as, is market sentiment moving away from telecoms and towards defensive stocks this month?

An 'almost never sell' policy also means that you are not continually distracted by the illusory greenness of the grass on the other side of the fence. If the company has passed the tests of the Valuegrowth method then it has many strengths, and you are unlikely to find alternative investments that possess all of these qualities. If you have held a stock for a long time you become familiar with the company, its management and its industry. You are able to follow the evolving story and become increasingly knowledgeable.

Also, a policy of short-term stock holding can result in very burdensome transaction costs and taxes. Plenty of other people become rich (e.g. brokers) while your wealth diminishes.

There are, however, times when it is necessary to sell a stock:

- When a mistake has been made in the original analysis – the factual background is significantly less favourable than believed at the time of purchase.

- The stock no longer qualifies under Valuegrowth investment rules. Through the passage of time, changes in the firm's competitive qualities, the industry, the management or its finances, mean that the stock fails to have clearly visualized potential for high return. The story is no longer sound relative to the price.

- An even better opportunity arises. This is very rare and the investor should be very sure before dropping a well-understood company for a new one where the negatives may be hidden from view.

CHARACTER TRAITS AND PERSONAL QUALITIES

To be successful investors we need to develop the ability to keep emotions from corroding the advantages brought by the Valuegrowth framework. The following qualities are needed:

- *Independence of mind* The market is full of beguiling rationales for the current consensus view. The Wall Street crowd has a tendency to follow a few lead steers like manic-depressive lemmings. Don't accept Mr

Market's judgement of value. Think independently. Gather facts, apply tests and standards, and critically evaluate the business using sound principles. If you do all these things you will have confidence and courage that comes from knowledge, experience and sober reflection. It does not matter that the popular view is different to yours. Be prepared to cut yourself off from the crowd and zig when the rest of the market is zagging. Be prepared to think and to act unconventionally – to go with your own reasoning. Be somewhere that allows you to ponder the really important issues – get away from the day-to-day stock market stimuli. Don't be intimidated by the 'professional investor'. Remember: the vast majority of 'professionals' fail to outperform their indices. The Valuegrowth investor is far superior to most Wall Street analysts.

- *Capacity for hard work* Valuegrowth investing requires full commitment. A good knowledge of strategic analysis, accounting, finance and economics are required. A willingness to spend time in scuttlebutt is necessary. The rewards of the Valuegrowth method are huge, but it asks for constant toil.

- *The ability to make decisions with incomplete information* In investment we are making judgements about the future. Owner earnings that are yet to occur cannot be stated with any great precision and yet we must still form a view. If you are uncomfortable with analysis based on shaky numbers and ball park figures; if you require facts that are provable before you can make a decision then you will not make a good Valuegrowth investor. Investment is a probability-based art form. The successful investors tilt the odds in their favour.

- *Resistance against the temptation to speculate* Discipline is needed to stick to sound investing criteria. This is especially the case in bull markets when you see speculators making vast returns. Don't be tempted to play catch-up hoping to get your money out before the crash and return to thorough-investigation-with-a-margin-of-safety-investing later. You are more likely to go down with the rest, as Fisher and Graham discovered in 1929. You must resist emotions and gut feelings. Like the dog in Aesop's Fable stick with what you know to be good rather than lose it trying to grab for deceptively better offerings. Buffett is content to aim for 15 per cent annual appreciation. Why should we think we can safely aim at more than that?

- *Patience, perseverance, fortitude and consistency* Valuegrowth investors are not impatient to buy stocks. Stand on the plate and let the bad pitches pass by. Do not drop your standards.

  Patience, perseverance and fortitude are also needed when the stock price falls after purchase. Doubts about the wisdom of the investment start to appear. If you have done your homework and you are convinced that the stock represents good value then a falling price creates buying opportunities if you hold your nerve. Market pessimism is the friend of the investor, but it takes a strong will to stand against the tide of opinion.

  Don't be impatient to sell – hold on to good stocks. It sometimes seems ages before the market recognizes the intrinsic value of a stock. If you hold on you can benefit from both rising earnings and an increase in the price-earnings ratio. On other occasions the price can rapidly appreciate and you are showing a good rate of return. The temptation is then to cash in your chips. This often needs to be resisted too. The best part of the return may yet be to come.

  The Valuegrowth investor is consistent in his or her investment activity. Do not switch investment styles. Have a regular routine of investment following best practice. Even following Valuegrowth investment principles there will be down years. In these periods resist the temptation to give up and try the latest fashion. Also, consistency is needed in continuing to follow the story of the company. On a regular basis investigate if the story is still strong enough for you to hold.

- *Willingness to admit and learn from mistakes* Mistakes are bound to occur in investment. It is impossible to be right about companies all the time. In fact, excellent performance only requires us to be right six times out of ten. When a mistake does occur don't sweep it under the carpet because you can't bear to look at it and be reminded of your 'failure'. Face up to it, examine it and learn from it. In this way the quality of your investment decisions will improve. Also, learn from the mistakes of others – 'you can't live long enough to make them all yourself' (Martin Vanbee).

KEY PRINCIPLES OF VALUEGROWTH INVESTING

Release time by avoiding expensive distractions:

- Don't trust the crystal ball gazers:
  - ignore macro economic forecasts
  - do not try to time the market
  - ignore charts and other technical analysis
  - do not engage in short-term selectivity.

- Don't touch the following types of companies:
  - hot stocks receiving lots of publicity
  - technology stocks
  - companies lacking a profit history and start-ups
  - turnaround stocks
  - new issue stocks.

- Don't manage your portfolio conventionally:
  - don't play the 'in-and-out' game
  - don't pull the flowers and water the weeds
  - don't use stop-loss orders
  - don't engage in simple contrarianism
  - don't accept consensus optimism or pessimism.

- Don't make investment too difficult:
  - don't use equations with Greek letters in them
  - don't use derivatives
  - don't continually try to go for home runs
  - don't confine yourself to high liquidity stocks.

The Valuegrowth model:

- Invest only in businesses you understand. Do not step outside your circle of competence.

- Honest and competent managers.

- Strong and durable economic franchise.

- Financial strength.

- The sum of discounted owner earnings equals intrinsic value.

- The discount rate used is very difficult to establish. Its value can be narrowed down to between the current risk free rate of return plus a risk premium of zero and the current risk free rate of return plus a risk premium of 5 per cent for US stocks.

- A high margin of safety between the price and intrinsic value should allow for errors made in judging a wide variety of vital inputs to the intrinsic value calculation.
- Do not diversify beyond a handful of stocks.
- Expect to hold stocks for a very long time.

Sell if:

- a mistake is made in analysis
- the stock no longer qualifies under the Valuegrowth investment rules
- a better opportunity arises.

Character traits and personal qualities:

- independence of mind
- capacity for hard work
- the ability to make decisions with incomplete information
- resistance against the temptation to speculate
- patience, perseverance, fortitude and consistency
- willingness to admit and learn from mistakes.

Notes

1   If you need your memory jogged you may find Chapters 2 (especially the appendix) and 17 of *Corporate Financial Management* by Arnold, G. (2002) London: F.T. Prentice Hall useful.
2   Dimson, E., Marsh, P. and Staunton, M. ABN Amro/LBS (2001).
3   Barclays Capital (2001).

APPENDIX 8.1: TWO STAGE GROWTH

The standard growth model is of practical use whether truly constant growth is anticipated or the growth rate is expected to vary around a trend rate. However, there will be cases when growth is expected to be very different for different periods of the future. For example, imagine that Cotillo has recently developed a new technology. Over the next three years it will be able to exploit an extraordinary competitive advantage and grow owner earnings at a rate of 25 per cent per year. Unfortunately, competitors are expected to respond and after the third year owner earnings growth will slow to 5 per cent per year, as similar and substitute products appear on the market. This 5 per cent rate is expected to continue to an infinite horizon. To calculate intrinsic value it is necessary to discount each of the first three years' owner earnings individually and then add the discounted value of all owner earnings for year 4 onwards see Table 8.7.

Table 8.7	Intrinsic value calculation with two stages of earnings growth

Year	Amount of owner earnings	Owner earnings discounted @ 10 per cent to Time 0 (now)
1	$15.965m x (1 + 0.25) = $19.956m	$\dfrac{\$19.956m}{1 + 0.1} = \$18.142m$
2	$15.965m x (1 + 0.25)^2 = $24.945m	$\dfrac{\$24.945m}{(1 + 0.1)^2} = \$20.616m$
3	$15.965m x (1 + 0.25)^3 = $31.182m	$\dfrac{\$31.182m}{(1 + 0.1)^3} = \$23.427m$
4 to infinity	First, calculate year 4 owner earnings: 31.182 x (1 + 0.05) = $32.741m Second, calculate intrinsic value of all the owner earnings from year 4 to infinity as though you were standing at time 3 (three years from now): $V_3 = \dfrac{\Omega_4}{k_e - g}$ Where Ω_4 = year 4's owner earnings, g = rate of growth in owner earnings, constant for all years to infinity, k_e = discount rate. $V_3 = \dfrac{\$32.741m}{0.1 - 0.05} = \$654.82$ Third, discount this value at time 3 to time 0:	$\dfrac{\$654.82m}{(1 + 0.1)^3} = \$491.976m$
	Total of discounted owner earnings for years 1, 2 and 3 plus the years 4 to infinity	$18.142 + $20.616 + $23.427 + $491.976 = **$554.161m**

APPENDIX 8.2: A DISCUSSION ON THE EFFECT OF TAXATION ON THE DISCOUNT RATE

Taxation complicates matters. Technically, because we are using the after-tax owner earnings figures we should also use the after-tax discount rate. The equity risk premium part of the discount rate is already calculated after-tax, as the dividends on shares have been taxed. If all investors are taxed on the returns received from long-term government bonds then the risk free rate should be expressed after the deduction of the tax payment. So, if bonds are paying 5.5 per cent pre-tax and the taxation rate is 30 per cent the post-tax rate is 3.85 per cent. The problem with using this figure is that many (most) financial securities are not taxed. This is usually because the institutions holding the security (e.g. a pension fund) are exempt from taxes. As a result we are left in a quandary as to what the effective after tax risk free rate is for an 'average' investor. Because of the difficulty we will err on the side of caution and use the current pre-tax risk free rate in our discount rate calculations.

9

The analysis of industries

There are two main influences on the strength and durability of an economic franchise. The first is the structure of the industry. The Value-growth investor should look for an industry in which companies generally exhibit high returns. There are some crucial factors that determine the average long-run rate of return on capital employed of firms in an industry. This chapter provides a framework for identifying these factors. The second, covered in Chapter 10, is the ability of a specific firm to rise above the others in its industry and generate exceptionally high long run rates of return on capital employed. This is determined by the possession of resources that give it a competitive advantage. A firm may have one or more of these extraordinary resources. Sometimes an extraordinary resource is tangible, such as ownership of the only rock pit in Brooklyn, but more often it is intangible, e.g. the quality of relationships with suppliers, customers and government that have been built up over many years, or the collective tacit knowledge held by the managerial team. Reputations, brands, attitude and competences can all contribute to a competitive edge. Chapter 10 provides a framework for examining the company so as to reveal those resources that give durable advantage (extraordinary resources) as well as those that give competitive parity (ordinary resources). The Valuegrowth investor is looking for a firm that is both in an industry with sustainable high returns on capital and one that possesses extraordinary resources that enables it to stand head and shoulders above its competitors or potential competitors in its industry, both now and for decades to come.

THE COMPETITIVE FLOOR[1]

In a perfectly competitive industry structure companies can only achieve a 'normal' rate of return. That is, where shareholders receive a rate of return that only just induces them to put money into the firm and hold it there. If returns dropped by 0.1 per cent then investors will withdraw capital from the firm and invest in an alternative with the same risk level providing the full 'normal' rate of return – eventually the firm will go out of business. With perfect competition the rate of return cannot rise above the normal level to give a supernormal return. Imagine if an industry did give a very high rate of return temporarily because of, say, a rise in the price of the product: new entrants to the industry or additional investment by existing competitors would quickly result in any supernormal return being competed away to take the industry back to the point where the return available is merely that appropriate for the risk level.

Obviously, a perfectly competitive industry is not attractive for investors. Valuegrowth investors need to search for an industry with a wide gap between the price of the product and its cost; producing a high rate of return. The problem is that competitive forces within industries tend to continually push for the gap between price and cost to narrow – toward the competitive floor – and thus put downward pressure on the rate of return on invested capital. However, there are some industries in which the competitive forces are weak permitting supernormal returns to persist over a long period. The Valuegrowth investor needs to search out those industries in which the average firm has a high degree of durable pricing power.

THE FIVE COMPETITIVE FORCES

Michael Porter produced a framework for analyzing the forces driving returns to the perfectly competitive level. It goes way beyond simply analyzing the degree of rivalry between existing competitors and the potential for entry of new competitors. He pointed out that customers, suppliers, and substitutes are also 'competitors' to the firms in an industry in the sense that they impose constraints on the firms achieving supernormal returns. For example, Heinz has few direct competitors because its brand sets it apart and it has an unrivalled distribution system. It faces little threat from the entry of new competitors because the new entrant would need decades to build the necessary brand image and distribution capability. However, Heinz's management are worried because of the increasing power of its customers, the major supermarket chains. The giant food retailers are in a position to ask for more of the value generated by the sale of the product – or put more crudely, they can hammer Heinz on price. Take another case: the distribution-of-music industry (record producers and retailers). Chief executives here are scared witless. It is not that particularly strong current competitors are taking greater market share and thereby becoming stronger. This is happening, but it is not the main cause of sleepless nights. Nor are they worried about the entry of new record labels and retail chains. These have come and gone before and industry returns have remained high. No, their nightmare comes in the form of a new technology that allows consumers to download music by file-swapping on the Internet for virtually nothing. Thus a substitute distribution system is a competitive threat to the entire industry.

In a perfectly competitive situation entry is free and existing firms have no bargaining power over suppliers or customers. In addition, rivalry between existing firms is fierce because products are identical. In reality, few industries resemble perfect competition. As J. K. Galbraith once observed, the greatest source of insecurity in business is competition and so managers strive constantly to move as far away from perfect competition as possible. How far they travel is determined by the strength of the five forces shown in Fig. 9.1.

The five forces determine the industry structure, which, in turn determines the long-run rate of return for the industry. Some industries have an

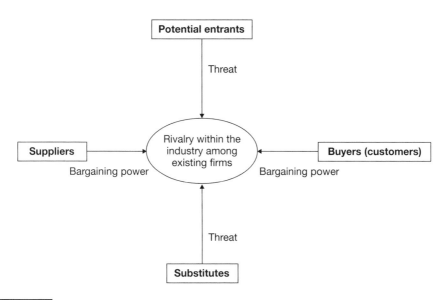

Figure 9.1 The five forces driving industry competition[2]

appalling position vis-à-vis the five forces and thus make very poor returns. Take steel production in Europe for example. Here are some of the largest and most efficient plants in the world. As things stand the steel firms could hire the best team of managers in the world but they would still not make good rates of return. All the five forces are against them. The suppliers of raw materials tend to be large groups with strong bargaining power (three producers dominate the world's iron-ore business, for instance). Many of their customers are enormous groups (particularly the big six car makers who are quite prepared to switch steel supplier unless the keenest prices are offered). There are dozens of low-cost new entrants in Asia and the Soviet Union chomping at the bit to take market share. Within Europe there is intense rivalry between the existing players because of the need for each participant to produce at a high volume due to the necessity of spreading high fixed costs. This is exacerbated by the difficulty of achieving exit from the industry: many companies are seen as national champions and important employers; they thus receive more than just a sympathetic ear from government. On top of all of this there is continual threat of substitutes, for example, the aluminium producers are a constant worry.

An industry that has proven to be even worse than steel is airlines. It is astonishing to discover that, after years of management initiatives, cost-cutting, mergers, massive marketing campaigns and all the rest, the cumulative earnings of the industry over its entire history are negative. The fact that passenger numbers grow at a rate other industries would die for (4–5 per cent p.a. in the 1990s) seems to count for nothing in terms of profitability. Suppliers are often powerful (e.g. pilot unions). Also, if an airline establishes a profitable market segment it is quickly swamped by new entrants, and by existing airlines moving planes from one part of the globe to another. Over-capacity and low prices are the result. Airlines find it difficult to shed capacity in a hurry; they buy aircraft that fly for decades. When passenger demand falls they simply cannot reduce the supply of aircraft. Exit from the industry is also inhibited by national pride being tied-up with the national flag carrier.

It is worth remembering two points before we look in more detail at the framework for the analysis of industry structure. The first is that industries can change. An industry with a poor industry structure offering low returns can be transformed into a high-rate-of-return-on-invested-capital-industry. This may come about for any number of reasons ranging from a technological innovation that alters the entire economics of the industry (e.g. mobile phones and Internet in telecommunications) to government policy (e.g. allowing mergers to take place in the airline industry that were previously prohibited). So, we need to obtain a dynamic rather than a static view when enquiring into an industry structure.

Second, when we are talking about rates of return on invested capital we are referring to the rate expected over the long term. Transient boosts or dampenings to profitability, from an economic boom, or recession, for example, should be distinguished from the long-term underlying nature of the industry and its consequent rate of return.

The strength of each of the five forces are influenced by a number of factors. The most important of these are discussed below. This discussion will provide a checklist of factors that the Valuegrowth investor needs to investigate.

THREAT OF ENTRY

If an industry is generating a return above that available in other industries (of comparable risk) it acts as a honey pot – a swarm of hungry insects will try to enter to take away some of the honey. New entrants add to the capacity of the industry as they make a grab for market share. The result is falling prices for every firm in the industry, or the costs of the original industry players rise as they try to maintain sales by spending on marketing, favourable credit terms for customers and so on.

> New entry is something that incumbent firms abhor.

New entry is definitely something that incumbent firms abhor. There are two things that can stop, or at least slow down, the advance of the insects to the honey pot. First, there could be barriers put in the path of the outsiders. Second, a clear message could go out to the aspiring entrant that if they did dare to cross the threshold then they will be subject to a massive retaliatory attack until they are driven out again. Of course, in many industries these two disincentives work in tandem.

Credibility is key to using the threat of retaliation to deter entrants. This credibility is enhanced if the incumbents:

- have shown themselves to be vigorous defenders of their honey pot in the past;

- have a large stock of resources with which to fight (cash, borrowing capacity, strong relationships or power over suppliers and customers, etc.);
- are clearly committed to the industry (e.g. the assets employed within it have few alternative uses).

Examples of industries with strong retaliatory threats include PC Software and soft drinks.

The barriers to prevent entry in the first place, come in a variety of forms – these may be used singly or in combination:

- *Large economies of scale and high capital costs* In some industries, firms operating on a small scale are at a competitive disadvantage because the average cost of their product is higher than for those companies producing at the most efficient scale. The aspiring entrant therefore knows that the only way it can survive in the industry is to invest massively. This narrows the field down to a few firms with the required financial resources. If one of these large firms did dare to commit so much money it would risk a severe reaction from the existing firms. Examples of industries protected to some degree by scale economies include brewing, aero engines and mid-market automobile assembly. To enter the aluminium industry on an integrated basis would cost several billion dollars – even then the entrant would probably have less than 5 per cent of worldwide demand. To overcome established brands such as McDonalds, Coca-Cola or the *Wall Street Journal* would cost a vast amount in marketing expense. The classic economy of scale driven industry are natural monopolies in which it doesn't make sense to have more than one producer, e.g. water supply to households.

  Some industries are also protected by economies of scope. That is, the ability to reap economies by sharing costs between a number of product lines. For example, food manufacturers can add additional product lines that make use of the same logistical network, influence with retailers and production equipment. This is one of the main motivators for mergers in this industry.

- *High risks associated with imitation* It is not always easy to identify how it is that a successful business manages to do what it does to elevate above the also-rans. The incumbent(s) may have special capabilities that are very difficult to emulate even if they could all be observed. The uncertainty of being able to imitate inhibits firms from entering the competitive arena. For example, it would be very difficult to imitate, in a credible fashion, the McKinsey method or the Goldman Sachs approach.

- *Access to distribution channels* The obvious distribution channels are usually tied-up by the existing firms. The newcomer will need to somehow break into these relationships to try to secure distribution for its product. This can be very costly. Buyers are likely to ask for substantial price-cutting and other benefits if they are to welcome a new supplier. New food manufacturers, for example, find it very difficult to attract the attention of the large retailers.

  Incumbents often have strong relationships and a long experience of adapting to customer demands to provide a specialist high quality service. This can form a very high barrier to entry. Often the only option open to an outsider is to find a completely new distribution channel. The potential for this has been enhanced significantly by the Internet (for some industries).

- *Switching costs* The buyers of a firm's output may have high costs of switching from one supplier to another. For example, the purchasers of aircraft spend a substantial amount training employees to fly and service the aircraft. They may invest in ancillary equipment to maintain and make best use of the planes. It would be costly to switch to another aeroplane manufacturer in terms of staff training and equipment. New entrants have to make an offer that is so good that it overcomes these switching costs. It would be very expensive for organizations to switch from using Microsoft's operating system and the Office Suite. Any potential entrant would need to offer something very special to encourage a switch. Merely slightly better performance and slightly lower price is not good enough.

- *Differentiation* Differentiation means that the product offers something of higher value than the competition. The additional features of the offer are valued more highly than the additional cost of those features which are charged to the customer. For example, there are many chocolate bars on the market but only one Hershey. There are many designers, but only one Stella McCartney. Even universities differentiate themselves on the basis of research and teaching excellence. Once a reputation is established it is very difficult for others to usurp that position.

- *Experience* Over time incumbents learn a great deal about their industry, their suppliers' and their buyers' industries. They develop specialist technical knowledge and a culture adapted to operating in the industry. The experienced firm can often make the product better or more cheaply than anyone else. For example, in the manufacture of aircraft the experience curve comes into play, in which a doubling of output reduces unit costs significantly. Workers and managers become more efficient by repeating a task. Specialized equipment and processes are developed to enhance efficiency. If the incumbents can keep to themselves the secrets of how cost is reduced by experience then they may create a very powerful entry barrier. Intel, for example, has decades of experience in developing micro-processors which makes it very difficult for new entrants to catch up.

• *Government legislation and policy* Patents are the most obvious barrier to entry erected by governments, but there are others. For example, restrictions on take off and landing slots at airports, controls on over-the-counter pharmaceuticals, tariff and quota barriers keeping out foreign competition, government subsidies to favoured sectors, licensing which forecloses entry, regulation of pricing, fishing quotas, purchase of defence equipment from domestic suppliers.

• *Control over raw materials or outlets* The firms in the industry may have favourable access or outright control over key inputs and outlets. For example, De Beers has tremendous power to insist that diamond miners sell through them. In this way they are able to control supply and thus prices in the consumer market. They have power over both suppliers and customers. A new entrant would find it difficult to challenge De Beers. However, recently, the mighty Russians and Australians have taken a defiant stand and are starting to chip away at its hegemony.

INTENSITY OF RIVALRY OF EXISTING COMPANIES

Valuegrowth investors must concern themselves with the degree of rivalrous behaviour between the existing industry competitors. The more in-fighting there is between the companies for market share and profits, the more rates of return will be depressed. Intense rivalry can erode profits in a number of ways. For example firms compete fiercely on price (any move made by one player is quickly matched by rivals); there is a tendency to spend a great deal on marketing; firms are impelled to improve the product regularly and to introduce new products to try and stay one step ahead.

In highly rivalrous industries there is always one maverick trying to get ahead of competitors. They see an opportunity and go for it with all their might. Unfortunately, the advantage is short-lived as other firms follow the price reductions, marketing innovation or new improved product with their own versions. At the end of the process the whole industry can end up less profitable than before.

In more concentrated industries competitors usually start to recognize their mutual interdependence and so restrain their rivalry. If the industry develops a dominant competitor rather than a set of equally balanced competitors rivalry is reduced – the dominant firm has a strong influence on industry prices and is able to discipline the mavericks. For highly rivalrous industries the financial press is likely to use phrases such as 'cut-throat competition' or 'price wars'. Less rigorous industries will be described as 'stable' even 'boring' or 'gentlemanly'. Some of the factors that intensify rivalry are:

- *Many equally balanced competitors* Where there is no dominant player there will be fierce fighting for market share and profits. When there are very large numbers of firms in the industry there will be one or two who try to steal a march on the others. Even if there are only a few, if they are evenly balanced in terms of resources and size they will often innovate, fight and retaliate dragging the rates of return for all firms down. This is great for customers, but the industry would be much more profitable with a dominant player.

- *Slow industry growth* When an industry is growing fast firms can increase sales without necessarily taking sales from other firms. In a slow growing industry there is a tendency to intense market share rivalry. The mass-market automobile industry is a prime example.

- *High fixed costs* High fixed cost firms need to have a high volume of output to spread costs over a lot of units. There is a high breakeven point. Rivals will cut prices to achieve the turnover required. Papermaking and steel manufacturers are industries that suffer from this problem. A similar tendency to slash prices to achieve rapid throughput is present in industries producing goods and services that are difficult to store, e.g. fruit, airline travel.

- *Products are not differentiated* If the product (or service) is seen as commodity-like (it is identical to that supplied by other firms) buyers will be attracted purely by price and ancillary services. Margins will be cut and rates of return constrained. Bricks, fertilizer and various plastics have been commoditized.

- *Extra capacity is added in large increments* In some industries small increases in capacity are not possible, e.g. bulk chemicals or steel. When a large scale plant is added, chronic industry disruption can occur. Companies are tempted to fill the capacity by reducing prices. Many industries are subject to recurring bouts of over capacity (e.g. paper, oil and plastics) as new plant is brought on stream – usually at the peak of business cycles.

- *When rivals have different strategies, origins, personalities and relationships* Firms in an industry may have completely different objectives, targets and strategies depending on their background, parent company goals and corporate personalities. What seems rational action to one appears irrational industry-damaging to others. In their competitive acts they 'continually run head on into each other in the process'.[3] Family owned firms may have a completely different attitude to public companies, or foreign rivals. Tacit collusion becomes extremely difficult as they have great difficulty reading each other's signals. Rules of the game do not become established to allow each firm to earn a high return. Some firms use the industry as an outlet for excess capacity elsewhere in the conglomerate, and then dump product, other firms are prepared to accept sub-normal rates of return as they see participation in the industry as part of a wider strategy, while others treat it as a cash-cow and try to gain maximum net cashflow, and so on.

- *High exit barriers* In a low return industry the logical response from managers should be to exit the market and use resources thus released in another competitive area where the returns are higher. The reduced supply will benefit the firms that remain and rates of return will rise. In reality, there are frequently factors that prevent the exit of firms despite sub-normal returns. Exit barriers come in many forms:

  – Specialized assets: If the assets of the business are useful in the one business but of no or little value in any other there may be little incentive to exit. Investment in plant, machinery, and so on may be regarded as sunk and therefore does not contribute to the economic cost of running the business. Under these circumstances firms may continue to produce for many years even if net cashflow is very low. Of course, when the assets need replacement, exit might occur. The textile industry in Europe and North America suffered from the unwillingness of firms to exit who were using increasingly old machinery – the 50-year shake out is continuing.

– Fixed costs of exit: There may be substantial costs imposed on firms when they exit an industry. For example, they may be obliged to pay large amounts under labour agreements (particularly the case in many countries in Europe); the divestment process itself is costly in terms of managerial time, lawyers and accountants; customers may have entitlement to after-sales service or spare parts for many years; employees may need to be retrained and reassigned; supplier compensation may be payable for broken contracts.

– Strategic loss: The business may be part of an overall strategic plan. Its removal might have a severe impact on other parts of the company. Perhaps the business, although not profitable in itself adds greatly to the image of the firm or the quality of its relationships with customers, suppliers or government, so it is well worth retaining. It may share facilities that would become uneconomic for the parent without the business. Key raw material suppliers to the group may become unwilling to supply in the absence of the business. The business may be an important link in a vertically integrated chain. For example, the major oil companies have exploration operations, extraction divisions, refining business and retail outlets. One of these businesses could be under performing (often the retail side), yet it is kept within the fold for wider strategic considerations.

– Emotional barriers: In a stand-alone business the managers will tend not to exit even in the face of economic adversity. They are likely to have an emotional attachment to the business. They take pride in the quality of the product and in the efficiency of the operation. It is a business they know and love – it often has a rich history and tradition. The managers realize that they are ill-suited for any other trade. These emotional ties can be especially strong in family-owned firms.

The blow to the pride of the managers of 'giving up' is too much to bear. Often their identity is tied-in with the work they do. One of the worst industries to be in is agriculture. Despite the hardships and the obvious economic logic of switching effort to more productive work many farmers grit their teeth and continue – or, at least, they do until they are forced to exit.

In large businesses it is often too much of a wrench for senior managers to close down the division that represents the corporation's origin despite poor prospects. This is often made more difficult if the CEO spent some of his or her career in that division and knows many of the families that will be badly affected by closure. It is possible for such divisions to be kept for emotional reasons and for their losses to be hidden in the corporate-wide reported figures for many years.

– Government and social barriers: Governments often step-in to prevent the closure of businesses because of their concern for jobs and the community. As a result the required capacity reduction in the industry does not take place and companies grimly hang on and battle away. The result is persistent low returns for the entire industry.

THE THREAT FROM SUBSTITUTES

The threat from substitutes dampens profit potential. Substitutes are products or services that perform the same function (at least in approximate terms). The returns available in the beverage packaging industry have a

> The threat from substitutes dampens profit potential.

ceiling because the buyers are able to switch between steel, aluminium, glass and plastic. Book retailers' margins are under threat because the Internet has promised a substitute method of obtaining books, e.g. Amazon.com. Postal service companies may regard e-mail as a troublesome substitute. The anti-ulcer treatment business, has been subject to regular substitution; Tagamet lost sales to Zantac, which, in turn, lost out to Losec and then Nexium.

The threat of substitutes is worse where:

• the cost to buyers of switching is low;

• the ratio of price to performance is better. That is, the substitute may not be as good at serving the function as the existing product or service, but it is a lot cheaper; or the substitute is slightly more expensive, but significantly more effective.

BUYER (CUSTOMER) POWER

Buyer power gives customers the potential to squeeze industry margins by forcing down prices, or pressing for higher quality or more services. Wal-Mart has achieved a great deal of buyer-power. It is able to exert huge pressure on the firms in the industries producing food, clothes, garden equipment and toys. Buyers are in a strong bargaining position if one or more of the following applies:

- *There is a concentration of buyers* If there are a few large firms responsible for the majority of market purchases then their power is likely to be enhanced vis-à-vis suppliers. The major automobile assemblers have a great deal of power over component suppliers. When there are few alternative buyers around the supplier is in a weak position. The supplier can be threatened with a loss of business if they refuse to co-operate. They are usually desperate to avoid losing a substantial proportion of their sales. The extreme case is monopsony – only one buyer but many sellers. This can occur in the defence field where the government is the only buyer.

- *The product is standardized or undifferentiated* If the product is much the same as that supplied by other companies then buyers will be confident that they will always be able to obtain the product if a particular supplier refused to reduce prices or add service features. They are then in a position to play one company against another. This is a particular problem for suppliers of some raw materials.

- *If the product accounts for a large proportion of the buyer's costs* Purchasers are likely to expend more energy driving down the price of larger-cost items than the price of a product that has an insignificant effect on their overall costs. Buyers are less price-sensitive with incidental products.

- *If the buyer has low switching costs* If it is costly for the buyer to change supplier then the supplier's bargaining power is enhanced.

- *The buyer suffers from low profitability* Car manufacturers frequently announce that they have developed a plan for survival and for a return to profitability. Invariably, as part of the package of measures they declare that they have reached an 'agreement' with their suppliers to cut the components bill by $1 billion, $2 billion or $5 billion. One can only guess at the negotiating stance taken but it probably goes along the line of 'if you don't reduce prices then we shut down plant, and even go bankrupt, and you lose an important customer. What'll it be punk?' If buyer firms are highly profitable they are less likely to be focused on cost cutting and may take a greater interest in preserving the long-run health of their suppliers.

- *If buyers can integrate backwards* If buyers can credibly threaten to make the product themselves they may have greater leverage over the suppliers. Paint manufacturers are often in a position to self-manufacture resin should they choose to do so. If the 'make-or-buy' decision is finely balanced, suppliers have little room for bargaining. Automotive component suppliers are frequently threatened with removal of business as the assemblers could produce for themselves if prices are not restrained.

- *If the consequence and risks of product failure are low* If the quality of the product is crucial to the buyer's system of operations then they are likely to pay less attention to finely tuning the price. For example, equipment that is used to prevent oil-rig blowouts is so vital and costs such a small amount compared with the costs of a blow-out that buyers are willing to pay a little extra to be absolutely sure of complete safety. Similar logic applies to medical equipment, legal advice and corporate finance guidance. If quality is unimportant the buyers will be more price-sensitive and shop around among suppliers.

- *The buyer has plenty of information* Buyer leverage can be enhanced if they know a lot about the supplier's margins, costs and order book. Suppliers will be unable to kid the buyers into thinking that they have inflicted real pain by bargaining down the price when in reality the price agreed is above the supplier's minimum bargaining price. The old lines such as 'you've cut my prices to the bone' and 'at this rate I'll be losing money on the deal' will not work if the buyer knows the reality of the supplier's costs.

SUPPLIER POWER

In many ways supplier power is the mirror image of buyer power. Powerful suppliers are able to set prices that are much greater than their production costs; they are able to appropriate a substantial proportion of the value created in the industries they serve. Suppliers exercise the power that they possess by raising prices or reducing the quality of purchased goods and services. Intel is a powerful supplier to the PC assemblers. Sports rights holders and hit TV show producers are powerful suppliers to the US TV networks, which are barely profitable. The following factors increase the power of suppliers to extract value from the industries they serve:

- *If supply is concentrated in a few hands (more so than the industry it sells to)* Coca-Cola, for example, sells to an industry (retailers) that is highly fragmented. Most of these buyers have very little power. A few of the large supermarket groups try to exert some authority but they are up against a powerful brand and a company used to deciding terms. You can test Coke's power for yourself. If you ever go to Paris, try buying a standard can of Coke for less than FFr 10 ($1.40) from the street vendors or the small shops. The same story applies in numerous capitals around the world – and numerous governments are trying to break Coke's power over the distribution chain. (Coke has over 50 per cent of the carbonated soft drinks market worldwide: in Greece is has an amazing 72.7 per cent, France 55 per cent, German 56.6 per cent, Spain 56 per cent and Italy 44.9 per cent).[4]

- *If there are no substitutes* The supplied item could be unique from a technical point of view and the customer unable to obtain an alternative that will perform the same task. On the other hand suppliers can lose power if they are faced with a viable substitute, e.g. Microsoft is concerned with the potential of Linux and Java.

- *If the industry is one of a large number supplied* If the industry accounts for a small fraction of sales, suppliers' fortunes are less tied in with the industry and supplier power is enhanced.

- *The product supplied is a very important input for the success of the industry* The buyer will be less price-sensitive if the product is crucial to the buyer's process or product quality (e.g. pilot unions are 'suppliers' to airlines – pilots are crucial to airlines and therefore are generously paid).

- *The supplier can forward integrate* If the supplier can credibly threaten to extend their operations to carrying out the tasks currently undertaken by their customers they can put a cap on the profitability of the industry. If profit margins become very wide the supplier may be tempted to enter the industry. The threat to do so encourages the industry participants to share the industry spoils with their suppliers.

- *Non-standard (differentiated) products are supplied* If a supermarket wants to sell a specific brand of baked bean then the supplier has more power than if they merely want to sell baked beans. Note that heavy advertising to consumers is to ensure that they put pressure on their supermarkets to stock the differentiated product as well as, or rather than, the generic product.

Supermarket chains are more or less obliged to stock Kellogg's breakfast cereals, Campbell's Soups and Pepsi's salty snacks. Branding leads to a shift in power between supplier and the industry.

- *If the industry firms face high switching costs* If the firms in the industry are geared-up to obtaining supplies from a particular source and there would be enormous cost of switching suppliers then the supplying firms have power. For example, Judge Thomas Penfield Jackson in his findings on Microsoft (1999) declared that:

  the cost of switching to a non-Intel compatible PC operating system includes the price of not only a new operating system, but also a new PC and new peripheral devices. It also includes the effort of learning to use the new system, the cost of acquiring a new set of compatible applications, and the work of replacing files and documents that were associated with the old applications ... users of Intel-compatible PC operating systems would not switch in large numbers to the Mac OS in response to even a substantial, sustained increase in the price of an Intel-compatible PC operating system.[5]

- *The industry firms are unable to withhold information* Information is power – the less your suppliers know about your costs and demand, the better.

INDUSTRY EVOLUTION

The five forces model is essentially static, whereas Valuegrowth investors need to develop a view of how favourable the industry structure will be years into the future. Industries change as companies, suppliers and buyers undertake strategic actions to enhance their respective degrees of power. They also change as new technology and government policy shifts the basic economic facts of life.

Having completed a static evaluation of the industry – a snapshot in time – the Valuegrowth investor must consider the factors that are likely to lead to the evolution of the industry. A firm that currently has strong pricing power can find it slipping away rapidly, e.g. IBM's slide in the late 1980s and early 1990s as the PC was exploited more effectively by competitors, or Chrysler's poor performance in the late 1990s and early 2000s as the early lead on SUVs was competed away when rivals caught up, or fixed-line telecom companies being out-witted by mobile companies.

If you have found an industry with excellent current characteristics then, when completing an industry evolution analysis, you will be looking for the potential for the industry to continue to produce high returns. Stability and invulnerability to attack and change are the desired qualities. On the other hand, if the industry has a 'poor' or 'fair' structure you would be interested in evaluating the potential for change to a durable high-return structure.

Long-range structural analysis is used to forecast the long-term rates of return of an industry. Its task is to examine the changing strength of each competitive force and to attempt the construction of a probable profit potential of the industry. Of course, this is easier in less complex industry environments. Value-growth investors should not try to analyze an

> Concentrate on industries that are relatively easy to follow.

industry with many highly uncertain variables. Concentrate on industries that are relatively easy to follow.

Changes in the environment of the industry are of significance if they affect the five forces. So the questions that will be asked are of the kind: will the change in technology or government regulations result in a rising or lowering of entry or exit barriers? Will a social trend result in more power accruing to buyers? The driving forces at the root of industry evolution can be classified under the following headings:

- technological change
- learning within the industry, and by suppliers, buyers and potential entrants
- economic change
- government legislation and policy
- social change.

Technological change

The most visible and pervasive form of change in society is the result of technological developments. New products, processes and materials directly affect people and alter the competitive forces within industries.

Just consider the last 100 years. Inventions and innovations in the fields of electricity, communication, transport, pharmaceuticals, computers and satellites, to name a few, have had profound effects on daily lives and industry structure. Indeed, most industries operating today did not even exist 100 years ago (e.g. telephone call centres, website designers, genomics, television programme production).

Given that there are more scientists alive today than have ever breathed in all the previous generations it seems reasonable to conclude that technological change is more likely to accelerate rather than decline. This presents a serious challenge to the Valuegrowth investor in trying to assess the durability of an industry's rate of return. If you really understand an industry subject to unusually rapid technological change such as one of the IT or biotechnology industries then by all means concentrate your resources on estimating likely future profitability. However, most of us will not be able to do this. For us the only hope is to focus on industries that are more predictable. These will still have technological (and social, economic, etc.) change and therefore need an evolutionary assessment, however, the pace of change is likely to be much slower in certain areas. For example, the industry structure for the extraction of rock and gravel is unlikely to alter greatly as a result of invention and innovation. Sure, new improved and specialist machinery will probably come along, but the seismic shifts that occur in other industries are unlikely in this one. The production and sale of old favourites such as the *Washington Post*, Coke or See's Candy is likely to continue much as it did before. It is true that all of these firms have to consider developments such as the Internet, but they will be able to adapt without fundamentally changing the method of doing business or, more importantly, the power structure within the industry. The *Washington Post* may develop its website but the paper version will still sell well. Coke may use the Internet to co-ordinate suppliers and drive down prices but will still sell through vending machines, stores and fast food outlets, over which it has tremendous power. See's Candy may start to sell world wide over the web but continue to serve its regular customers in San Francisco and so on. Its relationships with suppliers and customers is unlikely to change greatly. At least, that is, as far as we can see! Of course, we may be surprised by developments in the industry or in adjacent industries that lead to dramatic technological change, and in the five forces. Despite this problem, evolution analysis is still desirable. There are a number of ways in which technology can impact on industry structure:

- *It can affect the position of substitutes vis-à-vis the industry's product (or service)* The cost and quality of substitutes can change as a result of invention and innovation. This can affect the demand for the product if the cost falls or the quality improves sufficiently to overcome buyer-switching costs. Examples of such change include the switch from the purchase of air travel tickets from travel agents to the Internet, and the switch from traditional brokers to Internet brokers for the purchase of shares.

- *It can affect the position of complementary products* The sales achieved by a particular industry may be influenced by the cost, quality and availability of complementary products. If the complementary product is affected by technological change then the industry under examination may experience a shift in the five forces. For example, the development of broadband Internet services is influenced by the cost, quality and availability of optical-switching devices that allow for faster and more accurate transmission of data.

- *It can affect entry barriers* Entry barriers have been smashed in a lot of industries as a consequence of using Internet technology. Now small players can establish themselves as music or periodical publishers; a specialist producer of Stilton cheese in England can market the product worldwide, by-passing the powerful retail chains. Rapid and frequent product introduction may create barriers to entry because potential competitors are unable to keep pace with the incumbent firms (e.g. micro-processor design). Product developments could lead to higher economies of scale that acts as a barrier to potential entrants. For example, the costs of developing mid-range cars have become so great that output of over a million units is needed to spread the R & D cost.

- *A link in the value chain can be removed* The chain connecting the extraction of raw material through to the use of a final product to give value to a consumer can be shortened by the use of new technology. For example, insurance brokers, intermediaries acting between the client wanting insurance and the insurance companies covering the risk, are being squeezed by clients approaching insurance companies directly (disintermediation). This process has been assisted by the use of new technology (first the telephone and now the Internet) that makes the insurance company able to access consumers. Another example is in the PC market: a number of computer manufacturers sell direct to users, by-passing retailers.

- *The dependence on scarce or expensive complementary products may be reduced* For example, in many African countries mobile telephone operators have developed their own systems that avoid the need for using the cumbersome and corrupted government owned fixed-line systems.

- *Marketing innovation* Methods of marketing have changed significantly over the past 50 years. The use of flashing banner headlines on web pages is but the latest in a string of innovations. Firms that did not exist three or four years ago have worldwide exposure at a fraction of the cost of television, radio or print media advertising. This can be seen as a threat to local producers as global powerhouses invade industries that were once geographically bounded. Marketing innovations also permit the promotion of product differentiation, thus altering the producer-buyer power balance.

- *Process innovation* The methods of producing the output of the industry might change. These innovations can affect economies of scale, the cost structure (fixed versus variable) and the degree of vertical integration, which will influence the power relationships within the five forces. For example, the use of computer networks and computer design programming in architectural practices has enhanced the service offered by some practices (differentiation). The use of electronic data interchange by supermarkets and car manufacturers creates higher fixed costs but allows improved linkage between suppliers and firm. To be a supplier you need to be 'in the system'. This may reduce costs and response time but it may also mean ceding some power to the supermarket or assembler. Canon out-competed Xerox despite not being able to use methods patented by Xerox. It developed processes that avoided the patented approaches. Banks are switching increasing numbers of customers to Internet bank accounts. They are under attack from non-banking firms setting up Internet banking operations now that the barriers to entry have been lowered – an extensive branch network is not required.

- *The buyer segment served can be changed* Technological advancement may lead the industry to change the typical buyers that it serves. For example, mobile telephones were initially very expensive and useful only in a confined geographic area, such as the City of London. Target customers were high-income time-poor individuals. Now one of the largest target markets is children who value text messaging as well as chats. Technology that enables individuals to establish their location on the earth by the use of a global-positioning-system (GPS) was first used by the military. Today, production line automobiles are fitted with this technology.

The switch from one group of buyers to another can have serious consequences for the industry structure. Calculators began life as specialist differentiated products for scientists and engineers. Now industry rivalry is intense as the product has become commodity for the mass market and buyers have low switching costs.

• *Industry boundaries can be changed* Industry boundaries can be enlarged or contracted by the introduction of new technology. For example, the TV set is being used for communication and the Internet (particularly via cable systems). The convergence of telecommunications, computer technology and televisions will have a profound impact on the industry(ies) structure. New rivals appear; buyer power changes (as well as their demands); content provider power may be enhanced.

Learning

Over time the participants in an industry and those with an interest in an industry (e.g. suppliers) accumulate knowledge that can change the industry power balance. Through the regular purchase of a product, buyers develop knowledge of the product characteristics, qualities and cost of competing products. As buyers become more expert and the volume of sales increases a product can move from being unusual and differentiated to being more commodity-like. Buyers become increasingly demanding, looking for higher specification, additional service, and lower price. When personal computers were first marketed they were novel and differentiated. As more manufacturers extended the industry and buyers accumulated knowledge the PC became more and more a commodity item. Also, buyers insisted on even greater computing power, after-sales service and 'free' software.

Industry incumbents and potential entrants learn as an industry develops. New industries are often subject to much uncertainty. At first it is difficult to assess the size of the potential market, the likely buyer demand for particular product features, the characteristics of the buyers, and so on. As a result there is a tendency to have a wide variety of business models and a great deal of experimentation. Over time a selection process takes place as the industry characteristics take shape and companies learn the most appropriate strategies. Once the industry has settled into a more predictable pattern new entrants are attracted that were previously put off

> **New industries are often subject to much uncertainty.**

by the risk of selecting a wrong strategy. Of course, the Valuegrowth investor would not touch a very young industry subject to a very high level of uncertainty. Even those investors attracted to technological industries would confine themselves to those with some established analyzable industry structure.

Some industries are developed on the back of specialist knowledge of business processes or products. The firms in possession of this knowledge will guard it jealously to differentiate their product from the current competitors and to keep out potential entrants. However, gradually, as a technology becomes established, diffusion takes place. This may occur because other firms take apart the product and figure out how it was put together; it may be by poaching key staff; it may be deliberately leaked by customers to help create new suppliers.

Advantages based on the ownership of special knowledge are likely to be eroded. Advantages based on the ability to continually develop new special knowledge can be sustainable. There must be a dynamic managerial response. If a technology-led company is hiding behind patent protection and is not developing a stream of successor products it will not have the durable competitive advantage that the Valuegrowth investor is looking for.

Economic

An industry that is operating at a low volume and growing slowly may never change its method of production to achieve higher economies of scale. However, an industry that has a rapidly growing output may change its mode of operation and industry structure significantly. Companies operating on a large scale often substitute capital for labour, have very high capital investment requirements and large fixed costs. The switch from batch production to mass production or flow production creates a need to fill the capacity available. This has implications for the power relationships with buyers and suppliers.

The slowing of the growth rate of the industry can have a dramatic effect on the industry structure. This is a particular problem for durable goods producers. When a durable good is first invented there is initially a slow take up. There follows a rapid growth phase. This starts to tail off as penetration reaches saturation point. A slow down in the rate of growth is bad enough for firms that are accustomed to large year on year increases. But at least they are selling more each year so they continue to add capacity. Then, the crunch comes. Once satiation is reached sales can fall dramatically as consumers shift from first time buying to replacement purchase. With a durable good replacement can be put off for many years (even decades). This effect can be exacerbated by recession. The power balance in the growth phase can be completely different to that in the falling sales phase. During growth the industry can absorb entrants and still each firm remains profitable. The companies are less concerned with pushing down the price of components from suppliers than by reliability and speed of supply. In the downturn new entrants become a great danger to industry profitability. Suppliers are asked to bear a greater share of the burden of the crisis and buyers gain enormous power as they shop around for bargains.

Changes in the price of input costs as a result of economic developments can affect industry structure. For example, in the last 50 years the cost of shipping goods around the world has fallen a great deal. This has widened the potential market for some producers of exported goods and meant an influx of entrants in particular countries. The lowering of telecommunication costs has also had a significant effect on industries. For example India has an enormous software industry – code can be written in India at a fraction of the cost in Silicon Valley and transmitted instantly to anywhere in the world. Other examples of economic events that influence industry structure and the relative strength of the five forces include the liberalization of world trade, rise in labour costs and changes in exchange rates.

Government

Changes in government legislation and policy can lead to significant change in industry structure. The government's attitude toward competitive practices, for example, can vary over time. What is considered an acceptable level of concentration and power at one time is regarded as unacceptable at another, and companies are obliged to subject themselves to greater competition. There are some industries whose prices are regulated by governments or government appointed agencies. As California's electricity suppliers and consumers found in 2001 this regulation can be changed in perverse ways leading the industry down a disastrously unprofitable path. Governments also license some firms to enter industries. The other side of that coin is that they restrict the entry of other companies.

Product quality and safety is also influenced by government organizations, e.g. in food. The Kyoto conference in 1997 led a number of governments to impose legislation to curtail the emission of greenhouse gases. Industry structure can be immensely influenced by the imposition or removal of tariffs or import quotas. The effect of NAFTA and the EU single market has been highly significant for many industries. When China joins the World Trade Organization its industrialists will have to make major adjustments.

Governments can distort industry in an extreme form by operating a command economy. The shift of Eastern European countries and others to a more laissez-faire market-driven economy has profoundly altered the competitive environment and thus the power relationship within the five forces. Even western governments regularly intervene to distort markets, e.g. agricultural subsidiaries, grants to alternative energy suppliers. Taxation is a particularly common way of tilting the playing field for companies. For example, the price of fuel was hiked in Europe in the late 1990s by imposing high taxes. (In the UK, for example, four-fifths of the cost of petrol to the motorist is tax.) This had a great effect on the road haulage business. After a series of protests the policy of increasing fuel tax was reversed in 2000.

Industry structures are changed by a whole series of other government moves from labour law and privatization to patent law and information disclosure. The Valuegrowth investor has the difficult task of trying to evaluate the likelihood of a change in government policy having a significant influence on industry profitability through the power relationships of the five forces.

Social

Demographic change can influence the size of the buyer pool for an industry. For example, as the proportion of the population over the age of 50 increases in western countries so the demand for some products will rise (e.g. golf?) and others will fall (e.g. discos?). The ethnic mix of the population can alter the demand for products. Hispanics have become the largest minority group in the US. This may increase the demand for some products (e.g. certain foods) at the expense of others.

Values and cultures can change. Vegetarianism is growing in popularity, which is bound to affect the meat industry. There is greater equality between the sexes which will affect industries from employment agencies to childcare providers. Shifts are taking place in the perceived appropriate work-life balance affecting the demand for leisure activities.

Education and health levels can change over a relatively short period of time, particularly in countries with high economic growth. A more highly educated populace is likely to demand more newspapers, books, training courses. Health can rise in some regards, but decline in others, as incomes increase. Concern about weight has become a fixation – slimming foods and exercise gym businesses have been the beneficiaries.

Income distribution can change over time. For example, the redistribution of income toward the poor can reduce the demand for luxury goods but increase the demand for basics. Even a social issue as simple as this spread of English as the world language can influence industry structure. Film and television producers see their buyers and competitors as existing all over the world. Universities in the English-speaking countries compete for students from Asia.

KEY ELEMENTS OF INDUSTRY ANALYSIS

- Industries have a tendency to gravitate toward the competitive floor rate of return. But some industry structures permit barriers to be erected to prevent the loss of super normal rates of return.
- The five competitive forces are:
  - *Threat of entry*
    This can be reduced if one or more of the following applies:
    - credible threat of retaliation
    - large economies of scale and high capital cost
    - special capabilities that make imitation risky for entrant
    - access to distribution channels
    - high buyer switching costs
    - differentiation
    - experience curve effects
    - restrictive government legislation and policy
    - incumbents have control over raw materials and/or outlets.
  - *Intensity of rivalry of existing companies*
    This can be reduced if one or more of the following applies:
    - the industry is concentrated
    - there is a dominant player
    - there is fast industry growth
    - fixed costs are a small proportion of overall costs

- products are differentiated
- capacity can be added in small increments
- rivals have similar strategies and rationales for their actions
- exit barriers are low.

- *The threat from substitutes*
  This can be reduced if the cost to buyers of switching is high and/or the ratio of price to performance of the substitute is poor.

- *Buyer power*
  This can be reduced if one or more of the following applies:
  - there are a large number of buyers
  - the product is differentiated
  - the product is a small part of the buyer's costs
  - the buyer has high switching costs
  - the buyer has high profitability
  - buyers cannot easily integrate backwards
  - the consequences of the product failing when the buyer uses it are high
  - the buyer does not know much about the industry margins, costs and demand.

- *Supplier power*
  This can be reduced if one or more of the following applies:
  - supplies can be obtained from a wide variety of sources
  - there are substitutes with good price to performance ratios
  - suppliers supply only (or predominantly) this industry
  - the product supplied is unimportant for the success of the industry
  - the supplier is unable to credibly threaten to forward integrate
  - the supplied product is undifferentiated
  - there are low costs of switching suppliers
  - the supplier knows little about industry margins, costs and demand.

- Industry evolution analysis. The five forces, and therefore rates of return, can be influenced by the following types of change:
  - technological change
  - learning by industry firms, suppliers, customers and potential entrants
  - economic change
  - government legislation and policy changes
  - social change.

Notes

1   Much of the discussion that follows owes a great deal to Michael Porter's work, particularly *Competitive Strategy* (1980).

2   Adapted from Porter, M. (1980), p. 4.

3   Porter, M. (1980), p. 19.

4   Source: Willman, John and Blitz, James (1999) 'Coca-Cola's Style Offends European Regulators' Taste'. *Financial Times*, 22 July 1999, p. 2.

5   Penfield Jackson, T. (1999) http://usvms.Gpo.Gov

10

Competitive resource analysis

Identifying a good industry is only the first step. Valuegrowth investors need to seek out companies that beat the average rates of return on capital employed in a good industry. To beat the averages, companies need something special. That something special comes from the bundle of resources the firm possesses. Most of the resources are ordinary. That is, they give the firm competitive parity. However, the firm may be able to exploit one or two extraordinary resources – those that give a competitive edge. An extraordinary resource is one which, when combined with other (ordinary) resources enables the firm to outperform competitors and create new value generating opportunities. Critical extraordinary resources determine what a firm can do successfully.

It is the ability to generate value for customers that is crucial for superior returns. High shareholder returns are determined by the firm being able to either offer the same benefits to customers as competitors, but at a lower price; or being able to offer unique benefits that more than outweigh the associated higher price.

Ordinary resources provide a threshold competence. They are vital to ensure a company's survival. The problem is that mere competitive parity does not produce the returns looked for by the Valuegrowth investor. In the food retail business, for example, most firms have a threshold competence in basic activities, such as purchasing, human resource management, accounting control and store layout. However, the large chains have resources that set them apart from the small stores: they are able to obtain lower cost supplies because of their enormous buying power; they can exploit economies of scale in advertising and in the range of produce offered.

Despite the large retailers having these advantages it is clear that small stores have survived, and some produce very high returns on capital invested. These superior firms provide value to the customer significantly above cost. Some corner stores have a different set of extraordinary resources compared with the large groups: personal friendly service could be valued highly; opening at times convenient to customers could lead to acceptance of a premium price; the location may make shopping less hassle than traipsing to an out-of-town hypermarket. The large chains find emulation of these qualities expensive. If they were to try to imitate the small store they could end up losing their main competitive advantages, the most significant of which is low cost.

The extraordinary resources possessed by the supermarket chains as a group when compared with small shops are not necessarily extraordinary resources in the competitive rivalry *between* the chains. If the focus is shifted to the 'industry' of supermarket chains factors like economies of scale may merely give competitive parity – scale is needed for survival.

Competitive advantage is achieved through the development of other extraordinary resources, e.g. the quality of the relationship with suppliers, a very sophisticated system for collecting data on customers combined with target marketing; ownership of the best sites. However, even these extraordinary resources will not give superior competitive position forever. Many of these can be imitated. Long-term competitive advantage may depend on the capabilities of the management team to continually innovate and thereby shift the ground from under the feet of competitors. The extraordinary resource is then the coherence, attitude, intelligence, knowledge and drive of the managers in the organizational setting.

Many successful companies have stopped seeing themselves as bundles of product lines and businesses. Instead they look at the firm as a collection of resources. This helps to explain the logic behind some companies going into apparently unconnected product areas. The connection is the exploitation of extraordinary resources. So, for example, Honda has many different product areas: motor boat engines, cars, motorcycles, lawn mowers and electric generators. These are sold through different distribution channels in completely different ways to different customers. The common root for all these products is Honda's extraordinary resource which led to a superior ability to produce engines. Likewise, photo-copiers, cameras and image scanners are completely different product sectors and sold in different ways. Yet, they are all made by Canon which has extraordinary capabilities and knowledge of optics, imaging and microprocessor controls.

THE TRRACK SYSTEM

The Valuegrowth investor should not be looking for a long list of extra-ordinary resources in any one firm. If one can be found that is great – it only takes one to leap ahead of competitors and produce super-normal returns. If two are found then that is excellent. It is very unusual to come across a company that has three or more extraordinary resources. Coca-Cola is an exception with an extraordinary brand, distribution system with its connected relationships, and highly knowledgeable managers (knowledgeable principally about how to work the systems in countries around the world to keep the competition authorities off their backs while they tighten control over distribution and prices – allegedly).

To assist the thorough analysis of a company's extraordinary resource I have developed the TRRACK system. This classifies extraordinary resources into six categories – see Fig. 10.1.

T	**Tangible**
R	**Relationships**
R	**Reputation**
A	**Attitude**
C	**Capabilities**
K	**Knowledge**

Figure 10.1 The TRRACK system

Notice that the vast majority of extraordinary resources are intangible. They are qualities that are carried within the individuals that make up the organization or are connected with the interaction between individuals. They are usually developed over a long time rather than bought. These qualities cannot be scientifically evaluated to provide objective quantification. Despite our inability to be precise it is usually the case that these people-embodied factors are the most important drivers of value creation and we must pay most attention to them. Again, good investment hinges on good judgement rather than the ability to plug numbers into a formula.

Tangible

Occasionally physical resources provide a sustainable competitive advantage. These are assets that can be physically observed and are often valued (or misvalued) in a balance sheet. They include real estate, materials, production facilities and patents. They can be purchased, but if they were easily purchased they would cease to be extraordinary because all competitors would go out and buy. There must be some barrier preventing other firms from acquiring the same or similar assets for it to be truly valuable in the long run.

In many countries the dominant, usually previously state-owned, telephone company, has a valuable physical resource in the copper wire linking-up millions of houses and businesses. It would be uneconomic for a competitor to replicate such a network (however, this advantage is being eroded as alternative telecommunication systems are developed, e.g. cable, mobile phones). Microsoft's ownership of its operating system and other standards within the software industry gives it a competitive edge. McDonald's makes sure that it takes the best locations on the busiest highways, rather than settle for obscure secondary roads. Many smaller businesses have found themselves (or made smart moves to make sure) with the ownership of valuable real estate adjacent to popular tourist sites. Pharmaceutical companies, such as Merck, own valuable patents giving some protection against rivalry – at least temporarily. The port in Hong Kong owned by Hutchinson Whampoa has the extraordinary resource of being the major entry and exit point for goods in the region.

Relationships

Over time companies can form valuable relationships with individuals and organizations that are difficult or impossible for a potential competitor to emulate.

Relationships in business can be of many kinds. The least important are the contractual ones. The most important are informal or implicit. These relationships are usually based on a trust that has grown over many years. The terms of the implicit contract are enforced by the parties themselves rather than through the court – a loss of trust can be immensely damaging. Relationships generally 'rest on reputation and reciprocation'.[1] It is in all the parties' interests to co-operate with integrity because there is the expectation of reiteration leading to the sharing of collective value created over a long period.

Buyer-seller relationships differ in quality. Many are simply arm's length, adversarial and with serious bargaining. This may make sense when selling incidental items, say pencils, to organizations. It is not worth the expense of establishing a more sophisticated interaction. However, many firms have seen the value of developing close relationships with either their suppliers or customers. For example, Ikea and Wal-Mart are moving toward more collaborative relationships with suppliers to improve delivery mechanisms, through joint planning and scheduling, information system management and co-operation on quality and reliability advances.

South African Breweries (SAB) has 98 per cent of the beer market in South Africa. It has kept out foreign and domestic competitors because of its special relationships with suppliers and customers. It is highly profitable, and yet, for the last two decades it has reduced prices every year – the price of beer has halved in real terms. Most of South Africa's roads are poor and electricity supplies are intermittent. To distribute its beer it has formed some strong relationships. The truck drivers, many of whom are former employees, are helped to set up their small trucking businesses by SAB. *Shebeens* sell most of the beer. These are unlicensed pubs. Often, they are tiny – no more than a few benches. SAB cannot sell directly to the illegal shebeens. Instead it maintains an informal relationship via a system of wholesalers. SAB makes sure that distributors have refrigerators and, if necessary, generators. An entrant would have to develop its own special relationship with truck drivers, wholesalers and retailers. In all likelihood it would have to establish a completely separate and parallel system of distribution. Even then it would lack the legitimacy that comes with a long standing relationship.

Coca-Cola has special relationships with major fast-food chains such as McDonald's or Burger King. Coke has more than two-thirds of fountain sales through such outlets in the US. It demands that distributors handle only its products. Pepsi has been trying to win fountain sales through fast food outlets, but it keeps meeting the obstacle that the distributors are not allowed, under the terms of their agreement with Coke, to carry Pepsi as well. The fear of losing the right to distribute Coke keeps the distributors firmly committed to excluding other soft drinks. Supermarket chains in Europe have started to complain about the power Coke has. The relationship is such that it is alleged that Coke 'forces' supermarkets to give it the best positions in the stores. They claim that they are denied the discounts necessary to make a reasonable profit unless they give the company extra space, stock all its products and run promotions.[2] Other tactics are said to be loyalty discounts and sales targets that require distributors to sell less of competing products.

Famously Microsoft has a special relationship with the computer manufacturers. The recent court case focused on its ability to encourage

PC makers to include software particularly advantageous to Microsoft.

Most of the major car manufacturers and their suppliers share technical and development information in order to lower the cost of the vehicle and to try and achieve an advantage over competitors. The closer the relationships become the greater the pressure to reduce the number of first-tier suppliers; it is difficult to develop special co-operative relationships with hundreds of companies.

Accounting firms, management consultancies and investment banks are particularly keen on 'client-relationship management'. Frequently, it is the quality of the customer relationship that creates the real value for these types of organizations.

Relationships between employees, and between employees and the firm, can give a competitive edge. Some firms seem to possess a culture that creates wealth through the co-operation and dynamism of the employees. Information is shared, knowledge is developed, innovative activity flows, rapid response to market change is natural and respect for all pervades. General Electric has taken employee co-operation one-step further. It is the most highly valued company in the world with dozens of divisions, product lines and markets. It does not concentrate solely on employee co-operation and sharing of knowledge *within* divisions or countries. It has a culture that leads to the quick dissemination of best practice around the GE empire. If an idea worked in a manufacturing plant in France, it is shared with the rest of the group. Larry Johnson, head of the white good division says, 'Being a conglomerate like GE makes no sense unless you can leverage the size and diversity of the company and spread learning and best practices across the company'.[3] GE coined the term 'boundary-less selling' whereby managers from another part of the company are expected to help colleagues market completely different products and services:

> If we want to sell to a specific customer we pick the GE business that has the best relationship with this company and include representatives from this business in the team. We go to the company and say to the chief executive 'What are the four or five things that keep you awake at night. How can we help?'[4]

So, for example an executive who is usually engaged in selling aero engines might spend a few days a month helping a team trying to win an order from a major airline for an office lighting system.

The quality of the relationships with government can be astonishingly important to a company. Many of the defence contractors concentrate enormous resources to ensure a special relationship with various organs of government. The biggest firms often attract the best ex-government people to take up directorships or to head liaison with the government department. Their contacts and knowledge of the inside workings of purchasing decisions, with their political complications, can be very valuable. A similar logic often applies to pharmaceutical companies, airlines and regulated companies.

Reputation

Reputations are normally made over a long period. Once a good reputation is established it can be a source of very high returns (assuming that all the necessary ordinary resources are in place to support it). 'Reputation is the most important commercial mechanism for conveying information to consumers'.[5]

In the markets for goods and services consumers constantly come up against the difficulty of judging quality before purchase. This is an ancient problem. In medieval times craftsmen banded together in guilds which then sought to establish a quality reputation for every member of the group. If a member fell below the required standard he would be ejected to prevent the image of the group being sullied permanently. This type of arrangement exists today for builders, plumbers and cabinet-makers. Those that deal in gold and silver found, and still find it, worthwhile to spend time and money demonstrating the purity of the metal. They paid for systems to assay to the declared specification.

> **Reputations are normally made over a long period.**

Customers are willing to pay a premium for product quality assurance when they cannot easily monitor quality for themselves. This premium is not available to the suppliers in many markets – e.g. coal, electricity, sugar, paper – where the buyer is able to quickly and cheaply gauge quality. But in some industries customers will pay a price premium for the assurance of quality.

There are different types of good:

- search goods
- immediate experience good
- long-term experience good
- no-experience good.

Reputation is most important in the last two, but it has relevance to many immediate experience goods. Search goods are those for which the buyer can establish quality by inspection prior to purchase. So, for example, the quality of bananas or tomatoes can generally be observed in the store. It makes sense for the storekeeper to build up a reputation for quality as this will enable the store to remain on the list of retailers that consumers like to purchase from. But the retailer is generally unable to exploit this reputation to charge a significant price premium. If this was attempted, consumers would quickly switch to another store where they could easily assess the quality of the produce.

The second group of products are immediate experience goods. For these quality cannot be established by inspection. So the taste of a soup in a can or the flavour of canned vegetables is only learnt by the consumer after purchase. However, it does not take long to learn about the quality of Campbell's or Heinz's soup. Consumers soon develop a knowledge of a manufacturer's quality with immediate experience goods. Once learned there tends to be some degree of inertia leading to consumers being reluctant to switch brands (giving some pricing power).

The value of long-term experience goods can only be determined after extensive personal experience. For example, it takes a long time to establish whether a doctor is very able (given that most ailments clear up spontaneously). Only in the long term do you know, if you are relying on personal experience, whether the cancer treatment is working or the heart pills do not have unacceptable side effects. Reputation established with other patients may be key to your decision to accept the advice and treatment of a doctor. When companies are selecting auditing, accounting, and other professional services they rarely have the extensive history of dealing with a range of possible suppliers to be able to choose one on the basis of experience. They generally rely on reputation. To boost reputations, and increase (or at least maintain) the price premium they charge, a number of global professional services organizations spent vast sums on advertising and brand building campaigns in the late 1990s (KPMG spent $60 million, Ernst and Young had a $100 million campaign, Andersen Consulting spent $100 million, and then had to spend more when it changed its name to Accenture). It was perceived as being important to establish in the minds of chief executives that they need to pay a little extra for the peace of mind that comes with buying the best quality services and advice. 'For all the Big Five and the management consultancy businesses they have spawned, global brand building is critical as they try to change from networks of national firms into global organizations able to deliver consistent services to multinational companies.'[6] Another long-term experienced good is a video camera. Sony's reputation gives it the edge in the minds of consumers. The Sony offer carries more than a similar offer by a company with an obscure brand. With car hire in a foreign country the consumer is unable to assess quality in advance. Hertz provide certification for local traders under a franchise arrangement. These local car hirers would see no benefit to providing an above average service without the certification of Hertz because they would not be able to charge a premium price.[7] It is surprising how much more consumers are willing to pay for the assurance of reliable and efficient car hire when they travel abroad compared with the hiring of a car from an unfranchised local.

There are some goods that are only purchased once (or rarely). These are no-experience goods. For example, funeral services, swimming pools, construction, specialist legal services. Consumers tend to lean heavily on reputations established with other customers.

Companies pay a large premium to hire Goldman Sachs when contemplating an issue of securities or a merger. They are willing to pay for 'emotional reassurance'.[8] The CEO cannot be sure of the outcome of the transaction. If it were to fail, the penalty would be high – executives may lose bonuses, and, perhaps their jobs, shareholders lose money. The CEO therefore hires the best that is available for such once-in-a-lifetime moves. The cost of this hand holding is secondary. Once an adviser has a history of flawless handling of large and complex transactions it can offer a much more effective 'emotional comfort-blanket'[9] to CEOs than smaller rivals. This principle may apply to pension fund advisers, management consultants and advertising agencies as well as top investment bankers.

The ways in which buyers ascertain the quality of a good can strongly influence the potential for competitive advantage in an industry. The four types of goods and the importance of reputation in attaining reassurance on quality is shown in Table 10.1.

Branding is designed to represent and enhance reputations 'a brand is established when a branded item sells for more than a functionally equivalent product'.[10] The brand adds value to consumers, by providing information. Brands generally provide a degree of quality certification. For immediate experience and long-term experience goods, the brand provides the assurance of consistency. People buy branded beer because they expect that the next can will taste the same as the ones they bought

Table 10.1 Type of good and the importance of reputation

Type of good	Information on quality	Examples
Search	Obtained by inspection prior to purchase. Reputation of very little importance	Fresh fruit and vegetables Clothing Some furniture
Immediate experience	Obtained quickly after consumption. Reputation is of some importance	Tinned food and drink Newspapers Theme parks
Long-term experience	Obtained only after a long period of individual experience. Reputation is therefore very important	Professional advice Some medicines Investment advice
No experience	Not possible to obtain from individual experience. Reputation is therefore very important	Investment bank advice Funeral services Life assurance

before. In many product areas consumers are reluctant to take the risk of buying unbranded products, for fear of inconsistency of quality, e.g. hamburgers, soup, breakfast cereals and shampoo.

The promise of consistency provides a company with a competitive advantage, but the price premium that can be charged for this factor alone is limited because the consistency can be replicated by competitors. There are two other advantages of branded products that permit enhanced pricing power. These are shown in Fig. 10.2. A firm may have one, two or all three of these advantages. Naturally, the more the better.

Incumbency can be a powerful quality of a brand. Once a brand is established in the minds of consumers it is very difficult for a rival manufacturer to introduce an alternative product successfully, even if that product offered better value. For example, a rival to Hershey may offer a chocolate bar of equivalent quality at a lower price but few consumers will switch – at least not without a vast marketing spend, and a long period of time. Similarly, consumers are attached to dog food brands, ketchup brands and cleaning product brands. Consumer recognition and acceptance of a new product in the face of a well-establish incumbent is extraordinarily difficult. The combination of consistency and incumbency can lead to very high returns. Coca-Cola is aware of the role of these two

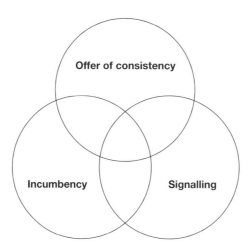

Figure 10.2 Three powerful advantages of brands

factors in their success – Douglas Daft, Chairman and Chief Executive, wrote, 'All our success flows from the strength of our brands, and our ability to relate to people. That's why we have to be the world's best marketers'.[11] He says that Coca-Cola should focus on becoming a 'pure marketing company' presumably this is to entrench the power of consistency and incumbency.

Consumers often use branded products to send signals to other people. Nike, Reebok, Levi's and a host of others exploit this element of human nature and receive a premium price. Signals of high status are generally expensive – Rolls Royce, Moet et Chandon, Burberry. De Beers is busy trying to set its brand as the most luxurious and highest quality in the world. They will rely on some element of truth, but mostly on perception.

Coca-Cola manages to score on this point as well: In many developing countries its American cultural associations mean that young people, in particular, will pay a premium. A similar advantage has accrued to Marlboro.

Attitude

Attitude refers to the mentality of the organization. It is the prevalent outlook. It is the way in which the organization views and relates to the world. Terms such as disposition, will and culture are closely connected

> .....**Attitude can become entrenched within an organization.** ....

with attitude. Every sports coach is aware of the importance of attitude. The team may consist of players with the best technique in the business or with a superb knowledge of the game, they may be the fastest and the most skilful, but without a winning attitude they will not succeed. There must be a will to win.

Attitude can become entrenched within an organization. It is difficult to shake off a negative attitude. A positive attitude can provide a significant competitive edge. Some firms develop a winning mentality based on a culture of innovation, others are determinedly orientated towards customer satisfaction while some companies are quality driven.

3M has a pervasive attitude of having-a-go. Testing out wild ideas is encouraged. Employees are given time to follow up a dreamed-up innovation, and they are not criticized for failing. Innovations such as 'Post-it' notes, have flowed from this attitude. Canon has the attitude of *Tsushin* – 'heart-to-heart and mind-to-mind communication' between the firm and its customers. In this way trust is developed.

Capabilities

Capabilities are derived from the company's ability to undertake a set of tasks. The term skill can be used to refer to a narrow activity or single task. Capability is used for the combination of a number of skills.[12] For example, a company's capability-base could include abilities in narrow areas such as market research, innovative design and efficient manufacturing that, when combined, result in a superior capability in new product development. Capabilities are 'complex combinations of assets, people, and processes that organizations use to transform inputs into outputs'.[13]

A capability is more than the sum of the individual processes – the combination and co-ordination of individual processes may provide an extraordinary resource. Frequently, it is extremely difficult for a firm to combine its process skills in such a way as to provide a superior capability. The mere fact that it is difficult gives a competitive advantage to a firm that has achieved it, as the combination becomes difficult for rivals to imitate. Static capabilities are less valuable than the ability to move quickly in product markets.

Sony developed a capability in miniaturization. This enabled it to produce a string of products from the Walkman to the Playstation. It grew by continually reinforcing the various skills needed for technological-based product innovation. This was complemented by marketing flair and strong brands.

McDonald's has developed a capability to deliver a high quality service in dispersed outlets. Merck has teams of people with extraordinary skills, knowledge and co-operative spirit: Raymond Gilmartin, Chief Executive, rejects the notion that scale of operation is the key to success in the pharmaceuticals industry. He said:

> We believe the only source of sustainable competitive advantage is to be able to discover breakthrough drugs. To get there is a question of insight, creativity and knowledge, not one of force … There have been some companies that have spent more R & D dollars than us. Yet I think we have been able to demonstrate that we can be quite creative and productive.[14]

In the 1940s Caterpillar developed a capability for building roads, airstrips and army bases for the US Department of War. They had to develop a wide range of skills as the military needed one supplier that would take on entire projects. Caterpillar offered a worldwide service and supply network for construction equipment at low cost. Having met the challenge set by the military Caterpillar was in an excellent position after the war to offer a capability rivals could not emulate. It became the dominant firm in the heavy construction equipment industry. Its ability to deliver any Caterpillar part to any location in the world in under two days was an unbeatable offer.

Nokia has taken world leadership in the manufacture of mobile telephones as a result of its capability in technical design and marketing.

In some industries the capability to be the lowest cost producer is vital for superior profitability. Cost leaders must exploit all sources of cost advantage. They tend to sell standard, undifferentiated products with few or no frills. They must be determined to be *the* lowest cost producer, not just one of many. This will require, for example, operating at the optimum efficient scale, unflagging attacks on the cost base, using the benefits of the experience curve. A cost minimizer is likely to be very cautious about spending in areas such as R & D and advertising. Above average returns will accrue to the low cost producer in an industry because average industry prices are set by the rivalrous behaviour of the other players – these will not fall beyond a certain point. Dell Computer is the classic industry cost leader. It is brutal in cutting prices in order to take market share. Higher market share leads to lower unit costs and widening gap between Dell and its smaller rivals. Its direct selling model gives a major cost advantage.

Knowledge

Knowledge is the awareness of information, and its interpretation, organization, synthesis, and prioritization, to provide insights and understanding. The retention, exploitation and sharing of knowledge can be extremely important in the achievement and maintenance of competitive advantage. All firms in an industry share basic knowledge. For example, all publishers have some knowledge of market trends, distribution techniques and printing technology. It is not this common knowledge that I am referring to in the context of extraordinary resources. If a publisher builds up data and skills in understanding a particular segment of the market say investments books, then its superior awareness, interpretation, organization, synthesis and prioritization of information can create competitive advantage through extraordinary knowledge. The company will have greater insight than rivals into this segment of the market.

There are two types of organizational knowledge. The first, *explicit* knowledge, can be formalized and passed on in codified form. This is objective knowledge that can be defined and documented. The second, *tacit* knowledge, is ill- or undefined. It is subjective, personal and context-specific. It is fuzzy and complex. It is hard to formalize and communicate. Examples of explicit knowledge includes costing procedures written in company accounting manuals, formal assessment of market demand, customer complaint data and classification. Explicit knowledge is unlikely to provide competitive advantage: if it is easily defined and codified it is likely be available to rivals. Tacit knowledge, on the other hand, is very difficult for rivals to obtain. Consider the analogy of a baseball: explicit knowledge of tactics is generally available; what separates the excellent from the ordinary player is the application of tacit knowledge, e.g. what becomes an instinctive ability to recognize types of pitches and the appropriate response to them.

Tacit knowledge is transmitted by doing, the main means of transferring knowledge from one individual to another is through close interaction to build understanding as in the master-apprentice relationship.

Nike was started by Phil Knight in 1964. He had a special knowledge of the needs of runners – in the 1950s he was a middle-distance runner in the

University of Oregon's track team. He felt that runners had been badly served by the existing manufacturers. He designed shoes using his special insight, but had no special knowledge of manufacturing and so this was contracted to Asian suppliers. His new designs were a great success. In the 1980s the company grew from the specialist sports shoe market to the fashion conscious teenage and young market. This required an additional set of knowledge attributes. As well as knowledge of how to create innovative sport shoes (e.g. Air Shoes) the company became very knowledgeable about its customers, marketing and its distributors. For example, image building was vital to sell to this type of consumer. Michael Jordan was featured in its advertising. The amount spent on sports marketing reached $1 billion in 1995. Tiger Woods and the whole of the Brazilian soccer team were signed up. The company's understanding of its target market was second to none. It projected an image that appealed to the young, cool and competitive. Its knowledge of product development was built on – in one year it launched 300 new designs! It developed a knowledge of new materials, and fabrics. The easily documented elements of Nike's knowledge base are the least important. The key elements are the knowledge that comes from day-to-day interaction between employees and with customers, suppliers and distributors. This knowledge builds up over time and is defused throughout the organization in the heads of thousands of individuals. In the pharmaceuticals sector GlaxoSmithKline has developed a deep explicit and tacit knowledge of drug development, regulatory environments and markets.

WHAT MAKES RESOURCES EXTRAORDINARY?

It is sometimes difficult to identify the extraordinary resources of a company, if indeed it has any at all. This section may help by summarizing the characteristics of extraordinary resources. To achieve *sustainable* competitive advantage the three characteristics must be durable. That is, it is expected that the above average return on capital will persist for a very long time because:

- the resource will be *demanded* (regarded as valuable) by customers far into the future;

- the resource will continue to be *scarce*. That is competitors will not be able to imitate the resource nor substitute alternative resources to satisfy customers needs; and

- as far as can be seen the additional net income generated by the use of the extraordinary resource is *appropriable* by the firm and not by another organization or individual(s).

The challenge for the Valuegrowth investor is understanding what distinguishes extraordinary resources from those that merely give competitive parity and to recognize when a resource switches from being extremely valuable to being pedestrian (and the likelihood of that switch occurring in the near future). For example, lower-priced Swiss watch manufacturers discovered that the extraordinary resources of knowledge accumulated over centuries and a high reputation were not enough to induce consumers to pay a premium when cheap digital watches became available. Similarly IBM found that it could not resist the onslaught in the PC market as the extraordinary resources it offered (technical design, reputation for bespoke solutions, etc.) became regarded as secondary when customers were offered cheaper PCs with a high specification produced as commodity type products.

Demanded

The first question to ask is: 'does the resource produce something of value to the customer, at a price the customer is more than willing to pay?' To be extraordinary the resource must fulfil a customer's need, and the customer must be prepared to pay a premium over the cost to obtain that benefit. At any one time, willingness to pay a premium will depend on the alternatives open to the customer. The resource has to meet current and projected needs that cannot be met by competitors.

Firms frequently see themselves as having extraordinary resources that are still demanded by customers but they are deluding themselves. This belief is often based on the observations of success in the past. For example, a manufacturer of metal vehicle bumpers may be the best in the world, with the greatest technical design, cheapest operating costs, brilliant plant managers and so on. However, if customer demand has moved from metal vehicle bumpers to compressible plastic, all those resources are no longer demanded and are therefore not valuable. The demand for the resources possessed by skilful tailors has declined, and all but disappeared, except for a few small niches, as people's demand for stylish well-fitting clothes is satisfied by mass production and mass distribution drawing on a different resource base.

The extraordinary resources that food stores once had in the days when sales assistants would weigh out sugar, flour and coffee (service culture, relationship with the customer) is no longer demanded as it has been replaced with the low-cost capability resource of the modern self service supermarket. People vote with their wallets in showing what they regard as a valuable resource. Domestic servants once offered the fulfillment of middle-class needs at a reasonable cost relative to the benefits. Over the first half of the 20th Century there was a gradual erosion of that extra-ordinary resource as labour costs rose and alternative methods of keeping a household comfortable became available (e.g. washing machines, vacuum cleaners, central heating). Railway companies around the world have discovered that the extraordinary resource they once had for being able to transport people and freight long distances quickly and comfort-ably had been eroded. At one time they could charge a premium because they offered so much more than the alternative (stagecoach or sea transport). Today, most railway operators fail to charge a price that covers their basic costs of operation let only receive a premium for offering an extraordinary good service compared with the competition (the internal combustion engine-based transport). Textile manufacturers of North America and Europe once thought that their technical ability and latest machinery would be so valuable that they could see off the competition from low wage economies. They were shown to be wrong as customers chose the low cost resource.

There are some resources which are more likely to have a long life than others. For example, Disney's extraordinary resource as a family-orientat-ed entertainment brand will, bar managerial stupidity or accident, pro-duce price premiums way into the future. Each of the leading characters – Mickey Mouse, Snow White etc. and the library of movies can be consid-ered extraordinary resources with a long shelf life. The theme parks have a special place in the hearts of many people – they are world-renowned lead-ers in the field. Each generation will want to share with their children the magic of Disney. They offer something special that competitors find hard to beat. The *Financial Times* or *The Economist* have powerful reputations that are likely to be long-lived because they offer to satisfy customer needs better than alternatives. Of course, the management will need to be vigi-lant and to invest to stay ahead, but they start from an excellent position.

Scarcity

If the resource is widely available it cannot be extraordinary. It must be in short supply to be valuable. If it is not rare then competitors will be able to acquire it and undercut the price premium. The company must have some protection against the actions of rivals attempting to either imitate its advantage or provide a substitute resource to steal away customers. It must have a deep moat around the competitive advantage to make it sustainable.

.... **If the resource is widely available it cannot be extraordinary.** ....

Resources that have built-in inhibitors to imitation fall into four categories:[15]

- *Physically unique* A company may have ownership of the best real estate. Rivals cannot imitate this. The firm may own the only possible rock pit in Brooklyn. It may have the mineral rights over a piece of land which contains the only economically viable quantity of a metal on a continent. It may own the best retail sites. Or, the firm may have bought the rights at auction to explore a region for oil and gas and ended up becoming the owner of the only gas field for 1,000 miles.

  Patent rights, e.g. for drugs, can prevent imitation for a while. However, the company must not rest on its laurels as patent rights can be by-passed by determined rivals fairly quickly. What is more likely to prove durable is the extraordinary resource to produce a *stream* of patentable products. That way competitors are always running to catch-up. So developing a capability and an attitude that allows rapid knowledge accumulation, innovative thinking, and quick development of products may be sustainable. We may stretch the definition of physical: the 'physical' asset of Bugs Bunny is extraordinary for Warner Brothers.

  The physical assets of firms are rarely inimitable. Gillette, for example, took ten years and spent $1 billion developing its Mach3 triple-blade razor. Within a few months, Asda, a British supermarket had produced its own triple-bladed razor, Tri-Flex, selling at a 40 per cent discount. The start up electronic traders such as Amazon.com, CDNOW, eToys and E*Trade thought they had developed a unique physical resource – a strong presence on the worldwide web. However, it has recently become apparent that the space they occupy can be invaded by the traditional retailers. Home Depot, Merrill Lynch, KMart and Wal-Mart have been able to imitate the electronic traders. They have found it relatively easy to occupy a 'site' adjacent to the brash up-starts. Furthermore, they are able to apply some other significant advantages such as exploiting relationships established with millions of customers over many years, a strong brand name, tried and tested distribution capability and good relationships with suppliers.

- *Path dependency* This is more likely to produce sustainable extraordinary resource than physical assets. Path dependent resources are created over a long period of time. They are created because of the route the firm took to get to where it is today.

  The history of some firms gives them the idiosyncratic attributes that makes them unique. Only they can offer the qualities demanded by the customer. So, a technology firm may develop an extraordinary resource in the creation and exploitation of breakthroughs in a scientific discipline. It is the long history of sequentially overcoming scientific barriers by a tight knit group of scientists that provides the firm with superior knowledge and capabilities leading to products that are cutting edge. Competitors may try to imitate by hiring hundreds of scientists and providing them with vast financial resources, but the new team will lack the long-term perspective, coherence and tacit knowledge of the established team.

  It takes a long time to develop strong and loyal networks of relationships with suppliers and customers. For example, South African Breweries is now in a strong position because, over many decades, it worked with suppliers and customers to make the distribution of beer possible in difficult circumstances.

  Brand name recognition is usually path dependent. Kellogg's and Heinz have taken over a century to establish themselves in the psyche of consumers. An imitator would find this very difficult to break. Coca-Cola's brand name recognition will not be replicated simply by rivals spending vast sums on marketing. Consumers have long experience of drinking Coke and their association of the drink with every stage of their lives, means that they have a path dependent attachment to it. This presents a deep moat to rivals.

  The unique organizational culture of GE has developed over many decades. Imitators may try to approach the degree of co-operation and mutual support between managers at GE, but they have to realize that it will take a very long time before it becomes second nature to everyone in the organization.

- *Causal ambiguity* There are two types of causal ambiguity. The first is that the potential imitator is unable to see clearly which resource is giving the sustainable competitive advantage. The second is that it is difficult to identify the way in which the extraordinary resource was created in the first place: the recipe is not obvious. If the sustainable competitive advantage is created by a single skill, relationship or a single capability then rivals will usually find it relatively easy to understand the causal mechanism leading to market-place success and abnormally high rates of return on capital used. However, in many cases the competitive advantage relies on a complex set of interacting factors and it is very difficult to disentangle the key elements that create resources and to identify those resources that raise the firm above competitive parity.

  With Sony, it is possible to observe the extraordinary resources; therefore, the first type of causal ambiguity is no problem. Sony has created a working environment that produces a seemingly never-ending stream of well-designed consumer-orientated innovations. It has also developed complementary extraordinary resources that lead to superior marketing and brands. While a rival can observe that Sony has these extraordinary resources, it cannot figure out how those resources were created in the first place. A multitude of factors embedded in the company's culture, personal interactions of employees, attitudes, and skills-base enter the melting pot to produce the special-something.

  It is usually the case that the firm with the causally ambiguous extraordinary resources does not itself understand what it is that gives it an advantage. If it did become obvious to those working for the company then rivals would be able to imitate by hiring away the well-placed knowledgeable managers.

  The most common reason for causal ambiguity is that the firm's resources are the result of complex social phenomena. The unique formal and informal social structures and interactions develop in that one environment. They are often influenced by the personalities of the participants today and by the culture created by their forebears (e.g. Sony's Akio Morita).

- *Economic deterrence* Rivals may be able to imitate but choose not to do so because they fear the consequences. For example, some industries consist of a few firms operating with very high fixed (and often sunk) costs in large-scale plant. A potential entrant could build a similar massive plant but that would add a lot of additional supply to the market and result in depressed prices. Furthermore, the existing players often have assets specific to that industry – they cannot be redeployed in another industry. The incumbents therefore offer a very credible threat of retaliation to a new rival as they are quite prepared, at least in the short run, to compete on the basis of marginal cost.

If a firm has one of the factors that deters imitation then that is good. Some firms can offer two or three – and that is great. For example, a company that has developed a knowledge and capability in bio-technological innovation may also, over time, have developed path dependent attitude and a co-operative, dynamic culture that leads to causal ambiguous resources.

The imitation of extraordinary resources by rivals is one problem; however, if rivals are unable to imitate they may go for a more viable alternative: they may substitute one extraordinary resource with another. For example, in the 1980s IBM dominated the computer business. It had a superb reputation, brand name, technical knowledge and organizational capabilities. However, in the late 1980s and early 1990s other PC manufacturers were able to imitate some of these qualities – e.g. technological prowess was emulated, helped by IBM's open standard. However, IBM's organizational culture, capabilities and attitude could not be imitated by the new PC manufacturers. Instead they substituted for IBM's extraordinary resources their own: dynamic entrepreneurialism, obsession with low-cost manufacture, a-change-the-world attitude, reputations for innovative design and rapid response to market demands.

Other companies have found, or ensured, that their extraordinary resources are largely unsubstitutable. Disney's reputation and its characters are strong barriers to substitution. Newspapers usually have some protection against substitution. It would be difficult for a rival to create an alternative set of resources to compete with the *Wall Street Journal*.

The Internet has created an opportunity for new entrants to substitute for traditional capabilities. For example, in book selling Amazon.com substituted easily manageable website navigation, internet-based marketing, large-scale warehousing and mail delivery systems capability for the traditional retailers' resources of high street location, immediate availability, friendly knowledgeable staff and an atmosphere in which browsing is encouraged. At the time of writing it is difficult to see whether the resources possessed by Amazon.com are enough to bring it to profitability: do its resources offer more additional value to consumers than the additional cost of their provision?

Appropriable

The resource that is supplying value must be one that allows *the company* to capture the value, rather than allow it to be captured by another organization or individual(s). In other words, the value is appropriable by the shareholders. For example, movies that are successful at the box office are often financially damaging to the studios. The leading actors are able to bargain for such high fees that they leave little for the company. A similar phenomenon occurs in sport where the clubs fail to hold on to the revenue generated as players appropriate a substantial proportion. In investment banking 'star' mergers and acquisition specialists, equity underwriters and bond managers can ask for multimillion dollar remuneration packages siphoning off much (or all) of the value they create. In the arts, Pavarotti is able to appropriate much of the revenue from a concert.

This distribution-of-rewards question will be resolved in favour of the company if the company, rather than an external party owns the property rights to the critical resource. For a football team the critical resource is the players' ability and therefore the sportsmen take much of the profit. For a company like Disney the critical resources are owned by the organization – Winnie-the-Pooh, reputation for family orientated entertainment, library of movies etc. – therefore the company will gain from the exploitation of the resource. Sure, from time to time a brilliant director, manager or 'imaginateer' will be found in the organization, but the value these individuals can pull away will be small beer compared with the organization in its entirety.

Another factor influencing appropriability is the degree of bargaining power. The firm's negotiating position will be enhanced if the supplier of a critical resource is one amongst many – then the company can shop around. (In contrast Intel and Microsoft are able to appropriate much of the value created by PCs. The manufacturers of PCs battle it out in a fierce market while these two companies coin it in.) Also, if the critical resource owner has few or no alternative uses for the skill, capability, knowledge or whatever, then the company may be able to lower the cost of using that resource.

Sometimes firms seem to give away the value derived from resources. Perhaps, they come under pressure to pay out the supernormal profits by making excessive payments for inputs. Alternatively, they create slack within the organization and slowly dissipate value. AT & T, owner of Bell

Laboratories, created the transistor radio. This invention made almost no money for AT & T. The company adopted a generous licensing strategy and the basic physics was in the public domain. Sony was able to leap in and develop the transistor radio and appropriate value – helped by the application of additional resources. In 2000 there was inflated talk about the future of the convergence of telecommunications, computer technology and the Internet. The major European telecommunication firms, such as British Telecommunication, Deutsche Telecom and France Telecom saw that high revenues could be expected by developing third-generation (3G) mobile telephone networks, that allowed the user to tap into the Internet as well as talk. They are right; value will be created by this new technology. What is doubtful is whether any of this value will be appropriated by the telecommunication companies. They have already committed themselves to paying over $130 billion to various European governments for licences to set up networks. They will have to spend the same amount again to build the networks. It is hotly debated as to whether all or most of the value to be created by 3G is to be captured by governments, consumers and equipment suppliers, with little or nothing going to the operators. It will be many years before the truth is known. However, share and bond investors have already reacted, pushing prices (and ratings) down sharply.

Two more examples of companies that appropriate the value of their extraordinary resources for shareholders:

- the *Washington Post* – its extraordinary resources – reputation, ethos etc. – are owned by the company. Outstanding individual contributors are valuable, but merely a drop in the ocean of quality reporting and analysis. Even star reporters can be fairly quickly replaced. Few readers would defect if dozens of journalists were replaced.

- Coca-Cola retains for itself the ownership of its key resources. It makes sure no supplier of an input has any real bargaining power to extract serious amounts of value. It controls the brand and the distribution system.

INVESTMENT IN RESOURCES

The Valuegrowth investor needs to investigate whether the firm is continuing to invest in the resource base. If it is reporting high current earnings because it is running down the resource base then the shares should be avoided.

A good company needs to maintain an approach of dynamic evolution with regard to its extraordinary resources. It has to recognize that it faces a never-ending struggle for competitive advantage. The firm can never rest from continually trying to offer better service to customers if it is to retain a large gap between price charged and cost. If it does not have this sense of urgency then rivals will soon take action to erode the firm's advantage.

> **A good company needs to maintain an approach of dynamic evolution.**

The resources of a firm have been likened to water in a bathtub. The water represents the current stock of resources. Unfortunately, there is a continual leakage from the bottom as resources depreciate (knowledge becomes less relevant, capabilities decline or reputations and brands become less appealing). It is necessary to continually pump in more to maintain the future value to be generated from a sustainable competitive advantage. Failure to spend more to top-up the resource-base (e.g. by not advertising the brand or cutting R & D) is perfectly possible for a number of years. Profits will receive a short-term boost. But eventually the tub runs out of water – the company has no extraordinary resources to offer customers. It is condemned to either limp along with low returns or head for corporate death.

Changing the metaphor might help to see what a truly good company looks like. Companies can be viewed as organizations existing in a Darwinian ecology of survival of the fittest and natural selection. Those that have reached the top have created extraordinary resources that enable them to dominate and exploit their part of the eco-system. They have developed superior ways of doing things. Their capabilities, knowledge, attitudes etc. allowed them to survive when less well-endowed rivals failed. But, the business world is susceptible to much more rapid change than the biological one. If the company becomes too rigid in relying on the ways of doing things that have stood it in good stead for much of its history then it becomes vulnerable to competitors who are better able to adapt to environmental change, ranging from new technology to social trends. Entire species of companies will die unless they adapt. Some are aware enough and able enough to respond, others die, sometimes slowly, sometimes quickly, but usually mystified as to why they are being out-competed when they used to be so strong.

Hilton Hotels, in the 1960s and 1970s built a high quality reputation. Then it let things slip. It wasn't long before it was no longer regarded as an up-market hotel chain. Its price premium disappeared. Microsoft has an uncanny ability to adapt. It built on its base of DOS PC operating systems to move into application software (Excel, Word etc.). More recently it spent hundreds of millions of dollars on research and development to adapt to Internet-based computing (this was after initially pooh-poohing the idea that the Internet was all that important, by the way). In the late 1990s, 2,000 of Microsoft's best programmers worked on the Explorer browser. The extraordinary resource of the power relationship with PC manufacturers contributed to the success of Microsoft's Internet strategy.

Consumer-electronics companies such as Matsushita are currently under threat from a shift in their environment. Their competitive advantage was based around analogue technology and large scale manufacturing in low cost locations around the world. Recently, a large number of electronic gadgets have been introduced to the market which are based on digital technology and are more closely related to, and interact with the PC. Personal digital assistants, recordable CD players, digital cameras, DVD drives, computer games consoles, MP3 players, personal video recorders and Internet radios are marketed as PC peripherals. Companies whose roots are in the PC industry have a great deal of credibility when selling these items.

Matsushita (Panasonic) has found its brand is not an extraordinary resource in these areas. Entry by digital-based companies has been relatively easy as the barrier of brand recognition has not been a problem. Hewlett-Packard offer digital cameras; Sonicblue, MP3 players; 3 Com, tabletop Internet radio. Even Intel is selling digital cameras and digital microscopes. The modern digital devices are not evolutions of the products produced by the old consumer electronic companies; they are completely new. The wisest of the Japanese firms have acknowledged a need to adapt and to add to their resource base. Many have built Silicon Valley research establishments. They have developed capabilities in digital product manufacture. Already Japanese firms dominate the digital camera market. They are combining their existing resources (e.g. their ability to produce innovative designs to make using electronic devices easy to use, their trusted brands and their extensive retail distribution relationships) with their newly developed digital-based resources to withstand the threat from the newcomers.

There are two types of resource investment:

- maintaining and upgrading existing resources; and
- adding new resources to the portfolio.

Existing resources may be enhanced by spending additional sums of money on them, e.g. Cadbury Schweppes spends $100 million on an advertising campaign. They can also be enhanced simply by the repeated use of them. For example, a firm that has an extraordinary resource in bringing new products to market will, probably, continually strengthen its capability in product development, if it continues to maintain an extensive programme. A firm that has a highly able, driven and cohesive management team would strengthen that extraordinary resource by setting the managers stretching tasks. Some resources do not get used up when they are employed – indeed they may grow stronger.

Companies may also need to invest in complementary resources to improve the firm's competitive advantage. Intel saw this in the 1990s. Its technological resources and reputation were enhanced by a big campaign to build a brand name. The 'Intel Inside' slogan and Pentium trademark must have cost hundreds of millions to promote. The reason for adding the power of a brand was that some competitors were imitating its technology or making use of credible substitute technology.

Sometimes the company needs to develop new resources that eventually move it out of its current competitive environment. This is a tricky one for the Valuegrowth investor. If the firm reasons that the industry structure is so unattractive that it needs to acquire new resources to allow it to move out then one has to query whether this investment should be held in the first place. Second, there are two dangers of such a radical move: the destination may not turn out to be as attractive on closer inspection (and a few years down the line) as first thought; the firm might go shopping for the new resources in an extravagant manner – it pays excessive prices in the belief that it is essential to have the new resource to allow survival, e.g. how many European telecom groups stopped to ask whether it would be better not to have the resource of a mobile phone licence? They all thought they must have one to stay in the game – the bidding in the auctions was then frenzied.

There are two dilemmas facing management when they are deciding the direction of, and extent of, their investment in resources:

- *Continuity versus adaptability* In a shifting environment do you stick with the resources that stood you in good stead for many years? Or, do you invest in alternative resources? For example, if you are a traditional bookseller do you continue to build up resources that reinforce your strengths in selling books the old way or do you develop the resources needed to set up an Internet based operation? There are risks on both sides. Sticking with the old can result in your being sidelined. Investing in the new can be expensive and the fundamental change is very disruptive and may destroy old strengths (it may also cannibalize sales). Some managers freeze when caught in the headlights of an environmental change and make no decision, or make it too late. The Valuegrowth investor needs to assess the ability of management to deal with this dilemma.

- *Commitment versus flexibility* When investing, the firm has to choose between resources that are specific to a particular strategy or those that are more flexible and can be useful for a number of alternative strategies (a policy of keeping options open). A concert violinist usually makes a commitment to deepen their talent with that one instrument early in their career. However, by focusing so intently the violinist sacrifices the ability to switch to other resources should the demand for excellent violinists decline. A firm that makes a strong commitment to particular resources can become locked in a strategy, which may later prove to be inappropriate. On the other hand, if flexibility is prized too highly the company could lose ground to a competitor that is more dedicated. Path dependent advantages may be lost for ever. The Valuegrowth investor is looking for firms that can strike the right balance in dealing with what usually ends up being a trade-off with no simple solution (but, then, if it was simple the opportunity for supernormal profit would quickly be competed away!).

LEVERAGING RESOURCES

Some companies have a powerful ability to leverage their resources into other segments or industries. For example, Disney has leveraged its characters into theme parks, promotions at McDonald's and websites amongst others.

Many resources not fully utilized in their original settings offer terrific opportunities for being applied to other fields. For example, a firm may have developed strong relationships and/or reputations with customers, governments and suppliers. These could be used by other parts of the organization at little additional cost and without impairing the resource. Likewise brands may be used for a wider range of products (e.g. a chocolate brand used for ice cream). Or knowledge could be leveraged, such as the use of technological innovation in more than one business sector. Or co-ordination of marketing strategies could create value, e.g. a film division uses music from the back catalogues of the music division. In the case of AOL Time Warner film, paper publishing, Internet and TV divisions can use each others' resources to benefit the whole firm.

McDonald's has extended its brand, location and food consistency resources to offer a range of new products as well as the hamburger.

Fiat, Italy's largest industrial group, is following a strategy of resource leverage. It is a world leader in businesses such as agricultural machinery and production systems. It is using the extraordinary resources developed in these areas to create value by offering related services. Its Iveco truck and bus division will move beyond selling vehicles to using its customer relationship resource to sell insurance and financial leases. A division, Comau, that manufacturers production and automation systems for large makers such as GM and Ford, will offer follow-up system servicing. The attraction of service businesses is the double-digit margins. Fiat envisages the day when over half of earnings come from service operations.

The Valuegrowth investor needs to watch out for companies diversifying beyond their extraordinary resource base. Between 1958 and 1974 BIC Pen Corporation had a great time leveraging its resources. It had the extraordinary resources of capability and knowledge in plastic injection moulding, mass marketing and a reputation through its strong brand. It leveraged from disposable pen production to disposable lighters and then to razors. This leveraging went well because the new product lines could make good use of all three of BICs extraordinary resources. Then, in 1974 it made a mistake. It entered the hosiery market. None of the extraordinary resources were any use at all in producing or selling hosiery. Their plastic manufacturing capability was not relevant, the product sold through completely different outlets and marketing a fashion item required a different approach to selling disposable pens, lighters and razors.

Also watch out for companies over-exploiting a resource. In 2000, William M. Mercer, the world's largest investment consultancy, wisely drew back from leveraging its resources to manage funds itself. Its traditional role is to advise pension funds on the best fund managers to run their money. If it had started to manage funds itself it would have destroyed the valuable resource of its integrity and impartiality.

Sotheby's and Christies have seriously damaged their extraordinary resource of reputation for honest dealing. In 2000 the US Justice Department announced the results of its three-year antitrust investigation. It is alleged that two organizations had colluded to set commission rates. The value of their brands went into freefall just as Sotheby's was about to leverage its brand for Internet auctioning. The companies have already paid out $512 million in compensation to former customers. Sotheby's has also paid a $45 million fine.

Gucci is a company that in the 21st Century realizes that one of its key resources is its rarity value. It is careful not to grow too big or to stretch the brand too far. Instead of increasing volume it has added new rarity value brands: Yves Saint Laurent, Bucheron Jewellery, Shoemaker Sergio Rossi and Alexander McQueen. Gucci had learnt the hard way that over exploitation of a brand is both possible and potentially fatal. In the 1980s it launched an aggressive strategy of rapid sales growth. It added lower priced goods to its product line and started to sell through department stores and duty-free shops. Its name appeared on a host of products from sunglasses to perfumes. Sales soared but its image fell, along with sales of the upmarket products, reducing overall profitability.

KEY ELEMENTS OF COMPETITIVE RESOURCE ANALYSIS

- Ordinary resources give a firm competitive parity, extraordinary resources give a competitive edge (to outperform competitors and create new value generating opportunities).

- It is the ability of firms to generate value for customers that is critical for high shareholder returns.

- Companies should be viewed as bundles of resources rather than bundles of product lines.

- TRRACK systems – a checklist for extraordinary resources:
  T   Tangible
  R   Relationships
  R   Reputation

A   Attitude
C   Capabilities
K   Knowledge.

- Factors making resources extraordinary:
  - demanded
  - scarce (inimitable, unsubstitutable)
  - appropriable.

- Imitation is inhibited by:
  - physical uniqueness
  - path dependency
  - causal ambiguity
  - economic deterrence.

- Investment in resources needs to be made by the company:
  - maintenance and upgrading investment
  - adding new resources to the portfolio.

- Two dilemmas facing managers making resource investments:
  - continuity versus adaptability
  - commitment versus flexibility.

- Companies that can leverage resources may develop sustainable competitive advantages in a number of markets.

- Diversifying beyond the extraordinary resource base is to be avoided.

- Over-exploiting an extraordinary resource is to be avoided.

Notes

1   Kay, J. (1993).
2   William, J. and Tucker, E. (1999).
3   Larry Johnson quoted in Marsh, P. (1999).
4   *Ibid.*
5   Kay, J. (1993), p. 87.
6   Kelly, J. (1998).
7   Kay, J. (1993).
8   Martin, P. (1998).
9   *Ibid.*
10 Kay, J. (1993), p. 258.
11 Daft, D. (2000).
12 De Wit, B. and Meyer, R. (1998).
13 Collis, D. J. and Montgomery, C.A. (1997).
14 Pilling, D. (2000).
15 Much of the section is inspired by work done by David Collis and Cynthia Montgomery, see Collis, D. J. and Montgomery, C. A. (1997) for more details.

Glossary

Administered prices Controlled by some authority, e.g. government.

Amortization of assets The reduction in book value of an intangible asset such as goodwill.

Appropriable resource The resource that is supplying value must be one that allows the company to capture the value rather than allow it to be captured by another organization or individual(s).

Asset allocation Investment methodology, which specifies the proportion of funds to be invested in different asset classes.

Asymmetry of information One party in a negotiation is not in the same position as other parties, being ignorant of, or unable to observe, some information which is essential to the contracting and decision-making process.

Barriers to entry The obstacles that a company entering a market for the first time has to overcome to do well in that market.

Batch production Producing in small quantities or groups.

Beta This measures the systematic risk of a financial security. In the capital asset pricing model it is a measure of sensitivity to market movements of a financial securities return, as measured by the covariance between returns on the asset and returns on the market portfolio divided by the variance of the market portfolio. In practice a proxy (e.g. S&P 500 index) is used for the market portfolio.

Bond A debt obligation with a long-term maturity, usually issued by firms and governments.

Book value Balance sheet value. Can be expressed on a per share basis.

Bubble stock Shares buoyed up by market optimism. Such optimism is not based on any rational standards of value.

Capitalization factor A discount rate.

Chartism Investment analysis that relies on historic price charts (and/or trading volumes) to predict future movements.

Churn Buying and selling shares frequently.

Circle of competence The business areas that an individual thoroughly understands and is equipped to analyze.

Cognitive Able to know and perceive.

Commodity product Undifferentiated in any customer-important way by factors such as performance, appearance, service support, etc.

Common stock Equity capital – ordinary shares.

Competitive advantage (edge) The possession of extraordinary resources that allow a firm to rise above the others in its industry to generate exceptional long-run rates of return on capital employed.

Competitive floor Where shareholders receive a rate of return that only just induces them to put money into the firm and hold it there.

Complementary product One that is generally used alongside the product in question.

Contrarians Taking the opposite to the generality of investors.

Convertible preferred stock A preferred share that can be changed into another type of security, e.g. an ordinary share.

Coupon An attachment to a bond or loan notes document which may be separated and serve as evidence of entitlement to interest. Nowadays it refers to the interest itself.

Causal ambiguity A potential imitator is unable to see clearly which resource is giving the sustainable competitive advantage, or it is difficult to identify the way in which the extraordinary resource was created in the first place.

Crack companies Those engaged in a combination of industrial and commercial activities which means they are difficult to classify. They fall between the cracks of standard institutional companies.

Current asset value (net) Current assets (cash, accounts receivable, inventory) minus current liabilities (also called working capital).

Cyclical companies (shares) Those companies in which profits are particularly sensitive to the growth level in the economy, which may be cyclical.

Debt maturity The length of time left until the repayment on a debt becomes due.

Default A failure to make agreed payments of interest or principal.

Defensive stocks Having a beta value of less than 1.

Derivative A financial asset, the performance of which is based on (derived from) the behaviour of the value of an underlying asset.

Differentiated product One that is slightly different in significant ways than those supplied by other companies.

Diminishing marginal attractiveness If stocks are listed in order of attractiveness based on the difference between their value and current price then the marginal (next stock) on the list would be attractive but not as attractive as the one before it.

Discounting The process of reducing future cashflows to a present value using an appropriate discount rate.

Discount rate The rate of return used to discount cashflows received in future years. It is the opportunity cost of capital given the risk class of the future cashflows.

Dividend yield Annual dividend divided by share price.

Dow or Dow Jones Industrial Average The best known index of movements in the price of US stocks and shares. There are 30 shares in the index.

Earnings per share Profit after tax and interest divided by number of shares in issue.

Earning power The earnings (profit) capacity of a business in a normal year. What the company might be expected to earn year after year if the business conditions continue unchanged.

Economic franchise Pricing power combined with strong barriers to entry. The strength and durability of an economic franchise is determined by (a) the structure of the industry, (b) the ability of the firm to rise above its rivals in its industry and generate exceptionally long-run rates of return on capital employed.

Economies of scale Producing a larger output results in lower unit cost.

Efficient market hypothesis The efficient market hypothesis implies that new information is incorporated into a share price (a) rapidly, and (b) rationally. In an efficient market no trader will be presented with an opportunity for making an abnormal return, except by chance.

Equity risk premium The additional average annual rate of return for an averagely risky share over the return on risk free asset as shown by historical data going back many decades.

Exclusive franchise See economic franchise.

Exit barrier A factor preventing firms from stopping production in a particular industry.

Experience curve The cost of performing a task reduces as experience is gained through repetition.

Extraordinary resources Those that give the firm a competitive edge. A resource, which when combined with other (ordinary) resources enables the firm to outperform competitors and create new value-generating opportunities. Critical extraordinary resources determine what a firm can do successfully.

Extrapolation To estimate the value beyond the known values by the extension of a curve or line.

Fixed cost A cost that does not vary according to the amount of goods or services that are produced.

Float (for insurance companies) A pool of money held in the firm in readiness to pay claims.

Flow production Producing by a continuous flow of product.

Free cashflow Cash generated by a business not required for operations or for reinvestment.

Free float The proportion of a company's shares available to general investors and not held by dominant shareholders or those close to the firm.

Free plus A return an investor enjoys over and above initial expectations.

Future A contract between two parties to undertake a transaction at an agreed price on a specified future date.

GAAP Generally accepted accounting principles.

GDP (nominal, real) Gross domestic product, the sum of all output of goods and services produced by a nation. Nominal means including inflation and real means with inflation removed.

Goodwill An accounting term for the difference between the amount that a company pays for another company and the market value of the other company's assets. Goodwill is thus an intangible asset representing things like the value of the company's brand names and the skills of its employees.

Greater fool investing The object is to pass on a share which is currently of great interest to the market speculators and traders after making a return on the 'investment' without really bothering to understand the fundamentals of the business.

Growth stock Where the company has performed better than average (in growth in earnings per share) for a period of years and is expected to do so in the future.

Hot shares/sectors Those currently receiving a lot of attention from the Press and investors.

Industry structure The combination of the degree of rivalry within the industry among existing firms; the bargaining strength of industry firms with suppliers and customers; and the potential for new firms to enter and for substitute products to take customers. The industry structure determines the long run rate of return on capital employed within the industry.

Inevitable A company likely to dominate its field for an investment life-time due to its competitive strength.

Institutional imperative An insidious and dangerous unseen force at work in companies. It is the tendency of organizations to stray from the path of rationality, decency and intelligence.

Intelligent speculation A focus on information that is quantifiable. Based on a calculation of probabilities. Keeping the speculative element within minor limits. The odds are strongly in favour of success.

Intrinsic value The discounted value of the cash that can be taken out of a business during its remaining life. It can never be precisely stated, it will be an estimate.

Investment operation One that, upon thorough analysis, promises safety of principal and a satisfactory return.

Lead steer A term used to describe a dominant person with the power to induce others to follow.

Liquidity The degree to which an asset can be sold quickly and easily without loss in value.

Liquidity-itis An obsession with shares that have a very active market to the point of neglect of shares in good companies but with low liquidity.

Long position A commitment to, or actual, buying of shares.

Macro economics The study of the relationships between broad economic aggregates: national income, saving, investment, balance of payments, inflation, taxation, etc.

Managementism Management not acting in shareholders best interests. There are three levels:
(a) dishonest managers
(b) honest but incompetent managers
(c) honest and competent but as humans are subject to the influence of conflicts of interest.

Margin of safety The value of a share must be well in excess of the price paid. A probability of protection against loss under all normal or reasonably likely conditions or variations.

Market capitalization The total value at market prices of the shares in issue for a company (or a stock market, or a sector of the stock market).

Market index A sample of shares is used to represent a share market's level and movements.

Market weightings The capitalization of all the firms in an industry as a proportion of the total capitalization of all the shares on the stock market.

Mass production The production of goods or services in large quantities and by a standardized process with the aim of appealing to a mass market.

Minority shareholder A shareholder who owns less than 50 per cent of a company.

Momentum investing Selecting shares that have experienced a rise.

Monetary policy The deliberate control of the money supply and/or rates of interest by the central bank.

Multi-bagger A share that rises to a multiple of the buying price.

Mutual fund A collective investment vehicle for shares or other financial securities. Many investors own stakes in the mutual fund which then invests in securities.

Niche company A fast growing small to medium-sized firm operating in a niche business with high potential.

Nifty fifty Fifty stocks declared in the late 1960s and early 1970s to have such a marvellous future that supposedly almost any multiple of current income could be justified as a share price.

Opportunity cost The value foregone by opting for one course of action; the next best use of, say, financial resources.

Option A contract giving one party the right, but not the obligation, to buy or sell a financial instrument, commodity or some other underlying asset at a given price, at or before a specified date.

Ordinary resources Those that give the firm competitive parity. They provide a threshold competence.

Over-capacity An industry or company has significantly more capacity to supply product than is being demanded.

Owner earnings Reported earnings plus depreciation, depletion, amortization and certain other non-cash charges less the amount of capitalized expenditure for plant and machinery and working capital etc. that a business requires to fully maintain its long-term competitive position, unit volume and investment in positive value projects.

Oxymorons (a contradiction in terms) A word used by Peter Lynch and Warren Buffett to describe 'professional investors'. Meaning that most professional fund managers fail to qualify as investors as Lynch and Buffett would describe the term.

Path dependent resources Firm resources that have been created because of the route that the firm took to get to where it is today.

Perfect competition Entry to the industry is free and the existing firms have no bargaining power over suppliers or customers. Rivalry between existing firms is fierce because products are identical. The following assumptions hold:

(a) there is a large number of buyers;

(b) there is a large number of sellers;

(c) the quantity of goods bought by any individual transactor is so small relative to the total quantity traded that individual trades leave the market price unaffected;

(d) the units of goods sold by different sellers are the same – the product is homogeneous;

(e) there is perfect information – all buyers and all sellers have complete information on the prices being asked and offered in other parts of the market; and

(f) perfect freedom of entry and exit from the market.

Price-earnings ratio

Historic Share price divided by most recently reported earnings per share.

Forward (prospective) Share price divided by anticipated earnings per share.

Price to book value The price of a share as a multiple of per share book (balance sheet) value.

Pricing power An ability to raise prices even when product demand is flat without the danger of losing significant volume or market share.

Primary equity market (new issue market) Where companies first sell shares to investors through a regulated exchange.

Promising company Companies with an ordinary earnings record where the investor *expects* it to do better than the average in the future.

Quantum analysis Quantitative based analysis

Quick asset value (net) Current assets minus inventory minus current liabilities.

Random walk The movements in share prices are independent of one another; one day's price change cannot be predicted by looking at the previous day's price change.

Return on equity Profit divided by the book value of equity ('shareholders funds' or 'net assets').

Risk free rate of return The rate earned on riskless investment, denoted r_f.

S&P 500 Standard and Poor's index of 500 leading US shares.

Scuttlebutt Obtaining knowledge about a company by talking to a wide range of people who have had dealings with the corporation: customers, suppliers, employees, ex-employees etc.

SEC, Securities and Exchange Commission The US federal body responsible for the regulation of securities markets (exchanges, brokers, investment advisers, etc.)

Shareholders' funds The net assets of the business (after deduction of all short- and long-term liabilities) shown in the balance sheet.

Short sales The selling of shares not currently owned by the seller in the expectation of buying at a lower price later.

Short-term selectivity The buying or selling of a financial security based on the analysis of a corporation's or an industry's near-term business prospects.

Sigma A measure of dispersion of returns, standard deviation.

Solvency The ability to pay debts as and when they become due.

Start-up companies Companies with a limited or non-existent trading history.

Stop-loss orders An order from an investor to a broker to sell if the share price breaches a lower threshold – used to limit possible losses.

Strategic analysis The analysis of industries served by the firm and the company's competitive position within the industry.

Subscription rights A right to subscribe for some shares.

Substitute Products or services that perform the same function (at least in approximate terms).

Sunk cost A cost the firm has incurred or to which it is committed that cannot be altered. This cost does not influence subsequent decisions and can be ignored in, for example, project appraisals.

Switching cost The cost of changing supplier.

Technical analysis *See Chartism*.

Tipsters People who put forward a view on the wisdom of buying or selling a stock – usually based on superficial knowledge.

Tracker An investment fund which is intended to replicate the return of a market index. Also called an index fund.

Time-loans Loan with a specific maturity.

Turnarounds Companies that have been going through a bad time and (it is hoped) will soon revive.

Undifferentiated product One that is much the same as that supplied by other companies.

Unintelligent speculation Buying and selling shares and other financial securities with a lack of proper knowledge and skill; risking more money than the stock picker can afford to lose; ignoring quantitative material; placing the emphasis on the rewards of speculation rather than on the individual's capacity to speculate successfully.

US long-term government bond These bonds are coupon paying securities issued with maturities over ten years.

Value chain The interlinking activities that take place within an organization or between organizations in the process of converting inputs into outputs. Identifying these activities and finding ways to perform them more efficiently is a way for companies to gain competitive advantage over their rivals.

Value investing The identification and holding of shares which are fundamentally undervalued by the market, given the prospects of the firm.

Working capital *See Current asset value.*

Bibliography

Achstatter, G. (1998) 'Fidelity's Peter Lynch. How He Conducted the Research That Made His Fund Best', *Investor's Business Daily*, 2 February.

Armstrong, W. (1848) *Stocks, and Stock-jobbing in Wall Street,* Pamphlet.

Arnold, G. (2002) *Corporate Financial Management*, second edition London: FT Prentice Hall.

Barclays Capital (2000) *Equity Gilt Study*, Barclays London: Capital.

Barclays Capital (2001) *Equity-Gilt Study 2001.*

Barnum, P. T. (1885) *The Life of P.T. Barnum*, New York: Redfield.

Bauer, P. E. (1986) *The Convictions of a Long-distance Investor.* Channels, November, p. 22.

Bianco, A. (1985) *Why Warren Buffett is Breaking His Own Rules, Business Week*, 15 April.

Buffett, W. E. (1967) Letter to Partners of Buffett Partnership Ltd. 9 October.

Buffett, W. E. (1977) Letter to shareholders included with the 1977 Annual Report of Berkshire Hathaway Inc. www.berkshirehathaway.com

Buffett, W. E. (1978) Letter to shareholders included with the 1978 Annual Report of Berkshire Hathaway Inc. www.berkshirehathaway.com

Buffett, W. E. (1979) Letter to shareholders included with the 1979 Annual Report of Berkshire Hathaway Inc. www.berkshirehathaway.com

Buffett, W. E. (1980) Letter to shareholders included with the 1980 Annual Report of Berkshire Hathaway Inc. www.berkshirehathaway.com

Buffett, W. E. (1981) Letter to shareholders included with the 1981 Annual Report of Berkshire Hathaway Inc. www.berkshirehathaway.com

Buffett, W. E. (1982) Letter to shareholders included with the 1982 Annual Report of Berkshire Hathaway Inc. www.berkshirehathaway.com

Buffett, W. E. (1983) Letter to shareholders included with the 1983 Annual Report of Berkshire Hathaway Inc. www.berkshirehathaway.com

Buffett, W. E. (1984) Letter to shareholders included with the 1984 Annual Report of Berkshire Hathaway Inc. www.berkshirehathaway.com

Buffett, W. E. (1985) Letter to shareholders included with the 1985 Annual Report of Berkshire Hathaway Inc. www.berkshirehathaway.com

Buffett, W. E. (1986) Letter to shareholders included with the 1986 Annual Report of Berkshire Hathaway Inc. www.berkshirehathaway.com

Buffett, W. E. (1987) Letter to shareholders included with the 1987 Annual Report of Berkshire Hathaway Inc. www.berkshirehathaway.com

Buffett, W. E. (1988) Letter to shareholders included with the 1988 Annual Report of Berkshire Hathaway Inc. www.berkshirehathaway.com

Buffett, W. E. (1989) Letter to shareholders included with the 1989 Annual Report of Berkshire Hathaway Inc. www.berkshirehathaway.com

Buffett, W. E. (1990) Letter to shareholders included with the 1990 Annual Report of Berkshire Hathaway Inc. www.berkshirehathaway.com

Buffett, W. E. (1991) Letter to shareholders included with the 1991 Annual Report of Berkshire Hathaway Inc. www.berkshirehathaway.com

Buffett, W. E. (1992) Letter to shareholders included with the 1992 Annual Report of Berkshire Hathaway Inc. www.berkshirehathaway.com

Buffett, W. E. (1993) Letter to shareholders included with the 1993 Annual Report of Berkshire Hathaway Inc. www.berkshirehathaway.com

Buffett, W. E. (1994) Letter to shareholders included with the 1994 Annual Report of Berkshire Hathaway Inc. www.berkshirehathaway.com

Buffett, W. E. (1995) Letter to shareholders included with the 1995 Annual Report of Berkshire Hathaway Inc. www.berkshirehathaway.com

Buffett, W. E. (1996) Letter to shareholders included with the 1996 Annual Report of Berkshire Hathaway Inc. www.berkshirehathaway.com

Buffett, W. E. (1997) Letter to shareholders included with the 1997 Annual Report of Berkshire Hathaway Inc. www.berkshirehathaway.com

Buffett, W. E. (1998) Letter to shareholders included with the 1998 Annual Report of Berkshire Hathaway Inc. www.berkshirehathaway.com

Buffett, W. E. (1999) Letter to shareholders included with the 1999 Annual Report of Berkshire Hathaway Inc. www.berkshirehathaway.com

Buffett, W. E. (2000) Letter to shareholders included with the 2000 Annual Report of Berkshire Hathaway Inc. www.berkshirehathaway.com

Buffett, W. E. (1984a) *The Superinvestors of Graham-and-Doddsville,* Transcript in *Hermes*, Magazine of Columbia Business School, autumn.

Buffett, W. (1994b) Speech, New York Society of Security Analysts, 6 December.

Buffett, W. E. (1995a) *Warren Buffett Talks Business*, The University of North Carolina, Center for Public Television, Chapel Hill.

Buffett, W. E. (1985a) 'Investing in Equity Markets', quoted in Columbia University Business School, Transcript of a Seminar held 13 March 1985, pp. 28–9.

Collis, D. J. and Montgomery, C. A. (1997) *Corporate Strategy: Resources and the Scope of the Firm*, New York: McGraw Hill, USA.

Daft, D. (2000) 'Back to Classic Coke', *Financial Times*, 27 March, p. 20.

Davis, L. J. (1990) 'Buffett Takes Stock', *New York Times Magazine*, 1 April, p. 16.

De Wit, B. and Meyer, R. (1998) *Strategy: Process, Content, Context.* 2nd edn. London: International Thomson Business Press.

Dickson, M. (1995) 'Lessons from History: On Berkshire Hathaway's Plan to Buy the Rest of Geico', *Financial Times*, 28 August.

Dimson, E., Marsh, P. and Staunton, M. (2001) *Millenium Book II: 101 Years of Investment Returns*, ABN Amro/LBS.

Dorr, R. (1977) 'Ex-Omahan Traded Law for Board Room'. *Omaha World-Herald*, 3 August, p. B1.

Dreman, D. (1998) *Contrarian Investment Strategies: The Next Generation*, New York: Simon and Schuster.

Duval Fromson, B. (1990) 'And Now, a Look at the Old One', Fortune 1990 Investor's Guide, p. 98.

Fisher, P. (1960) *Common Stocks and Uncommon Profits.* PSR Publications (originally published by Harper & Brothers in 1958). References are for 1996 reprinted Wiley Investment Classics book: *Common Stocks and Uncommon Profits*, New York: John Wiley and Son, Inc.

Fisher, P. (1975) *Conservative Investors Sleep Well.* Previously published by Business Classics. References are for 1996 reprinted Wiley Investment Classics book: *Common Stocks and Uncommon Profits*, New York: John Wiley and Son, Inc.

Fisher, P. (1980) *Developing an Investment Philosophy.* Financial Analysts Society and Business Classics. References are for 1996 reprinted Wiley Investment Classics book: *Common Stocks and Uncommon Profits*. New York: John Wiley and Son, Inc.

Graham, B. (1932) *Is American Business Worth More Dead than Alive? Inflated Treasuries and Deflated Stocks: Are Corporations Milking Their Owners?*, 1 June, Forbes. Reprinted in Lowe (1999).

Graham, B. (1932) 'Should Losing Corporations be Liquidated?, Forbes, 1 July. Reprinted in Lowe (1999).

Graham, B. (1946–7) 'Current Problems in Security Analysis', Lectures to the New York Institute of Finance. Excerpts reprinted in Lowe (1999).

Graham, B. (1952) 'Toward a Science of Security Analysis', Proceedings, Fifth Annual Convention, National Federation of Security Analysts. The *Analyst's Journal*, August. Reprinted in Lowe (1999).

Graham, B. (1955) 'Testimony Before the Committee on Banking and Currency, United States Senate: On Factors Affecting the Buying and Selling of Equity Securities', 11 March. Reprinted in Lowe (1999).

Graham, B. (1956) 'The Ethics of American Capitalism', Speech at University of California, Los Angeles Camp Kramer Retreat, 10 November.

Graham, B. (1959) 'Stock Market Warning: Danger Ahead!' Based on a speech delivered at UCLA. 17 December. *California Management Review*, Vol. 11, No.3, Spring, 1960. Reprinted in Lowe (1999).

Graham, B. (1973) *The Intelligent Investor*, Revised 4th edn. New York: Harper Business (reprinted 1997).

Graham, B. (1976) 'The Simplest Way to Select Bargain Stocks'. *Medical Economics*, 20 September. Reprinted in Lowe (1999).

Graham, B. (1996) *The Memoirs of the Dean of Wall Street*, New York: McGraw-Hill.

Graham, B. and Dodd, D. (1934). *Security Analysis*, New York: McGraw-Hill.

Grant, L (1991) 'The $4-Billion Regular Guy', the *Los Angeles Times*. Sunday, 7 April, p. 36.

Hagstrom, R. G. (1994) *The Warren Buffett Way*, Updated edition. New York: John Wiley and Sons Ltd.

Ineck, T. (1991) 'A Little "Dance" Music Lifts Son of Omaha Billionaire', the *Lincoln Journal and Star*, 8 August, p. 11.

Kay, J. (1993) *Foundations of Corporate Success*, New York: Oxford University Press.

Kelly, J. (1998) 'KPMG to spend $60m on Brand Building Campaign'. *Financial Times*, 7 September, p. 23.

Keynes, J. M. (1936) *The General Theory of Employment, Interest and Money*, New York: Harcourt, Brace Jovanovich.

Lenzner, R. (1993) 'Warren Buffett's Idea of Heaven: I Don't Have to Work With People I Don't Like', Forbes 400, 18 October.

Lenzner, R. and Fondiller, D. S. (1996) 'Meet Charlie Munger', Forbes, 22 January, p. 78.

Lenzner, R. and Fondiller, D. S. (1996), 'The Not-So-Silent Partner', Forbes, 22 January.

Lewis, W. (1998) 'The Dream Team's Realist', *Financial Times*, 13 May.

Loomis, C. J. (1988) 'The Inside Story of Warren Buffett' *Fortune*, 11 April, p. 26.

Lowe, J. (1997) *Warren Buffett Speaks*, New York: John Wiley and Sons Ltd.

Lowe, J. (1999) *The Rediscovered Benjamin Graham*, New York: John Wiley.

Lowenstein, R. (1995) *Buffett: The Making of an American Capitalist*, New York: Random House.

Lynch, P. (1990) *One Up on Wall Street* (with John Rothchild), New York: Penguin Books (Originally published by Simon and Schuster, 1989.)

Lynch, P. (1994) *Beating the Street* (with John Rothchild), Revised version of 1993 hardback publication. New York: Simon and Schuster.

Marsh, P. (1999) 'Original Thought Boosts the Many Interests of GE'. *Financial Times*, 23 November, p. 17.

Martin, P. (1998) 'Goldman's Goose', *Financial Times*, 11 August, p. 14.

McMorris, R. (1987) 'Leila Basks in Value of Son's Life, Not Fortune', *Omaha World-Herald*, 16 May, p. 17.

Munger, C. (1989) Wesco Financial Corporation Annual Report (1989).

Munger, C. T. and Koeppel, D. A. (1981) 1981 Annual Report of Blue Chip Stamps.

Munger, C. T. and Koeppel, D. A. (1982) 1982 Annual Report of Blue Chip Stamps.

Neff, J. (1999) *John Neff on Investing* (with S.L. Mintz), New York: John Wiley & Sons, Inc.

New York Post (1994), 'Warren Triples Profits', 14 May, p. D1.

Penfield Jackson, T. (1999) http://usvms.Gpo.Gov

Pilling, D. (2000) 'Making its Merck on its Own', *Financial Times*, 4 February, p. 28.

Porter, M. E. (1980) *Competitive Strategy: Techniques for Analyzing Industries and Competitors*. New York: The Free Press.

Porter, M. E. (1985) *Competitive Advantage: Creating and Sustaining Superior Performance*, New York: The Free Press.

Quirt, J. (1974) *Benjamin Graham: The Grandfather of Investment Value is Still Concerned. Institutional Investor*. April. Reprinted in Lowe (1999).

Rasmussen, J. (1994) 'Billionaire Talks Strategy With Students', *Omaha World-Herald*, 2 January, p. 17S.

Shefrin, H. (2000) *Beyond Greed and Fear*, Boston, Massachusetts: Harvard Business School Press.

Smith, A. (1972) *Super Money*, New York: Random House.

Train, J. (1980) *The Money Masters*, New York: Harper Business (reprinted 1994).

Train, J. (1987) *The Midas Touch*, New York: Harper and Row.

Urry, M. (1996) 'The $45bn Man Makes His Pitch'. *Financial Times* Weekend Money 11/12 May, p. 1.

US Office of Business Economics, *The National Income and Product Accounts of the United States, 1929–1965*.

Willman, J. and Blitz, J. (1999) 'Coca-Cola's Style Offends European Regulators' Taste', *Financial Times*, 22 July.

Willman, J. and Tucker, E. (1999) 'Space Invaders'. *Financial Times*, 21 October, p. 22.

Index